FamilyCircle®
healthy family dinners

More than 200 good-for-you recipes

WILEY

John Wiley & Sons, Inc.

For general information on our other products and services or
for technical support, please contact our Customer
Care Department within the United States at
(800) 762-2974, outside the United States at
(317) 572-3993 or fax (317) 572-4002.

Wiley also publishes its books in a variety of electronic
formats. Some content that appears in print may not be available in electronic books. For more information about Wiley
products, visit our web site at www.wiley.com.

Designed by Waterbury Publications, Inc., Des Moines, Iowa

Library of Congress Cataloging-in-Publication Data
Family circle healthy family dinners : more than 200 good-for-
you recipes.
    p. cm.
Includes index.
  ISBN 978-0-470-94502-5 (pbk.); 978-1-118-11941-9 (ebk.);
      978-1-118-11942-6 (ebk.); 978-1-118-11943-3 (ebk.)
  1. Dinners and dining. 2. Cookbooks. I. Family circle (Mount
Morris, Ill.)
  TX737.F2237 2011
  641.5--dc22
                    2010045227

Printed in the United States of America

Family Circle *Healthy Family Dinners*

Editor in Chief: Linda Fears

Food Director: Regina Ragone

Senior Food Editor: Julie Miltenberger

Contributing Writer: Georgia Downard

John Wiley & Sons, Inc.

Publisher: Natalie Chapman

Associate Publisher: Jessica Goodman

Senior Editor: Linda Ingroia

Production Director: Diana Cisek

Production Editor: Abby Saul

Manufacturing Manager: Tom Hyland

Design Director: Ken Carlson, Waterbury Publications, Inc.

Associate Design Director: Doug Samuelson, Waterbury
Publications, Inc.

Production Assistants: Mindy Samuelson, Waterbury
Publications, Inc.

Cover photo recipe: Penne with Sausage and Peas, page 60

contents

letter from the editor

I grew up with little to no junk food—my parents were early adapters of the health food trend—which meant I got my fix of Doritos and Snickers at friends' houses. Among the forbidden foods were most supermarket sweets. This didn't mean desserts were out of the question, but it was either ice cream or a cake or pie my dad bought from the local bakery.

My parents allowed us kids free reign over one food: breakfast cereal. Our cabinet resembled the shelf in Seinfeld's kitchen, with at least a half dozen varieties—including Frosted Flakes and Cap'n Crunch (my favorite). I think their theory was that if we liked our cereal, we'd get some nutrition and a serving of milk.

While I found the restrictions irritating at the time, they did make an impact. I've been raising my kids the same way: lots of fresh fruits and veggies (organic whenever possible), home-cooked dinners (with occasional takeout), no soda, limited processed foods, and any cereal they like (yes, even Frosted Flakes and Cap'n Crunch). As a result, my kids—who are now 13, 18, and 20— are really healthy eaters who don't have much of a sweet tooth. They drink milk or water with meals (at least at home) and generally make good eating choices when at school or a restaurant.

At *Family Circle*, we try to extend this message to our readers as well. We know there will always be times to indulge in our favorite treats—after all, we're only human. However, we want families to know that making good choices doesn't have to be boring or ultra-time consuming. Our hope is that you'll regularly reference *Healthy Family Dinners* in your kitchen—the good-for-you meals we've created will keep you and your family satisfied and energized for your busy lives.

Linda

Linda Fears, Editor In Chief

4

introduction

We all know that eating right is essential to leading a healthy lifestyle. Wherever we look nowadays there are constant reminders that a well-balanced diet, along with regular exercise, enhances physical and mental well-being. But for many of us the term "eating healthy" implies depriving yourself in some way. At *Family Circle* magazine we do not believe that you should ever be asked to give up your favorite foods. That is why *Healthy Family Dinners* celebrates the joy of eating delicious food—all foods. There's no sacrificing here because we know that enjoying a wonderful meal is one of life's greatest pleasures.

For me personally, cooking healthy, nutritious, delicious dishes has always been a way of life. I learned early from my mom—who was a dietitian and great cook—that the key to creating healthy meals was using flavorful, fresh ingredients (lots of vegetables, good fats, herbs, legumes and lean protein) and the right cooking techniques (for instance, sautéing in minimal amounts of oil, grilling and roasting). I brought that philosophy to the way we approach food here at *Family Circle*.

When I first joined the staff of the magazine a little over 20 years ago the trend toward lighter cooking was just beginning. Back then, it was all about eliminating as much fat as possible from a recipe. But over time we learned that this wasn't as beneficial as we thought it would be as it required substituting sugar for the lost fat. In the end, it didn't help any of our waistlines long-term.

Luckily, our understanding has improved over the years. The latest nutrition research shows us that a diet high in fruits and vegetables, small amounts of animal protein and less processed foods is best, but when you are cooking for a family on a budget—both of time and money—this is easier said than done.

We at *Family Circle* know that the most important thing we can do to help our readers is to provide recipes for quick and nutritious meals that their families will love eating. And number one is making sure the food tastes great. Our recipes will appeal to your entire family, but we wouldn't be surprised if you will want to serve them to company as well. While we've mostly relied on familiar ingredients, we've thrown in a few new ones that we hope will become additions to your pantry.

We know many of our readers lead very busy lives, balancing work, family and extra-curricular activities, so the majority of the recipes are for complete meals (and in many cases one-pot). Sometimes we suggest a side salad or starch—nothing time-consuming or complicated—to round out the dinner. And everything is simple to prepare, has short cooking times and involves minimal cleanup.

Since *Slow Cooker Solutions* is one of our most popular columns, we have devoted an entire chapter to delicious, satisfying meals that can be assembled in the morning and slow-cooked throughout the day. We think you will be surprised by the versatility of the recipe selection, and the dishes we've chosen have year-round appeal. After all, when isn't it a pleasure to be greeted at the end of the day by the satisfying aroma of a fabulous dinner ready to be enjoyed?

You'll also find sprinkled throughout the book tips from our kitchen staff on choosing, preparing and storing ingredients as well as how-to information on basic cooking techniques. There are step-by-step instructions for cutting up a chicken and mincing an onion, and the secrets to perfect sautéing. Along with the tips we have provided important food-related information including buying guidelines for fish, poultry and meat; safety measures for handling raw foods; glossaries for grains, pastas, herbs and greens; and a guide to setting up a pantry.

Most important, the recipes were created using the latest dietary and nutritional science available. Added fats and salts are kept to a minimum without sacrificing the flavor. Dinners were designed to be no more than 500 calories, and to have no more than 18 grams of fat and 800 milligrams of sodium. Fresh fruit is the best choice for dessert but sometimes we crave something special to satisfy a sweet tooth; for those times we've included some of our favorite desserts, each with less than 200 calories and 6 grams of fat per serving.

Healthy Family Dinners is more than a collection of recipes. It is an essential guide to cooking terrific meals that you can feel great about putting on your table. We have taken our years of experience and knowledge about healthy eating and combined it with our culinary know-how. And in so doing, we hope this cookbook will become an invaluable resource for preparing meals your entire family will love.

Regina

Regina Ragone, Food Director

Walk down the produce aisle of your local supermarket and you'll find a dizzying array of salad greens, herbs and vegetables—many of them prewashed and pre-sliced—ready for eating. This is just one reason we love salads—they're the answer to putting together a delicious dinner in no time.

The trick is not to load your healthy meal with unhealthy ingredients or dressings. Go easy on the croutons and high-fat cheeses and dressings. Instead build up your salads with vegetables, beans, whole grains and lean protein—all of which contain nutrients, fiber and protein that will help you feel full longer. Dried fruit, nuts and

main dish salads

crumbled low-fat cheeses are also a good add for a multi-textured, multi-flavored experience—just be sure to limit the amounts.

While we have included recommendations for low-fat dressings, making your own salad dressing is easy, better for you, and tastes fabulous. Our favorite version contains balsamic vinegar, mustard and extra-virgin olive oil—you need some healthy fat to increase absorbtion of important nutrients and to keep you satisfied.

The recipes that follow illustrate the variety of food combinations and flavor profiles you can use to create great-tasting main dish salads that are not only nutritious but fun to eat for the entire family.

Sure to please the entire family, this refreshing salad can be put together in minutes. If you don't have a can of butter beans in your pantry, chickpeas, kidney beans or cannellini beans may be substituted.

lemon-basil arugula & butter bean salad

MAKES 6 servings **PREP** 15 minutes

- 2 packages (5 ounces each) baby arugula
- ¼ pound small mozzarella balls, quartered
- ⅓ cup kalamata olives, halved
- ½ of a small red onion, thinly sliced
- 1 can (15.5 ounces) butter beans, drained and rinsed
- ½ cup fresh basil leaves
- ¼ cup lemon juice
- 2 tablespoons honey
- 1 tablespoon Dijon mustard
- ⅛ teaspoon salt
- ⅛ teaspoon black pepper
- 3 tablespoons extra-virgin olive oil
- ¼ cup French's fried onions

① In a large bowl, combine baby arugula, mozzarella balls, olives, red onion and butter beans.

② In mini chopper or blender, combine basil leaves, lemon juice, honey, mustard, salt and pepper. Pulse until basil is chopped and mixture is well combined. With blender running, add olive oil in a thin stream.

③ Toss dressing with salad; top with fried onions before serving.

PER SERVING 280 calories; 17 g fat (5 g sat.); 10 g protein; 24 g carbohydrate; 4 g fiber; 688 mg sodium; 13 mg cholesterol

A GUIDE TO HERBS

Basil – hints of pepper, cloves, anise and mint. **Uses:** pesto, tomato mozzarella salad, vegetable soup. **Tips:** Use fresh or freeze as pesto. Dried is more pungent.

Chives – mild and delicate, member of the onion family. **Uses:** egg dishes, salads, sauces. **Tips:** Cooking diminishes flavor, best added at end. Makes an elegant garnish; purple flowers are edible.

Cilantro – tangy, grassy scent with a suggestion of citrus. **Uses:** Tex-Mex dishes, chimichurri sauce, Thai curry, Asian soups. **Tips:** Do not rinse or remove roots until ready to use.

Dill – faint anise flavor, fresh smelling, lemony. **Uses:** salmon, boiled potatoes, mayonnaise-based salads. **Tips:** Dried is not very flavorful, so use fresh whenever possible.

Mint – refreshing, cool and sweet. **Uses:** lamb, iced tea, green peas, fruit salad. **Tips:** Generally used raw. Spearmint and peppermint are the most common; can be grown easily.

Oregano – peppery, marigold-like. **Uses:** Italian tomato sauce, pizza, grilled fish, Greek dishes. **Tips:** Can be used in place of marjoram; dried has a stronger flavor than fresh.

Parsley – fresh, green-grassy vegetable taste. **Uses:** boiled potatoes, gremolata, eggs, rice and pasta dishes. **Tips:** Flat leaf (also called Italian) is best for cooking, curly for garnishing. Sprinkle on at the end of cooking for a refreshing finish.

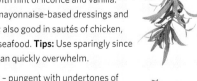

Rosemary – piney, bittersweet, tealike flavor. **Uses:** leg of lamb, roasted potatoes, pork, poultry and bean soups. **Tips:** Be sure to crush needles to release scent before using. Dried is as good as fresh.

Tarragon – bittersweet, warm, peppery scent with hint of licorice and vanilla. **Uses:** mayonnaise-based dressings and sauces; also good in sautés of chicken, fish or seafood. **Tips:** Use sparingly since flavor can quickly overwhelm.

Thyme – pungent with undertones of lemon and mint. **Uses:** soups, poultry stuffing, bean dishes, roasted or braised meats. **Tips:** Add to most herb mixes; flavor stands up to long cooking.

frisée with pears, cheddar & pecans

MAKES 6 servings **PREP** 15 minutes

2 ripe pears

2 tablespoons red wine vinegar

½ teaspoon Dijon mustard

¼ teaspoon salt

¼ teaspoon black pepper

4 tablespoons olive oil

2 large heads frisée, chopped (about 8 cups)

1 head (about ½ pound) radicchio, cored and thinly sliced

1 cup shredded reduced-fat cheddar cheese

¼ cup toasted chopped pecans

① Cut pears in half and core them. Peel 1 pear half, cut into chunks and place in blender with red wine vinegar, mustard, salt and pepper. Puree until smooth. With machine running, slowly pour in olive oil; set aside.

② Cut remaining pear halves into ¼-inch slices and place in a large bowl with frisée, radicchio, cheddar cheese and pecans. Drizzle with dressing and toss gently; serve immediately.

PER SERVING 264 calories; 17 g fat (4 g sat.); 10 g protein; 23 g carbohydrate; 12 g fiber; 378 mg sodium; 13 mg cholesterol

HOW-TO

Easy Toasting To give nuts a richer flavor cook them in a dry nonstick skillet over medium heat, shaking, for 4 to 5 minutes. Or bake at 350°F for 8 to 10 minutes.

panzanella

MAKES 4 servings **PREP** 10 minutes **BAKE** at 400°F for 10 minutes

1 baguette, cut into 1-inch cubes

¼ cup white wine vinegar

2 teaspoons Dijon or spicy brown mustard

½ teaspoon sugar

⅛ teaspoon salt

⅛ teaspoon black pepper

¼ cup olive oil

4 cups packed mixed baby greens

4 ounces tomato-basil cheddar cheese, cut into cubes

½ pound mixed heirloom cherry tomatoes, halved or quartered

① Heat oven to 400°F. Spread bread cubes onto a baking sheet and spritz with nonstick cooking spray. Bake at 400°F for 10 minutes or until lightly toasted. Remove from oven and let cool.

② In a small bowl, whisk together vinegar, mustard, sugar, salt and pepper. While whisking, add olive oil in a thin stream.

③ In a large bowl, toss together bread cubes, greens, cheese and tomatoes. Drizzle with dressing and toss to combine. Serve immediately.

PER SERVING 287 calories; 15 g fat (5 g sat.); 10 g protein; 30 g carbohydrate; 2 g fiber; 475 mg sodium; 20 mg cholesterol

TEST KITCHEN TIP

Perfect Dressing If you take the time to slowly emulsify a dressing, it will cling better. Whisk constantly as you pour the oil in a thin stream.

The addition of raspberry jam to the dressing gives it a slightly sweet-sour flavor that beautifully complements the remaining ingredients.

frisée, figs & prosciutto with walnut vinaigrette

MAKES 4 servings **PREP** 15 minutes

- 1½ tablespoons white wine vinegar
- 2 teaspoons raspberry jam
- 2 teaspoons minced shallot
- ½ teaspoon Dijon mustard
- ⅛ teaspoon salt
- ⅛ teaspoon black pepper
- 2 tablespoons walnut oil
- ½ tablespoon olive oil
- 2 large heads frisée, chopped (about 8 cups)
- ⅔ cup dried figs, cut into ¼-inch pieces
- ¼ cup toasted, chopped walnuts
- 2 ounces prosciutto, torn into long ribbons

① In a small bowl, whisk together vinegar, raspberry jam, shallot, mustard, salt and pepper. Slowly whisk in walnut and olive oils.

② In a large serving bowl, combine frisée, dried figs, walnuts and prosciutto. Toss with prepared dressing.

PER SERVING 328 calories; 16 g fat (2 g sat.); 12 g protein; 42 g carbohydrate; 18 g fiber; 634 mg sodium; 11 mg cholesterol

TEST KITCHEN TIP

Oil Know-How Store olive, nut or seed oils in the fridge to maintain freshness. Cloudiness will disappear at room temp.

If you're a bit skeptical about eating tofu, this salad will make you a fan. To optimize its appeal, we have drizzled it with a dynamite peanut butter sauce, guaranteed to please the kid in all of us.

crispy peanut tofu salad

MAKES 4 servings   **PREP** 15 minutes   **COOK** 12 minutes

- 3   tablespoons chunky peanut butter
- 2   cloves garlic, minced
- 1   tablespoon packed light-brown sugar
- 1   tablespoon rice vinegar
- 2   teaspoons low-sodium soy sauce
- ⅛   teaspoon red pepper flakes
- 1   large head iceberg lettuce, chopped (about 8 cups)
- 1   sweet red pepper, seeded and thinly sliced
- 1   bunch scallions, thinly sliced
- 1   package (14 ounces) firm tofu, drained and cut into 1-inch cubes
- ½   cup cornstarch
- 1   tablespoon vegetable oil

① In a small bowl, blend peanut butter, garlic, **2 tablespoons hot water,** light-brown sugar, rice vinegar, soy sauce and red pepper flakes.

② Place iceberg lettuce in a large bowl and add sweet red pepper and scallions.

③ Pat tofu dry with paper towels. Place cornstarch in a pie plate and coat tofu with cornstarch.

④ Heat oil in a large nonstick skillet over medium-high heat and cook tofu for 10 to 12 minutes, turning often, or until golden brown. Add tofu to bowl; drizzle with dressing.

PER SERVING 302 calories; 14 g fat (1 g sat.); 14 g protein; 31 g carbohydrate; 4 g fiber; 380 mg sodium; 0 mg cholesterol

NUTRITION NOTE

Look for "natural" peanut butter at your local supermarket—it is unprocessed and retains many of the beneficial nutrients found in the skins. Studies show that peanuts and their skins contain many families of antioxidants. According to USDA data, peanut skins are in the top 2% of foods with usable antioxidants. Once opened, store peanut butter in the refrigerator.

spinach niçoise

MAKES 6 servings **PREP** 10 minutes **COOK** 6 minutes

¼ cup olive oil

3 tablespoons red wine vinegar

1 shallot, minced

½ teaspoon Dijon mustard

¼ teaspoon salt

¼ teaspoon black pepper

10 ounces new potatoes, cut
    into ¼-inch-thick slices

12 ounces baby spinach

3 plum tomatoes, cut into
    ½-inch wedges

6 ounces green beans,
    steamed and halved

½ cup chopped black olives

4 cans (5 ounces each)
    albacore tuna in water,
    drained

3 hard-cooked eggs, peeled
    and cut into wedges

① In a small bowl, whisk together olive oil, red wine vinegar, shallot, mustard, salt and pepper.

② Bring a medium-size pot of salted water to a boil. Add potatoes to boiling water for 6 minutes, drain and run under cool water.

③ Place baby spinach in a large bowl with potatoes, tomatoes, green beans, black olives and 3 cans of tuna. Drizzle with dressing; toss well to coat.

④ Place salad mixture on serving platter and crumble 1 remaining can of tuna over top. Add eggs and serve immediately.

PER SERVING 295 calories; 15 g fat (3 g sat.); 23 g protein; 17 g carbohydrate; 5 g fiber; 371 mg sodium; 136 mg cholesterol

WHAT'S IN A NAME?

Olive oil is high in monounsaturated fatty acids, which help lower LDL (bad) cholesterol and raise HDL (good) cholesterol. It also contains antioxidants such as flavonoids and polyphenols that have anti-aging and other disease-fighting properties; polyphenols aid in lowering blood pressure as well. New varieties with added Omega-3s may help maintain a healthy heart. Here's how to decipher the labels:

Extra-Virgin Olive Oil Produced from the first cold pressing of olives that have been picked the same day. Best used for salads and as a condiment. This is the most expensive category and has the most pronounced flavor and fruitiness. Dark green in color.

Pure (Regular) Olive Oil Made with subsequent pressings of olives with some additional filtering and refining. Can be blended with extra-virgin olive oil to boost flavor lost in processing. Less expensive;

good choice for cooking. Golden yellow with green hues.

Light Olive Oil Does not mean light in calories (which is the same for all oils) but light in color, fragrance and flavor; it has been finely filtered. Suited for high-temperature frying due to its higher smoke point. Very pale yellow.

scallop & orange salad

MAKES 4 servings **PREP** 15 minutes **COOK** 13 minutes

2 small oranges

1 tablespoon olive oil

2 teaspoons low-sodium soy sauce

1 teaspoon honey

½ teaspoon salt

½ teaspoon black pepper

⅓ cup chopped walnuts

1 pound sea scallops

1 small red onion, thinly sliced

1 bag (6 ounces) baby spinach

① Grate zest from 1 orange into a small bowl. Cut peel from both oranges and slice flesh into segments; set aside. Squeeze juice from membranes into bowl with zest. Whisk in ½ tablespoon olive oil, soy sauce, honey and ¼ teaspoon *each* salt and pepper.

② Heat a large nonstick skillet over medium-high heat. Toast walnuts for 5 minutes or until fragrant; remove from heat.

③ Heat remaining ½ tablespoon olive oil in skillet over medium-high heat. Season scallops with remaining ¼ teaspoon *each* salt and pepper. Sauté 3 to 4 minutes per side. Remove from skillet; keep warm.

④ Toss orange segments, walnuts, red onion and spinach with dressing. Place 1½ cups salad on each plate and top with scallops.

PER SERVING 256 calories; 10 g fat (1 g sat.); 24 g protein; 19 g carbohydrate; 5 g fiber; 607 mg sodium; 136 mg cholesterol

HOW TO SEGMENT AN ORANGE

1. Cut stem and blossom ends from fruit to expose sections.

2. Slice off peel, following curve of fruit, removing white pith and leaving as much fruit as possible.

3. Holding fruit in your hand, carefully cut out each section, slicing close to membrane.

For simplicity and speed, this recipe calls for frozen popcorn shrimp. If you have fresh or thawed shrimp, eliminate baking shrimp and simply broil or grill it for 3 minutes on each side, or until browned and cooked through.

chinese shrimp salad

MAKES 4 servings **PREP** 10 minutes **BAKE** at 400°F for 13 minutes **BROIL** 3 minutes

- 2 **packages (8 ounces each) frozen popcorn shrimp**
- ½ **cup sliced almonds**
- ½ **head napa cabbage (about ¾ pound), cored and shredded**
- ½ **head green cabbage (about ¾ pound), cored and shredded**
- ⅓ **cup miso-sesame dressing (such as Masa's) or any low-calorie Asian dressing**
- ½ **cup crispy chow mein noodles**

① Heat oven to 400°F. Spread frozen popcorn shrimp on a large baking sheet; spread sliced almonds on medium-size sheet. Bake shrimp at 400°F for 13 minutes; bake almonds at 400°F for 3 minutes. Increase heat to broil. Broil shrimp 3 minutes or until browned and crispy.

② Meanwhile, in a large bowl, toss together napa cabbage, green cabbage, toasted almonds and miso-sesame dressing. Stir in hot shrimp, top with chow mein noodles and serve immediately.

PER SERVING 412 calories; 14 g fat (2 g sat.); 25 g protein; 48 g carbohydrate; 7 g fiber; 758 mg sodium; 91 mg cholesterol

TEST KITCHEN TIP

Napa Cabbage Also called Chinese cabbage, this crinkly, white-and-pale-green head has a mild, crunchy texture.

shrimp salad with scallion dressing

MAKES 6 servings **PREP** 10 minutes **REFRIGERATE** 1 hour **COOK** 6 minutes

Scallion Dressing:

- 4 scallions, trimmed and sliced
- 3 tablespoons fat-free low-sodium chicken broth
- 2 tablespoons olive oil
- 2 tablespoons white wine vinegar
- 1 tablespoon honey
- ¼ teaspoon salt
- ¼ teaspoon ground cumin
- ⅛ teaspoon black pepper

Marinade:

- 1 tablespoon lemon zest
- 2 cloves garlic, minced
- 2 teaspoons olive oil
- ½ teaspoon black pepper

Salad:

- 1½ pounds large shrimp, peeled and deveined
- ½ teaspoon salt
- 4 cups mixed baby salad greens
- 1 cup grape tomatoes, halved
- 1 large seedless cucumber, sliced

① Scallion Dressing: In a blender, combine scallions, broth, olive oil, vinegar, honey, salt, cumin and pepper and process until smooth, set aside.

② Marinade: In a resealable plastic food-storage bag, combine lemon zest, garlic, olive oil and pepper. Add shrimp and toss to coat evenly. Seal and refrigerate 1 hour.

③ Salad: Remove shrimp from marinade. Coat a large nonstick skillet with nonstick cooking spray. Add shrimp and cook over medium-high heat for 6 minutes or until cooked through, turning occasionally. Sprinkle with salt.

④ Arrange greens, tomatoes and cucumber on a large platter and toss with 3 tablespoons of Scallion Dressing. Top with shrimp. Drizzle with more dressing and serve.

PER SERVING 207 calories; 8 g fat (1 g sat.); 24 g protein; 9 g carbohydrate; 2 g fiber; 482 mg sodium; 172 mg cholesterol

Roasting foods concentrates their flavors, but it takes a little more time. To get dinner on the table faster, we call for grilling the shrimp while the vegetables roast. You can also grill the vegetables—about 15 minutes—and add the shrimp during the last 4 minutes of cooking time.

roasted vegetable & shrimp salad

MAKES 6 servings **PREP** 20 minutes **REFRIGERATE** 15 minutes **ROAST** at 450°F for 30 minutes **GRILL/BROIL** 4 minutes

2   large zucchini, cut into ½-inch slices on the diagonal

2   summer squash, cut into ½-inch slices on the diagonal

6   carrots, peeled and cut into ½-inch slices on the diagonal

2   sweet red peppers, cored, seeds removed and cut into ½-inch slices

10   tablespoons reduced-fat Italian dressing

½   teaspoon black pepper

¼   teaspoon salt

1½   pounds medium-size shrimp, peeled and deveined

6   cups watercress

3   ounces reduced-fat feta cheese, crumbled

① Heat oven to 450°F. Spray two 15 x 11-inch baking pans with nonstick cooking spray.

② Place zucchini, squash, carrots and red peppers in a large bowl. Toss with 2 tablespoons of dressing. Spoon vegetables evenly into prepared baking pans and season with pepper and salt. Roast at 450°F for 30 minutes, turning once after 15 minutes.

③ While vegetables are roasting, place shrimp in a resealable plastic food-storage bag with 2 tablespoons of dressing. Shake to coat. Marinate in refrigerator 15 minutes.

④ Grill or broil shrimp for 2 minutes per side. Set aside.

⑤ Evenly distribute watercress between 6 large salad plates and top with roasted vegetables. Drizzle each with 1 tablespoon of remaining dressing. Scatter cooked shrimp and feta over each salad. Serve immediately.

PER SERVING 214 calories; 5 g fat (2 g sat.); 22 g protein; 21 g carbohydrate; 6 g fiber; 762 mg sodium; 144 mg cholesterol

cobb salad

MAKES 4 servings **PREP** 10 minutes **COOK** 18 minutes

1 pound boneless, skinless chicken breasts

8 cups mixed salad greens

1 tomato (8 ounces), cut into ½-inch pieces

¼ cup light red wine vinaigrette

3 slices cooked bacon, crumbled

¼ cup crumbled blue cheese

3 hard-cooked eggs, peeled and chopped

① Heat a large pot of water to simmering. Add chicken, cover, and cook 18 minutes or until cooked through. Cool and cut into ½-inch cubes.

② Place chicken, greens and tomato in a large serving bowl and pour vinaigrette over top; toss to combine. Sprinkle each serving with equal amounts bacon, blue cheese and eggs.

PER SERVING 199 calories; 8 g fat (3 g sat.); 24 g protein; 7 g carbohydrate; 3 g fiber; 374 mg sodium; 160 mg cholesterol

TEST KITCHEN TIP

Dress for Success Making your own healthy salad dressing is a cinch to do, can save you a ton of money, and the taste is fantastic. The usual proportions are 3 parts oil to 1 part vinegar, but here's a lighter formula. Whisk together ½ cup balsamic vinegar, 2 tablespoons Dijon honey mustard and ¼ teaspoon *each* salt and black pepper; slowly add ½ cup extra-virgin olive oil, whisking continuously. Drizzle salad with about a tablespoon, which has 70 calories and 7 grams of fat, less than many store-bought brands. Store in a jar in fridge and shake before each use.

buffalo chicken salad

MAKES 4 servings **PREP** 15 minutes **COOK** 8 minutes

1 pound chicken breast tenders

3 tablespoons hot sauce (such as Frank's)

½ cup crumbled blue cheese

3 tablespoons reduced-fat sour cream

3 tablespoons 2% milk

3 tablespoons light mayonnaise

1 romaine heart, chopped

½ head iceberg lettuce, chopped

2 stalks celery, cut into ¼ x 2-inch matchsticks

1 cup shredded carrots

① Coat large nonstick skillet with nonstick cooking spray. Cook chicken breast tenders in skillet over medium heat about 8 minutes, flipping halfway, or until cooked through. Remove from heat and coat with hot sauce.

② In a small bowl, stir together blue cheese, sour cream, milk and mayonnaise.

③ In a large serving bowl, combine romaine and iceberg lettuces and add celery and carrots. Drizzle dressing over salad. Toss well to combine. Top with chicken.

PER SERVING 284 calories; 12 g fat (5 g sat.); 33 g protein; 11 g carbohydrate; 3 g fiber; 497 mg sodium; 89 mg cholesterol

NUTRITION NOTE

Light mayonnaise not only has half the calories and fat of real mayonnaise, it is naturally rich in Omega-3s.

mexican chicken salad

MAKES 12 servings **PREP** 15 minutes **REFRIGERATE** 1 hour **GRILL** 6 minutes

6 tablespoons extra-virgin olive oil

¼ cup lime juice

¼ cup chopped cilantro

2 cloves garlic, minced

1 shallot, minced

¾ teaspoon sugar

½ teaspoon cumin

1 pound thinly sliced chicken breast cutlets

3 hearts of romaine, chopped (about 10 cups)

3 plum tomatoes, seeded and cut into ¼-inch pieces

1 can (15.5 ounces) black beans, rinsed and drained

1 cup shredded Pepper Jack cheese

1 cup frozen corn, thawed

① In a small bowl, whisk together olive oil, lime juice, cilantro, garlic, shallot, sugar and cumin. Place 4 tablespoons in a large resealable plastic food-storage bag; set remaining dressing aside. Add chicken to bag; seal and squeeze to coat chicken. Refrigerate at least 1 hour.

② In a very large serving bowl, combine romaine, tomatoes, black beans, cheese and corn.

③ Heat grill to medium-high and grill chicken 3 to 4 minutes per side or until done; discard marinade. Chop chicken into 1-inch pieces and add to serving bowl. Drizzle with remaining dressing and toss well to combine.

PER SERVING 193 calories; 11 g fat (3 g sat.); 14 g protein; 10 g carbohydrate; 3 g fiber; 206 mg sodium; 30 mg cholesterol

HOW-TO

Making the Cut If you can't find extra-thin cutlets, it's no problem to make them yourself. Firmly press top of boneless skinless chicken breast, and, keeping blade of chef's knife parallel to cutting board, slice gently through center of chicken.

frisée with bacon & poached egg

MAKES 6 servings **PREP** 10 minutes **COOK** 11 minutes

1 tablespoon white wine vinegar

¾ teaspoon Dijon mustard

½ teaspoon light mayonnaise

⅛ teaspoon salt

⅛ teaspoon black pepper

3 tablespoons extra-virgin olive oil

4 slices turkey bacon

2 large heads frisée, chopped (about 8 cups)

5 ounces thinly sliced radishes (about 12)

6 eggs

① In a small bowl, whisk together white wine vinegar, Dijon mustard, light mayonnaise, salt and pepper. Slowly whisk in extra-virgin olive oil.

② Cut turkey bacon crosswise into ½-inch pieces and cook in a large nonstick skillet over medium-high heat for 7 minutes or until crispy; drain on a paper-towel-lined plate.

③ In a large serving bowl, combine chopped frisée, radishes and bacon. Drizzle with dressing and toss to coat. Divide salad among plates.

④ Bring a large skillet three-quarters full of water to a simmer. Crack eggs into separate measuring cups and pour separately into water; cook for 4 minutes. Remove eggs with a slotted spoon and place on top of individual servings.

PER SERVING 224 calories; 15 g fat (4 g sat.); 12 g protein; 10 g fiber; 13 g carbohydrate; 410 mg sodium; 224 mg cholesterol

TEST KITCHEN TIP

Storing Eggs Those indentations in your fridge aren't the best place to store eggs—the temperature there varies too much because of the opening and closing of the door. Leave them in their original container and keep on a shelf. This way you also have a record of the "best by" date. To test freshness, place eggs in a bowl of water. If they float, toss.

turkey waldorf salad

MAKES 6 servings **PREP** 10 minutes **REFRIGERATE** 1 hour

¾ cup low-fat ranch salad dressing

3 tablespoons cider vinegar

2 tablespoons sugar

¼ teaspoon black pepper

1 bag (16 ounces) coleslaw mix

1 bag (10 ounces) shredded carrots

1 package (9 ounces) precooked carved turkey pieces (such as Perdue Short Cuts), cut into ½-inch chunks

1 Fuji apple, cored and cut into ½-inch chunks

¾ cup chopped walnuts

① In a small bowl, stir together ranch dressing, vinegar, sugar and pepper; set aside.

② In a large bowl, combine coleslaw mix, carrots, turkey, apple and walnuts. Drizzle salad dressing mixture over top and toss well to combine. Refrigerate at least 1 hour before serving.

PER SERVING 268 calories; 14 g fat (2 g sat.), 15 g protein; 24 g carbohydrate; 5 g fiber; 615 mg sodium; 38 mg cholesterol

SWITCH IT UP

Substitute cooked chicken or ham for turkey.

steak salad

MAKES 6 servings **PREP** 10 minutes **GRILL** 12 minutes **LET REST** 5 minutes

1½ **pounds flank steak**

1 **teaspoon Italian seasoning**

½ **teaspoon garlic powder**

½ **teaspoon salt**

¼ **teaspoon black pepper**

Pinch cayenne pepper

2 **teaspoons olive oil**

1½ **packages (5 ounces each) baby arugula**

½ **pound bing cherries, pitted, or 2 cups strawberries, hulled and halved**

½ **cup crumbled blue cheese**

½ **cup low-fat blue cheese dressing (such as Bolthouse)**

① Heat grill or broiler. Spread flank steak on a cutting board.

② In a small bowl, combine Italian seasoning, garlic powder, salt, pepper and cayenne. Coat steak with olive oil and then rub spice mixture into steak.

③ Grill or broil for 6 minutes per side, turning once, for a total of 12 minutes. Transfer to a clean board and let rest 5 minutes.

④ Meanwhile, in a large bowl, combine arugula, cherries and blue cheese. Toss gently with blue cheese dressing. Slice steak against grain (starting on a small side), into thin slices. Toss with salad mixture. Serve immediately.

PER SERVING 288 calories; 15 g fat (6 g sat.); 29 g protein; 9 g carbohydrate; 1 g fiber; 503 mg sodium; 46 mg cholesterol

TEST KITCHEN TIP

If you don't have a jar of Italian seasoning on hand, make your own. Add a pinch *each* of oregano, basil, thyme, marjoram and crushed rosemary or any combination of the same.

A snap to prepare, this salad is equally good with leftover Thanksgiving turkey, cooked chicken or baked ham.

romaine with turkey & dried cranberries

MAKES 4 servings **PREP** 15 minutes

¼ cup whole-berry cranberry sauce

2 tablespoons light mayonnaise

1½ tablespoons red wine vinegar

2 teaspoons Dijon mustard

2 hearts romaine lettuce, chopped (about 8 cups)

8 ounces sliced smoked turkey, cut into strips

½ cup toasted pecans

½ cup dried cranberries

① In a small bowl, blend cranberry sauce, mayonnaise, vinegar and mustard.

② In a serving bowl, combine romaine, smoked turkey, pecans and dried cranberries. Drizzle with dressing and serve.

PER SERVING 293 calories; 16 g fat (2 g sat.); 13 g protein; 28 g carbohydrate; 5 g fiber; 683 mg sodium; 28 mg cholesterol

TEST KITCHEN TIP

To keep lettuce fresher longer, wrap a paper towel around the root end to absorb water, and store in a resealable plastic food-storage bag.

A GUIDE TO GREENS

The best salad includes a combination of flavors—mix up crunchy and tender and toss in a bit of bite.

CRUNCHY:

Iceberg Pair a wedge of this crisp option with strong-tasting dressings.

Romaine (*left*) Toss inner leaves with Caesar, but also miso or sesame-soy.

TENDER:

Green leaf Line plates with individual leaves, top with tuna or other salads.

Boston (*right*) Try a sharp berry-based vinaigrette for a contrasting flavor.

Bibb Be sure to include a tangy green with this buttery-textured variety.

Mâche Serve with a sampling of fresh herbs or a cream dressing.

Frisée (*right*) Serve as a bed for warm ingredients, such as Frisée with Bacon and Poached Egg (*page 31*).

PEPPERY:

Arugula (*right*) Let the smaller, bright-green leaves serve as a bed for grilled meats.

BITTER:

Green chicory Add to any mixture for a sharp bite or braise in olive oil.

COLORFUL:

Red leaf Use on a sandwich or to give a hit of bronze to bland combos.

vietnamese pork salad

MAKES 6 servings **PREP** 15 minutes **REFRIGERATE** 20 minutes **SOAK** 8 minutes **GRILL** 6 minutes

2 boneless, center-cut pork chops (about 1 pound)

⅓ cup rice vinegar

¼ cup mirin

2½ tablespoons fish sauce

1½ tablespoons olive oil

1½ tablespoons sugar

½ teaspoon Thai chili-garlic sauce (such as Sriracha)

3 ounces (from an 8-ounce package) rice vermicelli noodles

½ head napa cabbage, cored and sliced

½ cup cilantro leaves

½ cup mint leaves

2 scallions, sliced

① Slice pork chops in half horizontally to form 4 thin-cut chops. Pound to even thinness. In a small bowl, mix together rice vinegar, mirin, fish sauce, olive oil, sugar and Thai chili garlic sauce. In a resealable plastic food-storage bag, combine ¼ cup dressing with pork. Refrigerate 20 minutes.

② Following package directions, soak rice vermicelli noodles for 8 minutes. Drain and rinse.

③ Heat grill pan. Grill pork for 3 minutes, then flip and grill an additional 2 to 3 minutes. Remove to a cutting board and cut into thin strips.

④ In a large serving bowl, combine cabbage, cilantro leaves, mint leaves and scallions with noodles. Toss with remaining dressing and top with pork.

PER SERVING 226 calories; 5 g fat (1 g sat.); 20 g protein; 20 g carbohydrate; 2 g fiber; 730 mg sodium; 42 mg cholesterol

At the end of a long work or school day, what could be more satisfying than a bowl of mac 'n' cheese or plate of spaghetti and meatballs? For almost everyone, pasta is pure comfort food.

But ignore the carbophobes—pasta can truly be good for you. It provides the body with glucose—essential for energy—and can be a good source of fiber. Just control portion sizes (1/2 cup of cooked pasta is the recommended amount, about the size of a tennis ball) and add lean protein and vegetables.

pasta

Whenever possible, you should choose whole-grain varieties. They are nutrient-dense and fiber-rich, unlike the stripped-down version. And think beyond the spaghetti noodle—a wide range of shapes (bucatini, rigatoni, penne, rotini, farfalle, cellentani, orzo, etc.) are readily available. Take it even further and check out the Soba Noodles with Spicy Veggie Stir-Fry (page 52); the Japanese buckwheat pasta adds another flavor dimension to jazz up your dishes.

Tortellini and other filled pastas can transform a simple quick weeknight soup into something special. This one-pot meal lends itself to countless variations. If you're not a fan of spinach, add one or two of your favorite vegetables in its place.

tortellini soup

MAKES 4 servings **PREP** 15 minutes **COOK** 9 minutes

3   cups vegetable broth

½   teaspoon dried Italian seasoning

1   package (9 ounces) cheese-filled spinach tortellini

3   large carrots, peeled and sliced into thin coins

3   ribs celery, thinly sliced

¾   pound ripe plum tomatoes (about 4), seeded and chopped

1   bag (6 ounces) baby spinach

Grated Parmesan cheese (optional)

① In a large pot, bring broth, **3 cups water** and Italian seasoning to a boil. Add tortellini and simmer for 3 minutes. Add carrots and celery and simmer for an additional 4 minutes. Stir in tomatoes and spinach and simmer for 2 more minutes or until vegetables are tender and spinach is wilted.

② Ladle soup into bowls and serve with Parmesan cheese, if desired.

PER SERVING 272 calories; 6 g fat (3 g sat.); 12 g protein; 45 g carbohydrate; 7 g fiber; 741 mg sodium; 28 mg cholesterol

SWITCH IT UP

Substitute ravioletti for tortellini and chicken broth for vegetable broth, too.

penne with escarole, caramelized onions & chickpeas

MAKES 4 servings **PREP** 10 minutes **COOK** 34 minutes

2 tablespoons olive oil

1 large sweet onion (such as Vidalia; about 1 pound), thinly sliced

1 large bunch escarole (about 1½ pounds), washed and torn into pieces

¼ cup golden raisins

¼ teaspoon salt

½ pound (2⅓ cups uncooked) multigrain penne pasta (such as Barilla Plus)

1 can (15.5 ounces) chickpeas, undrained

Grated Parmesan cheese (optional)

① Heat oil in a 12-inch skillet over medium heat. Add onion and cook, stirring often, for 15 to 25 minutes or until golden. Lower heat if onion is browning too quickly.

② Add escarole and raisins to skillet. Cook, stirring occasionally, for about 6 minutes, until leaves are tender and stem ends are still crunchy. Sprinkle with salt.

③ Meanwhile, bring a large pot of salted water to a boil. Cook penne according to package directions, about 11 minutes. Drain, reserving ½ cup pasta water, and return pasta to pot.

④ Stir chickpeas into skillet with their liquid. Simmer, stirring occasionally, for 3 minutes or until heated through. Serve over pasta, adding reserved pasta water if needed to thin sauce. Sprinkle with grated cheese, if desired.

PER SERVING 487 calories; 10 g fat (1 g sat.); 19 g protein; 83 g carbohydrate; 16 g fiber; 540 mg sodium; 0 mg cholesterol

NUTRITION NOTE

Chickpeas are a good source of cholesterol-lowering fiber. When combined with whole grains such as multigrain pasta, chickpeas provide virtually fat-free, high-quality protein.

rigatoni alla siciliana

MAKES 6 servings **PREP** 10 minutes **COOK** 22 minutes

1	eggplant (about 1½ pounds)	1½	teaspoons dried oregano
3	cloves garlic, sliced	¾	teaspoon salt
3	tablespoons olive oil	¼	teaspoon red pepper flakes
1	can (28 ounces) fire roasted whole tomatoes (such as Muir Glen), or plain whole tomatoes	1	pound mini rigatoni pasta
		1	cup smoked mozzarella cheese or part-skim mozzarella cheese, shredded

① Trim eggplant and cut into ½-inch pieces. In a large skillet, cook eggplant and garlic in oil for 7 minutes over medium-high heat, stirring occasionally.

② Stir in tomatoes and break up with a wooden spoon. Add oregano, salt and red pepper flakes. Simmer for 15 minutes, stirring occasionally.

③ While sauce is simmering, cook pasta following package directions. Drain, reserving 1 cup of cooking water.

④ Toss drained pasta with sauce. Add reserved pasta water, in ¼ cup increments, until desired consistency.

⑤ Stir in mozzarella cheese and allow to melt slightly, then serve.

PER SERVING 451 calories; 13 g fat (3 g sat.), 16 g protein; 68 g carbohydrate; 6 g fiber; 706 mg sodium; 15 mg cholesterol

TEST KITCHEN TIP

Eggplant Look for firm, shiny fruit (yes, it's actually a berry) that's heavy for its size. The top should be green, not dried out. Store at room temperature or wrap loosely and place in a crisper drawer of your fridge for several days.

Packaged sauces, such as the pesto in this recipe, are a busy cook's best friend. A small amount of cream adds a silkiness to the dish. If you are on a restrictive diet, however, eliminate the cream and substitute ¼ cup pasta cooking liquid.

bow ties & veggies with pesto

MAKES 6 servings **PREP** 15 minutes **COOK** 8 minutes

12 ounces farfalle (bow tie) pasta

1 tablespoon extra-virgin olive oil

½ pound fresh green beans or asparagus, trimmed and cut into 2-inch pieces

1 yellow pepper, seeded and diced

1 small zucchini, trimmed, halved lengthwise and cut into ¼-inch half-moons

2 cloves garlic, sliced

½ cup purchased pesto

¼ cup heavy cream

1 cup grape tomatoes, halved

½ teaspoon salt

① Bring a large pot of salted water to a boil. Add pasta and cook following package directions for 8 minutes. Drain.

② Meanwhile, heat oil in a very large nonstick skillet over medium to medium-high heat. Add green beans and yellow pepper; cook for 5 minutes. Add zucchini and garlic. Cook for 2 minutes. Stir in pesto and cream; cook for 1 minute. Stir in tomatoes and salt. Remove from heat.

③ Add cooked bow ties to sauce; toss well to combine. Divide into bowls; serve.

PER SERVING 397 calories; 18 g fat (5 g sat.); 12 g protein; 50 g carbohydrate; 4 g fiber; 372 mg sodium; 19 mg cholesterol

TEST KITCHEN TIP

Green beans are a good source of folic acid and vitamins A and C. Buy pencil-thin beans that are crisp and snap easily; they should have a fresh, vivid color. Do not wash until ready to use; place in a plastic bag in the refrigerator for up to 1 week.

pasta primavera

MAKES 6 servings **PREP** 20 minutes **COOK** 16 minutes

½ **pound asparagus, trimmed and cut into 1-inch pieces**

½ **pound green beans, trimmed and cut into 1-inch pieces**

2 **sweet orange, red or yellow peppers, cored, seeded and cut into ¼-inch strips**

1 **pound spaghetti**

¾ **cup half-and-half**

¾ **cup chicken broth**

¾ **teaspoon salt**

¼ **teaspoon black pepper**

¼ **teaspoon ground nutmeg**

2 **tablespoons olive oil**

5 **cloves garlic, sliced**

2 **cups grape tomatoes, halved**

⅓ **cup grated Parmesan cheese**

¼ **cup flat-leaf parsley, chopped**

Shaved Parmesan cheese (optional)

① Bring a large pot of salted water to a boil. Add asparagus and green beans; cook 4 minutes. Add peppers and cook 1 more minute. Scoop out vegetables with a large slotted spoon and place in a colander. Rinse under cold water.

② Add pasta to boiling water and cook following package directions, about 9 minutes. Drain; return to pot.

③ While pasta is cooking, place half-and-half, chicken broth, salt, pepper and nutmeg in a small saucepan. Bring to a simmer over medium heat.

④ Heat a large nonstick skillet over medium-high heat. Add olive oil and garlic and cook 30 seconds. Add cooked veggies and tomatoes. Cook, stirring a few times, about 1 minute, 30 seconds. Spoon into pasta pot. Stir grated cheese into half-and-half mixture. Add to pasta and gently stir in parsley until all ingredients are combined. Allow to stand for 5 minutes. Shave Parmesan cheese on top, if desired.

PER SERVING 425 calories; 11 g fat (5 g sat.), 17 g protein; 67 g carbohydrate; 6 g fiber; 447 mg sodium; 18 mg cholesterol

TEST KITCHEN TIP

Pepper Power Raw, sautéed or roasted, peppers add color and vitamins to any dish. Select peppers that are smooth, shiny and firm, without any soft spots or bruises. Refrigerate for up to 5 days.

cheesy meximac

MAKES 10 servings **PREP** 10 minutes **COOK** 11 minutes **BAKE** at 350°F for 25 minutes

1 box (16 ounces) rotini pasta

2 scallions, trimmed and sliced

½ sweet red pepper, cored and diced

½ green bell pepper, cored and diced

1 tablespoon unsalted butter

1 tablespoon all-purpose flour

1½ cups milk

¼ teaspoon salt

⅛ teaspoon black pepper

16 ounces Pepper Jack cheese, shredded

1 can (10 ounces) Mexican-flavored corn, drained

Pinch chili powder

① Heat oven to 350°F. Coat an 11 x 7 x 2-inch baking dish with nonstick cooking spray. Bring a large pot of lightly salted water to a boil. Add rotini and cook 5 minutes.

Add scallions and both peppers and cook an additional 2 minutes. Drain and set aside.

② In a medium-size saucepan, melt butter over medium heat. Whisk in flour until smooth. Gradually add milk, whisking constantly, until smooth. Stir in salt and pepper; bring to a simmer. Cook, simmering, 4 minutes. Remove from heat.

③ Add half of shredded cheese to milk mixture; whisk until smooth. Stir in corn, then combine in a large bowl with pasta, scallions and peppers. Pour half into prepared dish; top with half of remaining cheese. Repeat, ending with cheese. Sprinkle top with chili powder.

④ Bake at 350°F for 25 minutes. Cool slightly before serving.

PER SERVING 401 calories; 17 g fat (10 g sat.); 18 g protein; 43 g carbohydrate; 2 g fiber; 507 mg sodium; 55 mg cholesterol

NUTRITION NOTE

Find a way to work vegetables into every meal. Stir chopped peppers and onions or spinach into eggs for a veggie omelet. Slip sliced cucumbers into sandwiches. Set out baby carrots, cherry tomatoes and pepper strips with dip for snacking.

Although lower in fat and calories than the classic, this mac and cheese tastes decadently good. It's also a great way to sneak vegetables into a family favorite. If the kids don't like broccoli, substitute peas, carrots or their favorite vegetable.

reduced-fat mac

MAKES 6 servings   **PREP** 5 minutes   **COOK** 10 minutes

1   box (13.25 ounces) whole-grain penne pasta

4   cups broccoli florets (about 2 stalks)

1   cup fat-free milk

1   tablespoon all-purpose flour

1   teaspoon Dijon mustard

½   teaspoon salt

¼   teaspoon black pepper

    Pinch cayenne pepper

8   ounces 2% sharp cheddar cheese, grated (2 cups)

① Bring a large pot of salted water to a boil. Add pasta and cook 6 minutes. Add broccoli and cook an additional 4 minutes. Drain.

② Meanwhile, in a small saucepan, whisk milk and flour together. Bring to a simmer over medium heat; simmer 3 minutes until thickened. Remove from heat and whisk in mustard, salt, pepper and cayenne.

③ Add grated cheddar cheese to saucepan, whisking constantly until melted. Transfer pasta and broccoli to serving bowl. Pour cheese sauce over pasta-broccoli mixture and stir until coated.

PER SERVING 294 calories; 8 g fat (4 g sat.); 18 g protein; 37 g carbohydrate; 4 g fiber; 449 mg sodium; 21 mg cholesterol

HOW-TO

Cut Broccoli into Florets With a sharp knife cut off head of broccoli so that large individual florets fall away as you cut. Cut each large floret in half and cut each half into quarters.

rotini with eggplant, tomato & fresh basil sauce

MAKES 6 servings **PREP** 20 minutes **COOK** 18 minutes

- 3 tablespoons olive oil
- 1½ pounds eggplant, ends trimmed and cut into ½-inch cubes
- 1 medium-size onion, halved and thinly sliced
- 3 cloves garlic, chopped
- 1 teaspoon salt
- ½ teaspoon red pepper flakes
- 1 can (28 ounces) diced tomatoes in juice
- 1 pound rotini pasta
- 1 cup packed basil, torn into pieces
- 1 tablespoon fresh oregano, chopped
- 3 tablespoons snipped chives
- 6 tablespoons part-skim ricotta cheese

① Heat oil in a large skillet over medium-high heat. Add eggplant, onion, garlic and ½ teaspoon of salt. Cook 8 minutes, stirring occasionally, until eggplant softens.

② Add red pepper flakes, tomatoes with juice and remaining ½ teaspoon salt. Bring to a simmer. Lower heat to medium-low; cook for 10 minutes or until eggplant is very soft.

③ While sauce is simmering, cook pasta following package directions. Drain.

④ Stir most of basil, oregano and chives into sauce; toss with pasta. Serve with dollops of ricotta cheese and reserved herbs on top.

PER SERVING 398 calories; 9 g fat (2 g sat.); 13 g protein; 67 g carbohydrate; 8 g fiber; 581 mg sodium; 5 mg cholesterol

TEST KITCHEN TIP

Local Time

When food isn't flown or trucked thousands of miles, it's almost always fresher, tastier and more nutritious—and less of a drain on the environment.

Localharvest.org

Enter your zip code to see nearby farmers' markets, grocery stores and restaurants that sell local and sustainable fare.

Sustainabletable.org

Read up on why you should eat food grown in your area and check out the blog for easy tips and tricks for getting started.

fingerling potato & green bean pasta

MAKES 6 servings **PREP** 15 minutes **COOK** 29 minutes

¾ **pound fingerling potatoes (or small white potatoes)**

1 **pound spaghetti**

¾ **pound green beans, trimmed and cut into 1-inch pieces**

⅔ **cup prepared basil pesto**

½ **cup grated Parmesan cheese (optional)**

① Place potatoes in a large pot of lightly salted water. Bring to a boil. Reduce heat and simmer for 15 to 20 minutes or until just tender. With a slotted spoon, remove potatoes and keep warm.

② Into simmering water, add spaghetti and boil for 4 minutes. Add green beans and cook for an additional 5 minutes or until tender. Drain, reserving 1 cup of cooking liquid.

③ Return spaghetti and green beans to pot. Cut cooked potatoes into bite-size pieces and add to pot. Stir in pesto and about ¾ cup of reserved cooking liquid. Add more cooking liquid if necessary to evenly coat all pasta.

④ Serve immediately with grated Parmesan cheese, if desired.

PER SERVING 500 calories; 16 g fat (4 g sat.); 18 g protein; 73 g carbohydrate; 6 g fiber; 361 mg sodium; 15 mg cholesterol

TEST KITCHEN TIP

This Spud's for You At only 1 to 3 inches long, what fingerling potatoes lack in size, they make up for in flavor. Better still, they're versatile and packed with fiber and vitamin C. Choose from these varieties: Russian Banana, French Fingerling, Purple Peruvian or Ruby Crescent.

soba noodles with spicy veggie stir-fry

MAKES 4 servings **PREP** 10 minutes **COOK** 29 minutes

- 3 tablespoons low-sodium soy sauce
- 2 tablespoons light-brown sugar
- 1½ teaspoons Thai chili-garlic sauce (such as Sriracha)
- 1 tablespoon grated fresh ginger
- ½ cup cornstarch
- 1 block (14 ounces) firm tofu, drained and cut into 1-inch cubes
- 1 tablespoon vegetable oil
- 2 large sweet red peppers, seeded and chopped
- 1 cup baby carrots, cut diagonally into thirds
- 4 ounces snow peas, trimmed and halved diagonally
- 6 cups fresh spinach, stems removed
- 8 ounces soba noodles, prepared according to package directions

① In a small bowl, blend soy sauce, sugar, chili-garlic sauce, ginger and 1 tablespoon of cornstarch.

② Pat tofu dry. Place remaining 7 tablespoons cornstarch in a pie plate; coat tofu on all sides.

③ Heat oil in a large nonstick skillet over medium-high heat. Add tofu to skillet in 2 batches; cook each 10 minutes or until lightly browned. Remove from skillet.

④ Add red pepper, carrots, snow peas and **3 tablespoons water** to skillet and cover; cook 6 minutes or until tender. Add spinach; cover. Cook 1 minute. Stir in soy sauce mixture; cook 2 minutes or until thickened. Stir in tofu; serve with noodles.

PER SERVING 482 calories; 9 g fat (0 g sat.); 20 g protein; 81 g carbohydrate; 8 g fiber; 404 mg sodium; 0 mg cholesterol

BEYOND SPAGHETTI

Start with soba noodles or rice sticks for a fast, totally different dinner and introduce your family to a whole new world of flavors.

Rice Noodles Made from a dough of rice flour and water; available in a variety of shapes. Soak in hot water for about 10 minutes before stir-frying. Substitute: fettuccine.

Cellophane Noodles The same bean that's sold as sprouts is ground and turned into fine white noodles that are used in stir-fries, soups or salads. Substitute: angel hair or vermicelli.

Rice Sticks Another name for rice noodles; the thin variety is common in soups and salads. Soak in hot water before using, unless deep-frying. Substitute: capellini or vermicelli.

Chinese Noodles Made with wheat flour; available in varying thicknesses and shapes. Boil until tender, then add to stir-fries or soups. Substitute: fettuccine or spaghetti.

Soba Noodles These Japanese noodles have a nutty taste from buckwheat flour; often served cold. Boil 3 minutes, stirring to keep from sticking. Substitute: whole-wheat spaghetti.

Lo Mein Noodles A popular shape of Chinese wheat noodles; flat and wide, they are cooked, then stir-fried with other ingredients. Substitute: linguine.

linguine with clam sauce

MAKES 8 servings **PREP** 10 minutes **COOK** 14 minutes

1 pound linguine

1 tablespoon olive oil

1 medium-size onion, chopped

3 cloves garlic, chopped

3 cans (6.5 ounces each) chopped clams

1 tablespoon dried parsley

½ teaspoon dried oregano

½ teaspoon dried basil

¼ teaspoon red pepper flakes

¼ teaspoon salt

⅛ teaspoon black pepper

¼ cup plain bread crumbs

① Bring a large pot of salted water to a boil, add linguine and cook 11 minutes. Drain and return to pot.

② Meanwhile, heat ½ tablespoon oil in a 10-inch nonstick skillet over medium heat. Add onion and garlic; sauté 5 minutes.

③ Strain liquid from clams and add liquid to skillet, reserving clams. Add parsley, oregano, basil, pepper flakes, salt and pepper to pan. Simmer 5 minutes then stir in clams; cook 2 minutes. Stir into pasta pot; toss to mix. Cover to keep warm.

④ Heat remaining ½ tablespoon oil in a small skillet over medium-high heat and add bread crumbs. Cook, stirring, for 2 minutes or until lightly browned. Sprinkle over pasta and gently toss. Serve immediately.

PER SERVING 361 calories; 4 g fat (1 g sat.); 18 g protein; 65 g carbohydrate; 3 g fiber; 739 mg sodium; 17 mg cholesterol

SUPPER SOLUTIONS

No last-minute shopping on the way home. Everything you need for dinner is right in your kitchen. Turn basics like potatoes, pasta and beans into meals that taste anything but ordinary. The trick is to keep surprising go-to items like canned clams, jarred roasted red peppers, dried mushrooms and chiles on hand.

ALL-PURPOSE PANTRY STAPLES:

Assorted vinegars, including balsamic, white wine and cider; roasted red peppers; dried mushrooms; assorted pasta; onions; potatoes; canned whole and chopped tomatoes; hoisin sauce; assorted beans, such as kidney, white and black; chickpeas; lentils; a variety of canned seafood, including salmon, tuna and clams.

light fettuccine alfredo with shrimp

MAKES 6 servings **PREP** 10 minutes **COOK** 6½ minutes

1 pound egg fettuccine or a combination of egg and spinach

2 cups fat-free half-and-half

2 tablespoons cornstarch

¾ teaspoon garlic salt

¼ teaspoon ground nutmeg

½ cup shredded Asiago cheese

1 tablespoon Dijon mustard

1 cup frozen peas, thawed

2 tablespoons olive oil

1¾ pounds jumbo shrimp, shelled and deveined

Additional Asiago cheese and fresh basil for garnish, if desired

① Bring a large pot of salted water to boil. Prepare pasta following package directions, stirring frequently. Drain.

② Meanwhile, in a small bowl, mix ¼ cup of half-and-half with cornstarch; stir well and set aside. In a medium-size saucepan, add remaining 1¾ cups half-and-half and place over medium-high heat. Stir in ½ teaspoon of garlic salt and nutmeg. Bring to a simmer and stir in cornstarch mixture; cook for 30 seconds or until slightly thickened.

③ Take sauce off heat and whisk in Asiago cheese and mustard until smooth. Stir in peas. Keep warm.

④ Heat olive oil in a large skillet over medium-high heat. Add shrimp and remaining ¼ teaspoon garlic salt; cook for 3 minutes per side until cooked through. Stir cream sauce into skillet with shrimp; add pasta and toss to coat. Serve immediately with additional Asiago cheese. Garnish with basil, if desired.

PER SERVING 445 calories; 10 g fat (2 g sat.); 31 g protein; 56 g carbohydrate; 3 g fiber; 733 mg sodium; 170 mg cholesterol

SWITCH IT UP

Substitute Parmesan, Pecorino Romano or dry Jack for Asiago.

creamy salmon & rotini

MAKES 6 servings **PREP** 10 minutes **BAKE** at 450°F for 12 minutes **COOK** 10 minutes

½ **pound salmon fillet (1 piece)**

1 **box (14.5 ounces) Omega-3-enriched rotini pasta (such as Barilla)**

2 **cups fat-free half-and-half**

2 **teaspoons cornstarch**

¼ **teaspoon salt**

¼ **teaspoon ground nutmeg**

⅛ **teaspoon cayenne pepper**

1 **box (10 ounces) frozen peas, thawed**

½ **cup grated Parmesan cheese**

⅓ **cup toasted walnuts, coarsely chopped**

① Heat oven to 450°F. Coat a small baking pan with nonstick cooking spray. Add salmon to pan and bake at 450°F for 12 minutes or until fish flakes easily when tested with a fork. Keep warm.

② Meanwhile, cook pasta following package directions, 15 minutes. Drain and return to pot.

③ While pasta is cooking, in a medium-size bowl, whisk together half-and-half, cornstarch, salt, nutmeg and cayenne. Place in medium-size saucepan and bring to a boil. Simmer on low for 1 minute until sauce thickens. Add peas and simmer for an additional minute until peas are heated through. Remove from heat; stir in ¼ cup of Parmesan cheese.

④ Stir sauce into drained pasta. Remove skin from salmon and discard. Flake salmon into bite-size pieces and gently stir into pasta. Top with remaining ¼ cup cheese and nuts and serve.

PER SERVING 479 calories; 11 g fat (2 g sat.); 29 g protein; 63 g carbohydrate; 8 g fiber; 359 g sodium; 30 mg cholesterol

NUTRITION NOTE

Why look for foods with Omega-3s? These polyunsaturated fatty acids may prevent coronary artery disease. Omega-3-enriched pasta also has 4 more grams of protein and 3 more grams of fiber than regular pasta.

warm sweet & savory pasta salad

MAKES 6 servings **PREP** 15 minutes **COOK** 11 minutes

8 ounces multigrain rotini pasta (such as Barilla Plus)

1 small red onion, thinly sliced

3 tablespoons finely chopped fresh oregano

½ cup low-sodium chicken broth

3 tablespoons white balsamic vinegar

2 cups cooked, shredded chicken breast

1 can (15.5 ounces) black beans, drained and rinsed

¼ cup chopped green olives

① Bring a large pot of salted water to a boil. Cook pasta according to package directions, about 11 minutes. Drain, reserving ½ cup pasta water. Return pasta to pot.

② While pasta is cooking, heat a large nonstick skillet over medium heat. Add onion and oregano; coat generously with nonstick cooking spray. Cover and cook, stirring occasionally, for 3 minutes.

③ Stir broth and vinegar into skillet. Stir in chicken, beans and olives; cook for 2 minutes or until heated through. Toss with pasta and serve, adding reserved pasta water if too dry.

PER SERVING 304 calories; 5 g fat (0 g sat.); 25 g protein; 38 g carbohydrate; 7 g fiber; 496 mg sodium; 40 mg cholesterol

NUTRITION NOTE

Whole-grain pasta is the best and healthiest choice. Because it includes the entire grain seed, it retains the vitamins, minerals and fiber lost in the refining process when pasta is made from processed flour.

penne with sausage & peas

MAKES 6 servings **PREP** 10 minutes **COOK** 12 minutes

4 cups whole-wheat penne pasta (12 ounces)

2 tablespoons olive oil

1 package (12 ounces) fully cooked roasted garlic chicken sausage, sliced on the diagonal

2 cloves garlic, chopped

1 pound tomatoes, seeded and chopped

¼ teaspoon salt

½ cup low-sodium, 99% fat-free chicken broth

1 cup frozen peas, thawed

2 tablespoons freshly grated Parmesan cheese

① Bring a large pot of salted water to a boil. Add pasta and cook according to package directions, 12 minutes. Drain.

② Meanwhile, heat 1 tablespoon of oil in a large nonstick skillet over medium-high heat. Add sausage and cook 3 minutes, turning a few times, until browned. Scoop out sausage with a slotted spoon onto a plate.

③ Reduce heat to medium and add remaining 1 tablespoon oil and garlic. Cook 30 seconds. Stir in tomatoes and salt and cook 2 minutes. Stir in chicken broth, peas and browned sausage. Heat through.

④ Place cooked pasta in a large bowl. Add sausage mixture and 1 tablespoon of Parmesan cheese. Toss to combine. Top with remaining tablespoon Parmesan cheese and serve warm.

PER SERVING 350 calories; 10 g fat (2 g sat.); 20 g protein; 50 g carbohydrate; 7 g fiber; 561 mg sodium; 62 mg cholesterol

HOW-TO

Perfect Pasta Every Time:

1. For 1 pound of dried pasta, bring at least 6 quarts of salted water to a boil.

2. Add all of the pasta. With wooden spoon, stir once or twice to prevent sticking.

3. Check at suggested time; if cooked properly, there will be no white inside.

quick meat sauce & shells

MAKES 6 servings   **PREP** 15 minutes   **COOK** 23 minutes

1   pound lean ground beef

1   large sweet red pepper, cored, seeded and diced

1   large green bell pepper, cored, seeded and diced

1   medium onion, peeled and chopped

2   cloves garlic, peeled and chopped

2   cans (14.5 ounces each) diced tomatoes with Italian seasoning

1   teaspoon sugar

½   teaspoon salt

¼   teaspoon black pepper

1   pound medium pasta shells

1   cup part-skim shredded mozzarella cheese

① Coat a large nonstick skillet with nonstick cooking spray; heat over medium-high heat and add crumbled ground beef, peppers, onion and garlic. Cook for 8 minutes, stirring occasionally.

② Stir in tomatoes, sugar, salt and pepper. Cover and simmer on medium-low for 15 minutes, stirring occasionally.

③ While sauce is simmering, cook pasta following package directions. Drain.

④ Spoon sauce over pasta. Top with shredded mozzarella cheese and serve.

PER SERVING 486 calories; 9 g fat (4 g sat.); 33 g protein; 68 g carbohydrate; 5 g fiber; 697 mg sodium; 57 mg cholesterol

TEST KITCHEN TIP

Cook once, eat twice. Make a double batch of sauce and freeze half for a quick dinner.

cavatappi with chicken & vegetables

MAKES 8 servings   **PREP** 15 minutes   **COOK** 8 minutes

1   pound cavatappi or other corkscrew-shaped pasta

1   tablespoon olive oil

1½   pounds boneless, skinless chicken breasts, cut into 1-inch pieces

1   yellow pepper, cored and diced

1   bunch (1 pound) asparagus, trimmed and cut into 2-inch pieces

1   pint cherry tomatoes, halved

1   package (5.2 ounces) spreadable herb cheese (such as Boursin)

¼   teaspoon salt

¼   teaspoon black pepper

① Bring a large pot of salted water to a boil. Add pasta and bring back to a boil. Cook 6 minutes.

② Meanwhile, heat a large nonstick skillet over medium-high heat. Add olive oil and tilt pan to coat. Add chicken. Cook 6 minutes, stirring occasionally. During last minute of cooking, add yellow pepper to skillet. Remove from heat.

③ Once pasta has cooked for 6 minutes, add asparagus pieces and cook an additional 2 minutes. Scoop out ¼ cup pasta water, then drain.

④ In a large bowl, toss together hot pasta and asparagus, chicken and pepper, tomatoes, herbed cheese, reserved pasta water, salt and pepper until well blended and cheese is melted.

PER SERVING 395 calories; 10 g fat (5 g sat.); 30 g protein; 47 g carbohydrate; 3 g fiber; 248 mg sodium; 74 mg cholesterol

TEST KITCHEN TIP

Getting Asparagus Ready for Cooking Is a Snap—Literally! For most stalks, all you need to do is break off the woody bases where the spears snap easily. Peeling is optional—you may wish to do so with thicker stalks that can have a tough outer layer.

The combination of garlic and olive oil is a marriage made in heaven. Add pasta and chicken and you have pure comfort food at its best. For variety, substitute asparagus or green beans for the broccolini and whole-wheat fettuccine or tubular pasta for the linguine.

chicken & broccolini aglio e olio

MAKES 4 servings **PREP** 15 minutes **COOK** 20 minutes

1 bunch broccolini (about 1 pound), cut into thirds (or use regular broccoli)

½ pound whole-wheat linguine

1½ pounds boneless, skinless chicken breasts, cut into 1-inch pieces

¼ cup all-purpose flour

½ teaspoon salt

¼ teaspoon black pepper

4 tablespoons extra-virgin olive oil

4 to 6 cloves garlic, thinly sliced

2 tablespoons capers and 1 tablespoon of the brine

¼ teaspoon red pepper flakes

2 tablespoons chopped parsley

① Bring a large pot of salted water to a boil. Add broccolini; boil 3 minutes. With slotted spoon, remove broccolini to a bowl. Add pasta to pot. Cook following package directions. Drain, reserving ½ cup of cooking water.

② While pasta is cooking, coat chicken pieces with all-purpose flour, shaking off excess. Season with ¼ teaspoon of salt and pepper.

③ Heat 3 tablespoons of olive oil in a large skillet over medium-high heat. Add chicken and cook 3 to 4 minutes per side or until cooked through. Add garlic, capers, brine and red pepper flakes. Cook for 1 minute. Add cooked broccolini and reserved pasta water. Bring to a simmer. Add pasta and remaining ¼ teaspoon salt. Stir to combine and coat pasta with liquid.

④ Transfer to a large platter and drizzle with remaining 1 tablespoon olive oil. Sprinkle with parsley. Serve immediately.

PER SERVING 500 calories; 16 g fat (2 g sat.); 39 g protein; 55 g carbohydrate; 9 g fiber; 561 mg sodium; 66 mg cholesterol

NUTRITION NOTE

Aside from its tender texture and bright-flavored buds, broccolini is rich in many vitamins and minerals. It contains high amounts of vitamin C, potassium, iron, fiber and vitamin A.

chipotle chicken wagon wheels

MAKES 6 servings **PREP** 15 minutes **COOK** 12 minutes

- 1 tablespoon vegetable oil
- 1½ pounds boneless, skinless chicken breasts, cut into 1½-inch pieces
- ½ red onion, thinly sliced
- 2 cloves garlic, peeled and chopped
- 1 can (14.5 ounces) diced tomatoes, drained
- ¾ cup fat-free half-and-half
- 2 chipotle peppers in adobo, seeded and chopped
- ¾ teaspoon salt
- 2 tablespoons chopped cilantro
- 1 pound wagon wheel pasta

① Heat a large nonstick skillet over medium-high heat. Add oil and chicken. Cook 5 minutes, turning after 3 minutes. Add onion and garlic; cook 3 minutes. Stir in tomatoes, half-and-half, chipotle and salt. Simmer, uncovered, 4 minutes, stirring occasionally. Add cilantro.

② Meanwhile, cook pasta following package directions, about 12 minutes. Drain, reserving ½ cup of pasta water.

③ Toss pasta with sauce. Add reserved water as needed to thin out sauce.

PER SERVING 467 calories; 5 g fat (1 g sat.); 38 g protein; 65 g carbohydrate; 4 g fiber; 615 mg sodium; 7 mg cholesterol

TEST KITCHEN TIP

Chipotle We're hot for this chile—adding it is a simple, affordable way to spice up any dish. As a ripe jalapeño pepper, smoked and dried to give it a rich, smoky flavor, it's a must-have pantry staple.

penne & turkey sausage

MAKES 6 servings **PREP** 10 minutes **COOK** 15 minutes

12 ounces whole-wheat penne pasta

1 large head escarole

2 tablespoons olive oil

1 small onion, chopped

1 pound hot Italian turkey sausage

¼ teaspoon garlic salt

½ teaspoon black pepper

1 can small white beans, drained and rinsed

Parmesan cheese (optional)

① Bring a large pot of salted water to a boil. Add pasta and cook 12 minutes. Clean, trim and chop escarole.

② While pasta cooks, heat olive oil in a large skillet over medium heat. Add onion and cook 3 minutes, stirring occasionally. Remove sausage from its casing and crumble into pan. Cook 5 minutes, breaking apart with a spoon.

③ Drain pasta, reserving 1 cup pasta water. Keep warm. Increase heat under skillet to medium-high. Add escarole, garlic salt and pepper. Cook 3 minutes, until greens are wilted. Add beans and ½ cup of pasta water (if necessary). Add drained pasta to pan and toss to combine. Garnish with Parmesan cheese, if desired.

PER SERVING 404 calories; 10 g fat (2 g sat.); 27 g protein; 58 g carbohydrate; 10 g fiber; 800 mg sodium; 53 mg cholesterol

HOW-TO

Clean Escarole Fill a large bowl or the sink with water, then swish greens around with your hands. The grit should sink to the bottom; lift escarole out of bowl and spin dry.

mediterranean orzo

MAKES 6 servings **PREP** 10 minutes **COOK** 12 minutes

12 ounces onion-and-garlic or Italian-flavored chicken sausage (such as Al Fresco), halved lengthwise and cut into ½-inch-thick half-moons

1 pint grape tomatoes, halved

3 tablespoons red wine vinegar

1 teaspoon canola oil

¾ teaspoon dried oregano

8 ounces orzo

8 ounces green beans, trimmed and cut in half

½ cup crumbled fat-free feta cheese

1 tablespoon fresh chopped parsley

2 teaspoons olive oil

① Heat a large nonstick skillet over medium-high heat. Add sausage to skillet and cook, stirring occasionally, for 5 minutes. Add tomatoes, 1 tablespoon of vinegar, canola oil and ½ teaspoon of oregano to pan; cook 2 minutes. Place sausage mixture in a large serving bowl.

② Meanwhile, bring a large pot of salted water to a boil. Cook orzo according to package directions. Add green beans to pasta pot for final 5 minutes of cooking time. Drain and rinse under cold water.

③ Place pasta mixture in serving bowl with sausage mixture and add remaining 2 tablespoons vinegar, ¼ teaspoon oregano, feta, parsley and olive oil. Stir to combine and serve.

PER SERVING 301 calories; 7 g fat (2 g sat.); 22 g protein; 36 g carbohydrate; 3 g fiber; 562 mg sodium; 48 mg cholesterol

Your family will never guess this is a slimmed-down version of the classic. High in flavor with a creamy texture, it's every bit as good as its high-calorie cousin.

pasta carbonara

MAKES 6 servings **PREP** 10 minutes **COOK** 22 minutes

¾ **pound gemelli pasta**

1 **pound asparagus, trimmed and cut into 1-inch pieces**

12 **slices turkey bacon (6 ounces), cut crosswise into thin strips**

1¼ **cups fat-free half-and-half**

3 **egg yolks**

½ **teaspoon dried basil**

¼ **teaspoon salt**

⅛ **teaspoon black pepper**

⅛ **teaspoon ground nutmeg**

⅓ **cup plus 1 tablespoon grated Parmesan cheese**

① Bring a large pot of salted water to a boil. Add pasta and cook following package directions. Add asparagus to pasta water for last 4 minutes of cooking time. Drain and keep warm.

② While pasta is cooking, place bacon in a medium-size nonstick skillet and cook over medium-high heat about 8 minutes, stirring occasionally, or until slightly browned and crisp. Remove from pan with a slotted spoon and drain on a paper-towel-lined plate.

③ In a small saucepan, whisk half-and-half and egg yolks. Cook over medium heat about 8 minutes, whisking constantly, until temperature reaches 160°F on an instant-read thermometer. Stir in basil, salt, pepper and nutmeg.

④ Add bacon to cooked pasta and asparagus. Stir in creamy egg mixture. Stir in ⅓ cup of Parmesan cheese.

⑤ Spoon pasta into a serving bowl and sprinkle remaining 1 tablespoon Parmesan cheese on top. Serve immediately.

PER SERVING 386 calories; 11 g fat (4 g sat.); 19 g protein; 51 g carbohydrate; 4 g fiber; 648 mg sodium; 137 mg cholesterol

SWITCH IT UP

Substitute fusilli, rigatoni, radiatore, penne or macaroni for gemelli.

All'Amatriciana is a traditional pasta sauce originating in the town of Amatrice, Italy. Traditionally it combines pancetta with tomatoes, onion and Pecorino Romano cheese. We have substituted smoked bacon for the pancetta with delicious results.

all'amatriciana

MAKES 6 servings   **PREP** 10 minutes   **COOK** 15 minutes

1 tablespoon olive oil

6 slices thick-cut smoked bacon (about 5 ounces total), cut into ¼-inch strips

1 medium onion, halved and thinly sliced

1 can (15 ounces) tomato puree

1 tablespoon red wine vinegar

¼ teaspoon red pepper flakes

¼ teaspoon salt

1 pound bucatini or perciatelli pasta

½ cup grated Romano cheese

¼ cup basil leaves, coarsely chopped

Fresh black pepper, if desired

① Bring a large pot of salted water to a boil.

② Heat olive oil in a large skillet over medium heat. Add bacon and cook 5 minutes until bacon just begins to turn brown, stirring occasionally. Remove bacon with slotted spoon and reserve.

③ Add onion and cook in bacon drippings 7 minutes, stirring occasionally. Stir in reserved bacon, tomato puree, vinegar, red pepper flakes and salt. Simmer for 3 minutes on medium-low heat.

④ While sauce is cooking, prepare pasta following package directions until al dente. Drain.

⑤ Toss pasta with sauce. Stir in ¼ cup of Romano cheese and basil. Serve with extra cheese on the side and pepper, if using.

PER SERVING 443 calories; 10 g fat (4 g sat.); 16 g protein; 70 g carbohydrate; 6 g fiber; 782 mg sodium; 619 mg cholesterol

TEST KITCHEN TIP

Al Dente Pasta "To the tooth," the Italian translation, refers to cooked pasta that's tender yet still firm.

Cellentani pasta, also known as cavatappi, is a tubular pasta resembling a corkscrew. It has a nutty flavor which makes it a popular choice for a variety of dishes.

cellentani with ham & greens

MAKES 6 servings **PREP** 10 minutes **COOK** 12 minutes

1 pound cellentani (such as Barilla) or cavatappi

2 tablespoons unsalted butter

1 medium onion, chopped

⅓ pound thinly sliced Virginia ham, cut into ½ x 2-inch ribbons

1 package (10 ounces) frozen chopped kale, thawed according to package directions

3 tablespoons all-purpose flour

1 can (14 ounces) low-sodium chicken broth

Grated Romano cheese (optional)

① Bring a large pot of salted water to a boil. Cook cellentani according to package directions, about 12 minutes. Drain and return to pot.

② Meanwhile, melt butter in a large nonstick skillet over medium-high heat. Cook onion, ham and kale in skillet for 8 minutes. Reduce heat to medium and add all-purpose flour. Cook, stirring constantly, for 1 minute.

③ Add chicken broth to skillet and cook, stirring occasionally, for 3 minutes or until sauce has thickened slightly. Pour contents of skillet over pasta and stir to combine. Top with Romano cheese, if desired.

PER SERVING 376 calories; 5 g fat (3 g sat.); 16 g protein; 65 g carbohydrate; 4 g fiber; 460 mg sodium; 21 mg cholesterol

NUTRITION NOTE

Kale is a great source of two kinds of antioxidants—believed to be a major player in the battle against cancer, heart disease and certain age-related chronic diseases.

rotini with broccoli rabe & sausage

MAKES 4 servings **PREP** 10 minutes **COOK** 13 minutes

2   tablespoons olive oil

½   pound sweet Italian sausage, crumbled

4   cloves garlic, thinly sliced

1   large bunch broccoli rabe, stems trimmed, rinsed and cut into 2-inch pieces

½   teaspoon salt

½   teaspoon dried oregano

¼   teaspoon black pepper

1   package (12 ounces) tri-color rotini pasta

Grated Asiago cheese (optional)

① Heat oil in a large nonstick skillet over medium-high heat. Add sausage and cook 5 minutes, stirring occasionally. Stir in garlic during last minute of cooking time. Add broccoli rabe, salt, oregano and pepper. Cook, uncovered, 8 minutes or until tender, stirring occasionally. If mixture gets too dry, add a few tablespoons of water.

② Meanwhile, cook pasta following package directions, about 7 minutes. Drain, reserving ½ cup of pasta water.

③ Add pasta water to sausage mixture to create a sauce, then stir together with pasta. Serve immediately with grated Asiago cheese, if desired.

PER SERVING 494 calories; 13 g fat (3 g sat.); 25 g protein; 72 g carbohydrate; 3 g fiber; 656 mg sodium; 17 mg cholesterol

TEST KITCHEN TIP

To store broccoli rabe, wrap in plastic and place in the crisper section of your refrigerator for up to 7 days.

spaghetti with basic marinara

MAKES 6 servings **PREP** 5 minutes **COOK** 30 minutes

2 tablespoons olive oil

1 medium onion, peeled and chopped

2 cloves garlic, peeled and chopped

1 can (28 ounces) whole tomatoes

1 can (8 ounces) no-salt-added tomato sauce

1 teaspoon Italian seasoning (or ½ teaspoon dried oregano plus ½ teaspoon dried basil)

1 teaspoon sugar

½ teaspoon salt

¼ teaspoon black pepper

1 pound spaghetti

① Heat oil in medium-size saucepan over medium-low heat. Add onion and garlic and cook, stirring occasionally, 10 minutes.

② Add tomatoes and their liquid, tomato sauce, dried herbs, sugar, salt and pepper. Using clean kitchen scissors, cut tomatoes into bite-size chunks in pan. Bring sauce to a simmer over medium-high heat, then reduce heat to medium and simmer 20 minutes.

③ Meanwhile, in a large pot of salted water, cook spaghetti according to package directions. Drain pasta and serve topped with marinara sauce.

PER SERVING 370 calories; 6 g fat (1 g sat.); 11 g protein; 67 g carbohydrate; 4 g fiber; 400 mg sodium; 0 mg cholesterol

TEST KITCHEN TIP

Jazzing Up Marinara This everyday sauce can be perked up with any of the following: smashed capers, chopped black olives, flaked tuna, chopped fresh mozzarella, sautéed zucchini coins, crisp bacon bits or slivers of prosciutto.

quick hearty lasagna

MAKES 8 servings **PREP** 20 minutes **COOK** 5 minutes **BAKE** at 350°F for 50 minutes **LET STAND** 10 minutes

1 jar (28 ounces) sausage-flavored pasta sauce

1 tablespoon vegetable oil

½ package (20 ounces) frozen sausage breakfast blend (such as Jimmy Dean)

1 package (8 ounces) shredded Italian 5-cheese blend

1 container (15 ounces) part-skim ricotta cheese

12 no-boil lasagna noodles (such as Barilla, from a 9-ounce box)

① Heat oven to 350°F. Coat a 13 x 9 x 2-inch baking dish with nonstick cooking spray. Spread ½ cup of sausage-flavored pasta sauce over bottom of prepared dish. Heat oil in a large nonstick skillet over medium-high heat. Add sausage breakfast blend to skillet and cook, stirring, 5 minutes. Remove from heat and stir in remaining pasta sauce.

② In a medium-size bowl, stir together ¾ cup of shredded cheese, ricotta cheese and **2 tablespoons water.** Spread 3 noodles over sauce in dish (do not overlap). Top with half of ricotta mixture, then 3 more noodles. Repeat layering with half of pasta sauce, 3 noodles, remaining ricotta mixture, 3 noodles, remaining sauce and cheese.

③ Cover dish with nonstick foil; transfer to oven. Bake at 350°F for 30 minutes. Uncover and continue to bake an additional 20 minutes until bubbly. Let stand 10 minutes before serving.

PER SERVING 386 calories; 17 g fat (9 g sat.); 21 g protein; 39 g carbohydrate; 4 g fiber; 800 mg sodium; 76 mg cholesterol

TEST KITCHEN TIP

Make Ahead Assemble lasagna a day ahead, cover with plastic wrap and chill. When ready to cook, add an additional 10 minutes to baking time.

ravioli with spinach & squash

MAKES 6 servings **PREP** 10 minutes **COOK** 9 minutes

2 **packages (9 ounces each) light four-cheese ravioli (such as Buitoni)**

1 **bag (6 ounces) baby spinach**

2 **medium yellow summer squash (about 7 ounces each), cut into ¼-inch-thick half-moons**

1 **medium zucchini (about 8 ounces), cut into ¼-inch-thick half-moons**

1 **package (4.4 ounces) light spreadable herb cheese (such as Boursin Light Garlic & Fine Herbs)**

½ **teaspoon salt**

½ **teaspoon black pepper**

① Cook ravioli according to package directions, about 9 minutes. Add spinach during final minute.

② Meanwhile, heat a large nonstick skillet over medium-high heat. Coat skillet with nonstick cooking spray; add squash and zucchini to pan. Lightly coat squash mixture with nonstick spray. Cover and cook, stirring occasionally, for 6 to 7 minutes or until tender.

③ Drain pasta, reserving ½ cup pasta water; return pasta mixture to pot. Stir herb cheese into pasta mixture until well blended. Gently stir in squash, salt and pepper. Stir in pasta water by the tablespoonful if mixture becomes too dry.

PER SERVING 291 calories; 7 g fat (4 g sat.); 15 g protein; 43 g carbohydrate; 5 g fiber; 790 mg sodium; 51 mg cholesterol

TEST KITCHEN TIP

Summer Squash and Zucchini Choose young, small and firm squash with no blemishes or soft spots. Store unwashed in a plastic bag in the refrigerator up to 4 days.

Grains are making a major comeback—and for good reason. They're economical, easy to prepare and full of flavor. Adults should be consuming approximately 6 ounces of grains daily, half of those coming from whole grains, to help fight high blood pressure, weight gain and heart disease.

Once you know how, it's easy to incorporate 3 servings of grains into our daily diet. Begin your day with a whole-grain muffin, cereal or oatmeal. On weekends, with the kids, whip up a batch of buckwheat pancakes and top them with fruit. For a quick on-the-go snack or as an after-school treat, combine whole-grain cereal,

⋯⋯⋮⋗ grains

fat-free popcorn and a sprinkling of nuts and dried fruit. Instead of potatoes or white rice, serve risotto or pilaf made with such whole grains as brown rice, wild rice, whole-wheat couscous, barley or quinoa. Stir cooked barley, brown rice or bulgur into soups, stews and casseroles. And when combined with lean protein and legumes, grains make great stuffings for whole vegetables, like in Kasha Picadillo Stuffed Peppers (page 98).

Also check out our homemade version of Pork Fried Rice (page 82) or an update on Turkey Alfredo (page 87). Your family will never guess it's good for them.

This recipe lends itself to endless variations. Substitute chicken breast for the pork and frozen carrots, succotash or stir-fry vegetables for the peas. It's also perfect for using leftover rice as well as cooked chicken, meat and vegetables.

pork fried rice

MAKES 4 servings **PREP** 10 minutes **COOK** 6½ minutes

1 egg, lightly beaten

1 pound boneless, center-cut pork chops, fat trimmed and cut into ¼-inch strips

2 scallions, trimmed and sliced

2 packages (8.8 ounces each) fully cooked brown rice

1 cup frozen peas, thawed

¼ cup low-sodium soy sauce

2 teaspoons sesame oil

① Coat a 12-inch nonstick skillet with nonstick cooking spray and heat over medium heat. Add beaten egg and let cook, undisturbed, for 1 minute. Use a large silicone spatula to flip over egg and cook an additional 30 seconds, until cooked through. Transfer to a cutting board and cut into 2 x ½-inch strips.

② Increase heat under skillet to medium-high and add pork. Cook 3 minutes, until no longer pink, then add scallions, brown rice and peas. Cover and cook an additional 2 minutes. Stir in egg, soy sauce and sesame oil and heat through. Serve warm.

PER SERVING 442 calories; 11 g fat (2 g sat.); 33 g protein; 42 g carbohydrate; 4 g fiber; 493 mg sodium; 123 mg cholesterol

GRAIN FACTS:

QUINOA

• More protein per serving than any other grain

• Considered "complete" because it contains all 8 essential amino acids

• Can be easily added to soups, salads and baked dishes

BARLEY

• Chewy, mild taste

• Protein-rich and contains a type of fiber called beta-glucan, which helps lower cholesterol

BROWN RICE

• Rice that is stripped of its inedible outer husk but retains its vitamin-rich bran layer

• Has a nutty flavor and a chewy texture

• Takes longer to cook than white rice but is available parboiled or precooked

BULGUR

• Made from wheat kernels that have been steamed, dried and crushed

• Has a tender, chewy texture

• Versatile

• Cooks quickly

WHOLE-WHEAT COUSCOUS

• Made of granular semolina flour

• Cooks in 5 minutes

• Can be made to be sweet or savory as it has a mild flavor

mediterranean bulgur with chickpeas

MAKES 4 servings **PREP** 15 minutes

1 cup bulgur (cracked wheat)

2 plum tomatoes, cut into ¼-inch pieces

1 small zucchini, cut into ¼-inch pieces

3 tablespoons chopped fresh parsley

1 can (15.5 ounces) chickpeas, drained and rinsed

¾ cup crumbled feta cheese

¾ teaspoon grated lemon zest

2 tablespoons lemon juice

2 tablespoons olive oil

① In a large serving bowl, combine bulgur, tomatoes, zucchini and parsley. Pour in **1½ cups boiling water** and cover tightly with foil for 12 minutes or until liquid is absorbed and bulgur is tender.

② Stir in chickpeas, feta, lemon zest, lemon juice and olive oil. Serve warm.

PER SERVING 434 calories; 15 g fat (5 g sat.); 14 g protein; 62 g carbohydrate; 12 g fiber; 665 mg sodium; 25 mg cholesterol

NUTRITION NOTE

A little bit of feta goes a long way toward great cheese flavor. Containing a third less calories and fat than standard cheddar cheese, it's the ideal healthy choice for those who want the taste of real cheese without the extra fat.

bulgur-stuffed squash

MAKES 6 servings **PREP** 5 minutes **COOK** 5 minutes **LET STAND** 30 minutes **BAKE** at 400°F for 45 minutes

3 small acorn squash, halved
and seeded

¾ cup bulgur (cracked wheat)

2 hot Italian sausages,
casings removed

½ teaspoon garlic powder

1 small sweet red pepper,
seeded and diced

2 tablespoons chili sauce

¼ teaspoon salt

2 tablespoons maple syrup

PER SERVING 274 calories; 7 g fat (2 g sat.);
9 g protein; 50 g carbohydrate; 12 g fiber;
455 mg sodium; 13 mg cholesterol

NUTRITION NOTE

High in protein and low in fat and calories,
bulgur is also a powerhouse in terms of
fiber content.

① Heat oven to 400°F. Place squash halves, cut-side down, on a 15 x 10 x 1-inch baking pan. Add **2 cups water,** and transfer to oven. Bake at 400°F for 35 minutes.

② Meanwhile, put bulgur in a medium-size bowl. Pour ¾ **cup boiling water** over bulgur; cover with plastic wrap. Let stand 30 minutes.

③ Once bulgur is softened, heat a nonstick skillet over medium-high heat. Add sausage; cook 2 minutes. Stir in garlic powder and red pepper; cook 3 minutes. Remove from heat. Stir in bulgur, chili sauce and ⅛ teaspoon of salt. Remove squash from oven; pour off water. Flip over squash; brush with maple syrup. Season with remaining ⅛ teaspoon salt. Spoon filling in squash; return to oven. Bake 10 minutes.

quinoa & red bean burritos

MAKES 8 burritos **PREP** 15 minutes **BAKE** at 350°F for 12 minutes **MICROWAVE** 45 seconds

1 cup quinoa

2 teaspoons smoked paprika

1 can (15 ounces) red kidney beans, drained, rinsed and lightly mashed

1½ cups jarred salsa, plus more for serving

8 whole-wheat tortillas

1 cup shredded Mexican cheese blend

① Place quinoa and paprika in a saucepan and cook following package directions. Once cooked, stir in beans and 1 cup of salsa.

② While quinoa is cooking, heat oven to 350°F. Coat large baking sheet with nonstick cooking spray.

③ Heat tortillas in microwave for 45 seconds to soften. Place ½ cup of quinoa mixture in center of each tortilla and fold like a package. Place seam-side down on baking sheet.

④ Lightly coat burritos with nonstick cooking spray and top with remaining salsa and Mexican cheese blend, dividing equally. Bake burritos at 350°F for 12 minutes until heated through, with cheese melted. Serve with additional salsa.

PER BURRITO 315 calories; 8 g fat (4 g sat.); 14 g protein; 47 g carbohydrate; 8 g fiber; 734 mg sodium; 13 mg cholesterol

Note: Quinoa is found in the rice and dried bean aisle of the supermarket.

HOW-TO

Fold A Burrito

1. Place filling slightly above center and fold both sides into middle.

2. Carefully fold over top, keeping filling in place with fingers.

3. Continue to roll until wrap is completely sealed, making sure filling stays in place.

turkey quinoa alfredo

MAKES 4 servings **PREP** 5 minutes **BAKE** at 350°F for 50 minutes

1 cup quinoa

1 cup jarred reduced-fat
   Alfredo sauce

1 box (10 ounces) frozen
   Brussels sprouts, thawed
   and halved

1 package turkey cutlets
   (about 1 pound)

¼ cup grated Parmesan cheese

   Freshly ground black pepper

   Chopped fresh parsley

① Heat oven to 350°F. Coat a
2½-quart baking dish with nonstick
cooking spray. Set aside.

② In a large bowl, stir together
quinoa, **1 cup water,** Alfredo sauce
and Brussels sprouts. Pour into
prepared dish.

③ Top quinoa mixture with
turkey cutlets, spacing them
slightly apart so they do not touch.
Sprinkle with grated Parmesan
cheese and pepper.

④ Cover with nonstick foil and
bake at 350°F for 35 minutes.
Carefully remove foil and continue
to bake an additional 15 minutes.
Cool for 10 minutes; sprinkle with
chopped parsley before serving.

PER SERVING 442 calories; 15 g fat (6 g sat.);
40 g protein; 39 g carbohydrate; 6 g fiber;
698 mg sodium; 97 mg cholesterol

SWITCH IT UP

Substitute frozen green beans, asparagus
or broccoli for Brussels sprouts.

pork with quinoa pilaf

MAKES 6 servings **PREP** 10 minutes **COOK** 25 minutes

1½ pounds pork tenderloin

¾ teaspoon lemon-pepper seasoning

¾ teaspoon salt

1 tablespoon canola oil

1 medium red onion, chopped

1 medium-size Granny Smith apple, peeled, cored and diced

1 cup quinoa

2 cups chicken broth

2 medium-size carrots, peeled and shredded

¾ cup dried cranberries

½ cup walnuts, chopped

½ cup crumbled reduced-fat feta cheese

   Steamed green beans (optional)

① Season pork tenderloin with ½ teaspoon of lemon-pepper seasoning and ½ teaspoon of salt. Heat oil in 12-inch nonstick skillet over medium-high heat. Brown pork 4 minutes, turning until golden. Remove.

② In same skillet, reduce heat to medium. Sauté onion and apple for 5 minutes or until tender. Add quinoa; cook, stirring, 1 minute to toast. Add broth, carrots, cranberries and remaining ¼ teaspoon lemon-pepper seasoning and ¼ teaspoon salt; mix well.

③ Place pork on top of quinoa mixture in skillet. Cover; bring to a boil. Reduce heat to medium low; simmer about 15 minutes until pork registers 145°F on instant-read thermometer, liquid is absorbed and quinoa is tender. Remove pork from skillet; let rest for 5 minutes. Thinly slice pork. Stir walnuts and feta cheese into quinoa mixture. Place ¾ cup quinoa pilaf onto each plate; fan sliced pork on top. Serve with steamed green beans, if desired.

PER SERVING 409 calories; 18 g fat (3 g sat.); 32 g protein; 37 g carbohydrate; 4 g fiber; 565 mg sodium; 77 mg cholesterol

NUTRITION NOTE

Keen on Quinoa Considered "ancient" because it hasn't been genetically changed since it was a staple in the Incas' diet centuries ago, quinoa (KEEN-wah) is an excellent source of protein, B vitamins, calcium and magnesium. This quick-cooking superfood can be used as a side dish or added to soups, salads and baked goods, such as muffins and cakes.

chicken & barley salad

MAKES 4 servings **PREP** 5 minutes **COOK** 10 minutes

1 cup quick-cooking barley

2 cups broccoli florets

½ cup sweetened dried cranberries

1 large boneless, skinless chicken breast (9 ounces), grilled and sliced into strips, or 1 package fully cooked, grilled chicken strips (such as Perdue)

½ cup walnuts, chopped

⅛ teaspoon salt

¾ cup raspberry vinaigrette dressing (such as Wish-Bone Bountifuls)

① Bring **3 cups water** to a boil in a medium-size saucepan.

② Stir in barley, reduce heat to medium-high and cook 6 minutes. Add broccoli, and continue to cook for 3 minutes. Stir in cranberries, cook 1 minute, then drain.

③ Transfer barley mixture to a serving bowl, and stir in chicken pieces, walnuts and salt. Pour vinaigrette over salad and gently stir to combine. Serve slightly warm or at room temperature.

PER SERVING 412 calories; 12 g fat (1 g sat.); 23 g protein; 56 g carbohydrate; 7 g fiber; 445 mg sodium; 41 mg cholesterol

SWITCH IT UP

Substitute cooked turkey, ham or shrimp for chicken.

shrimp with barley pilaf

MAKES 4 servings **PREP** 15 minutes **REFRIGERATE** 20 minutes **COOK** 10 minutes **GRILL** 9 minutes

1¼ **pounds shrimp, peeled and deveined**

⅓ **cup plus ½ cup light lime vinaigrette**

1⅓ **cups quick-cooking barley**

1 **sweet red pepper, diced**

2 **carrots, peeled and diced**

2 **ribs celery, trimmed and diced**

① Combine shrimp and ⅓ cup of vinaigrette in a large resealable plastic food-storage bag. Marinate in refrigerator for 20 minutes.

② Meanwhile, soak 8 bamboo skewers in warm water. Bring a medium-size pot of lightly salted water to a boil. Add barley and cook 10 minutes. Drain and rinse with cool water.

③ Heat a grill pan. Thread shrimp onto skewers, about 3 or 4 per skewer. Discard shrimp marinade. Grill shrimp 7 to 9 minutes, turning once. While shrimp grills, in a large bowl, combine barley, red pepper, carrots, celery and remaining ½ cup dressing. Toss to combine and coat all ingredients with dressing.

④ Spoon about 1 cup barley salad onto a plate. Top with two shrimp skewers. Serve hot or at room temperature.

PER SERVING 365 calories; 5 g fat (1 g sat.); 34 g protein; 50 g carbohydrate; 6 g fiber; 695 mg sodium; 215 mg cholesterol

NUTRITION NOTE

In addition to its high fiber content, barley is low in fat, cholesterol-free and contains antioxidants, phytochemicals, vitamins and minerals.

Spices such as paprika, cumin and turmeric complement chickpeas, sweet golden raisins and honey to give this dish a North African flavor. Your kids won't miss the meat—and they'll have fun eating both the stuffing and its tomato container.

moroccan-style stuffed tomatoes

MAKES 6 servings **PREP** 15 minutes **COOK** 5 to 6 minutes **LET STAND** 5 minutes

6 large ripe tomatoes, red, yellow or a mix (about 10 ounces each)

2 tablespoons olive oil

½ small yellow onion, chopped

½ large green pepper, seeded and chopped

2 cups vegetable broth

1 can (15 ounces) chickpeas, drained and rinsed

½ cup golden raisins

1 teaspoon paprika

¾ teaspoon salt

½ teaspoon ground cumin

½ teaspoon black pepper

¼ teaspoon turmeric

1 tablespoon honey

1 cup whole-wheat couscous

2 tablespoons sliced almonds, toasted

① Cut tops off tomatoes and reserve. Gently squeeze out seeds and discard. Scoop out most of pulp using a melon baller or spoon and reserve 1 cup. Place tomatoes, cut side down, on a paper-towel-lined baking sheet; allow to drain.

② Heat oil in a medium-size saucepan over medium heat. Add onion and green pepper; cook, stirring occasionally, for 5 minutes, until softened. Add broth, chickpeas, raisins, paprika, salt, cumin, pepper and turmeric. Chop reserved tomato pulp; add to pan. Bring to a boil. Stir in honey.

③ Stir in couscous. Remove from heat. Cover and let stand for 5 minutes.

④ Fluff couscous filling with a fork. Divide filling among tomatoes. Top with toasted almonds, replace tomato tops and serve.

PER SERVING 332 calories; 8 g fat (1 g sat.); 10 g protein; 59 g carbohydrate; 7 g fiber; 736 mg sodium; 0 mg cholesterol

TEST KITCHEN TIP

Pantry Perfect Couscous is a great staple to have on hand. Sold in a variety of flavors, it pairs well with vegetables, chicken and meat.

scallop couscous paella

MAKES 6 servings **PREP** 15 minutes **COOK** 11 minutes **LET STAND** 5 minutes

1 tablespoon olive oil

2 sweet red peppers, cored, seeds removed, cut into ½-inch pieces

1 large onion, chopped

4 cloves garlic, chopped

1 can (14.5 ounces) reduced-sodium chicken broth

½ teaspoon turmeric

½ teaspoon black pepper

¼ teaspoon salt

¼ teaspoon red pepper flakes

1¼ pounds sea scallops, rinsed

1 package (10 ounces) frozen peas, thawed

2 chipotle chorizo or jalapeño-flavored fully cooked chicken sausages from a 12-ounce package (such as Al Fresco), cut into ½-inch coins

1 can (6½ ounces) chopped clams

3 cups whole-wheat couscous

1 lemon, cut into wedges (optional)

① Heat oil in a large nonstick skillet over medium-high heat. Add red peppers, onion and garlic. Cook 6 minutes, stirring occasionally. Add broth, **1 cup water**, turmeric, pepper, salt and red pepper flakes. Bring to a simmer and add scallops. Simmer, covered, 3 minutes. Stir in peas, sausage and clams with their liquid. Simmer, covered, 2 minutes.

② Turn off heat and stir in couscous. Cover and allow to stand 5 minutes.

③ Fluff couscous with a fork. Serve with lemon wedges for squeezing, if desired.

PER SERVING 460 calories; 8 g fat (2 g sat.); 36 g protein; 64 g carbohydrate; 11 g fiber; 772 g sodium; 57 mg cholesterol

risotto with sugar snap peas & ham

MAKES 4 servings **PREP** 10 minutes **COOK** 34 minutes

½ pound sugar snap peas, trimmed and cut in half on the diagonal

3½ cups low-sodium chicken broth

2 teaspoons olive oil

4 leeks, cleaned and thinly sliced

2 cloves garlic, minced

1 cup arborio rice

4 ounces cubed ham (half of an 8-ounce package, such as Cumberland Gap)

½ cup grated Parmesan cheese

¼ teaspoon black pepper

① Cook peas in boiling water about 4 minutes or until crisp-tender. Drain and rinse with cold water and set aside.

② Pour broth into a medium-size saucepan and bring to a simmer over medium heat; reduce heat to low and keep broth warm.

③ Heat oil in a large saucepan over medium heat. Add leeks and cook 6 minutes, stirring frequently, or until softened. Add garlic and cook 1 minute. Stir in rice and cook 1 more minute. Stir in broth, ½ cup at a time. Stir frequently until liquid is absorbed before adding next ½ cup (about 20 minutes total); rice should be tender yet firm to the bite.

④ Add peas and ham and cook, stirring constantly, 2 minutes or until peas are heated through. Stir in Parmesan cheese and pepper.

PER SERVING 421 calories; 9 g fat (4 g sat.); 20 g protein; 65 g carbohydrate; 4 g fiber; 771 mg sodium; 13 mg cholesterol

HOW TO MAKE RISOTTO

1. Stir in rice and cook 1 minute.

2. Add ½ cup broth and stir frequently until liquid is absorbed before adding the next.

3. Continue to stir in broth, ½ cup at a time, until rice is tender yet firm to the bite.

chickpea & brown basmati curry

MAKES 6 servings **PREP** 20 minutes **COOK** 45 minutes

1¼   cups brown basmati rice

2   tablespoons canola oil

1   large onion, chopped

1½   pounds all-purpose potatoes, peeled and cut into 1-inch pieces, ½-inch thick

2   sweet peppers, cored, seeded and thinly sliced

3   teaspoons mild curry powder

1   teaspoon ground ginger

¼   teaspoon ground cinnamon

1   can (14.5 ounces) vegetable broth

1   can (8 ounces) no-salt-added tomato sauce

2   cans (15 ounces each) chickpeas, drained and rinsed

½   teaspoon salt

1   bag (6 ounces) baby spinach

¼   cup sliced almonds, toasted

① Cook rice following package directions, about 45 minutes.

② Meanwhile, heat oil in a large nonstick skillet over medium-high heat. Add onion and potatoes. Cook, uncovered, 10 minutes until lightly browned. Stir frequently.

③ Add peppers, curry powder, ginger and cinnamon. Cook 1 minute. Stir in broth, tomato sauce, chickpeas and salt. Scrape up any browned bits from bottom of skillet. Simmer, covered, for 15 minutes, or until potatoes are tender. Stir occasionally.

④ Gradually stir in spinach and allow to wilt into mixture.

⑤ Spoon rice onto a large platter and spoon curry on top. Scatter nuts over curry.

PER SERVING 469 calories; 9 g fat (1 g sat.); 14 g protein; 86 g carbohydrate; 13 g fiber; 797 mg sodium; 0 mg cholesterol

kasha picadillo stuffed peppers

MAKES 6 servings **PREP** 20 minutes **MICROWAVE** 5 minutes **COOK** 19 minutes **BAKE** at 350°F for 15 minutes

3 large green peppers (about 12 ounces each), cut in half from stem to bottom, seeds and membrane removed

1 tablespoon olive oil

1 large onion, chopped

½ pound ground pork

3 cloves garlic, chopped

1 teaspoon dried oregano

1 teaspoon ground cinnamon

½ teaspoon ground cumin

1 can (14.5 ounces) no-salt-added diced tomatoes

½ cup raisins

½ cup pimiento-stuffed olives, halved

½ teaspoon salt

½ teaspoon black pepper

1 can (14.5 ounces) reduced fat and sodium beef broth

1 egg

1 cup kasha

Cilantro (optional)

① Place pepper halves, cut side down, in a microwave-safe glass dish. Pour ¼ **cup water** into dish and cover with plastic wrap, venting at one corner. Microwave for 4 to 5 minutes until tender. Microwave in batches if necessary. Place, cut side up, in a 13 x 9 x 2-inch baking dish and set aside.

② Heat oil in a large nonstick skillet over medium-high heat. Add onion and cook 3 minutes. Crumble in pork and cook 3 minutes. Stir in garlic, oregano, cinnamon and cumin; cook 1 minute.

③ Stir in tomatoes, raisins, olives, ¼ teaspoon of salt and ¼ teaspoon of pepper. Simmer, covered, for 12 minutes, stirring occasionally. Heat oven to 350°F.

④ While tomato and raisin mixture is simmering, make kasha. In a small saucepan, bring broth and remaining ¼ teaspoon salt and ¼ teaspoon pepper to a boil. In a medium-size bowl, lightly beat egg and stir in kasha until kernels are coated. In a medium-size saucepan, cook kasha over medium-high heat until egg has dried on kasha and kernels are separate. Quickly stir in boiling broth. Cover and simmer 9 to 10 minutes, until kasha is tender and liquid is absorbed. Stir kasha into mixture in skillet.

⑤ Place a cup of kasha mixture into each pepper half and cover baking dish with foil.

⑥ Just before serving, heat stuffed peppers in 350°F oven 10 to 15 minutes. Garnish with cilantro, if desired. Heat any remaining kasha mixture and serve alongside.

PER SERVING 358 calories; 15 g fat (4 g sat.); 14 g protein; 44 g carbohydrate; 6 g fiber; 718 mg sodium; 62 mg cholesterol

NUTRITION NOTE

Kasha (buckwheat groats) is one of the oldest known foods in Eastern European cooking. Although it looks and tastes like a grain, it's actually the seeds of buckwheat. Since it's gluten-free, it's ideal for people with allergies to gluten. High in iron, full of B vitamins and rich in phosphorous, potassium and calcium, 1 cup of buckwheat kasha contains more than 20% of the recommended daily intake of fiber.

wheat berry salad cups

MAKES 6 servings (12 cups) **PREP** 15 minutes **SOAK** overnight **COOK** 1 hour, 15 minutes

2 cups wheat berries

2 large portobello mushroom caps, stemmed, and gills removed, thinly sliced

4 ribs celery, thinly sliced

½ red onion, peeled and chopped

4 scallions, trimmed and chopped

1 large Fuji apple, cored and diced

3 tablespoons extra-virgin olive oil

3 tablespoons balsamic vinegar

1 teaspoon salt

½ teaspoon black pepper

1 head Bibb lettuce, trimmed, rinsed and dried

4 ounces goat cheese, crumbled

⅓ cup chopped toasted walnuts

① Place wheat berries in a large bowl and cover with water. Allow to soak overnight. Drain and place in a large pot and add **4 cups water**. Cover and bring to a boil over medium-high heat. Reduce heat to medium-low and simmer, covered, for 70 to 75 minutes or until tender. Stir occasionally.

② While wheat berries are simmering, coat a large nonstick skillet with cooking spray. Add mushrooms and cook over medium-high heat about 4 minutes or until tender. Remove from heat and reserve.

③ Drain wheat berries and place in a large bowl. Add mushrooms, celery, onion, scallions and apple. Stir to combine. Whisk together olive oil, balsamic vinegar, salt and pepper. Add to wheat berry mixture and stir to coat.

④ Form lettuce leaves into cups and fill with wheat berry mixture. Top each with some of the crumbled goat cheese and walnuts.

PER SERVING 424 calories; 16 g fat (4 g sat.); 14 g protein; 54 g carbohydrate; 9 g fiber; 489 mg sodium; 7 mg cholesterol

NUTRITION NOTE

Wheat berries are whole, unprocessed wheat kernels that are high in protein and fiber.

wild rice & tofu toss

MAKES 6 servings **PREP** 20 minutes **COOK** 45 minutes **GRILL** 4 minutes

2 cups wild and brown rice mix (such as RiceSelect)

½ cup dried apricots, thinly sliced

7 tablespoons reduced-sodium soy sauce

4 tablespoons apricot preserves

12 ounces extra-firm tofu, sliced into eight ½-inch-thick slices, from short side

1 tablespoon canola oil

1 large onion, chopped

3 ribs celery, chopped

1 bunch scallions, rinsed and cut into 1-inch pieces on the diagonal

4 ounces shiitake mushrooms, stemmed and sliced

1 sweet red pepper, cored, seeded and chopped

1 can (4½ ounces) diced water chestnuts, drained

2 teaspoons sesame oil

① Cook wild rice mix following package directions, about 45 minutes. Stir in apricots during last 5 minutes of cooking.

② In a small bowl, whisk together soy sauce and apricot preserves until smooth. Set aside.

③ Meanwhile, lightly grease a grill pan and heat over medium-high heat. Brush both sides of tofu slices with 2 tablespoons of soy sauce mixture. Grill for 2 minutes per side. Remove to a plate and keep warm.

④ Heat oil in a large nonstick skillet over medium-high heat. Add onion, celery, scallions and mushrooms. Cook 8 minutes, stirring occasionally. Add red pepper and water chestnuts; cook for 2 minutes. Stir in rice, remaining soy sauce mixture and sesame oil. Cut tofu into bite-size pieces and gently fold in.

⑤ Gently heat, if necessary, and serve immediately.

PER SERVING 458 calories; 8 g fat (1 g sat.); 14 g protein; 81 g carbohydrate; 9 g fiber; 739 mg sodium; 0 mg cholesterol

smoky beef & hominy stew

MAKES 6 servings (12 cups) **PREP** 20 minutes **COOK** 1 hour 35 minutes

6 tablespoons all-purpose flour

1 to 1½ teaspoons chipotle chile powder, depending on taste

¼ teaspoon salt

1 pound beef chuck, cut into 1-inch cubes

1 tablespoon canola oil

1 large onion, peeled, halved and thinly sliced

3 cloves garlic, peeled and coarsely chopped

3 cups reduced-sodium beef broth

1 can (14.5 ounces) no-salt-added stewed tomatoes

¾ teaspoon dried oregano

2 cans (15 ounces each) hominy, drained and rinsed

1 bag (1 pound) peeled baby carrots, sliced

1 large green pepper, cored, seeded and thinly sliced

3 tablespoons chopped cilantro

4½ cups cooked brown rice (1½ cups uncooked)

① In a shallow dish, whisk together flour, 1 teaspoon of chile powder and salt. Coat beef cubes with flour mixture; reserve unused flour.

② Heat oil in a large pot or Dutch oven over medium-high heat. Add beef and cook, turning, until all sides are browned, about 5 minutes. Remove to a plate and reserve.

③ Add onion and garlic to pot and cook over medium heat, stirring to keep garlic from burning, about 4 to 5 minutes. Add ¼ **cup water** if needed to avoid burning. Scrape up any browned bits from bottom of pot.

④ Stir in beef and any juices, reserved flour mixture, broth, tomatoes, **1 cup water** and dried oregano. Bring to a boil. Reduce heat to medium-low and gently simmer 1 hour, stirring occasionally.

⑤ Add hominy, carrots, green pepper and remaining ½ teaspoon chile powder, if desired. Simmer, covered, for 20 to 25 minutes or until carrots are tender.

⑥ Stir in cilantro and serve with cooked brown rice.

PER SERVING 469 calories; 7 g fat (2 g sat.); 26 g protein; 72 g carbohydrate; 44 g fiber; 797 mg sodium; 33 mg cholesterol

TEST KITCHEN TIP

Hominy is more tender and has a creamier texture than regular corn. It can be served in many of the same ways as potatoes.

The easiest way to feed your family great meals for less is to go meatless, at least a few days a week. Study after study has demonstrated that eating a plant-based diet—one high in fruits, vegetables and whole grains—is the key to good health, including preventing childhood obesity. Vegetables, beans and lentils are all low in fat and full of fiber.

vegetarian

One of the simplest and most delicious ways to transition your family into trying meat-free meals is to serve ethnic dishes like the ones in this chapter. Serve up Harvest Chili (page 120) for Tex-Mex Night, Eggplant Rollatini (page 118) for an Italian feast and Vegetable Curry (page 136), complete with condiments, for an Indian buffet. With dishes like these, no one will ask, "Where's the meat?"

easy minestrone

MAKES 6 servings **PREP** 10 minutes **COOK** 13 minutes

1   cup chopped onion

3   cloves garlic, sliced

2   tablespoons olive oil

2   cans (14.5 ounces each) vegetable broth

1   jar (16 ounces) marinara sauce

1   can (15 ounces) red kidney beans, drained and rinsed

3   ribs celery, sliced

1   box (10 ounces) frozen mixed vegetables

1   cup ditalini pasta

    Grated Parmesan cheese (optional)

    Basil

① In a large nonstick pot, cook onion and garlic in olive oil for 3 minutes over medium-high heat. Add vegetable broth, marinara sauce, kidney beans, celery and frozen mixed vegetables.

② Bring to a boil and add ditalini pasta. Cook, covered, with lid slightly ajar, for 10 minutes, stirring occasionally. Serve immediately with grated Parmesan cheese, if desired. Garnish with basil.

PER SERVING 284 calories; 9 g fat (2 g sat.); 11 g protein; 42 g carbohydrate; 11 g fiber; 730 mg sodium; 0 mg cholesterol

red lentil soup

MAKES 6 servings **PREP** 10 minutes **COOK** 20 minutes

2 tablespoons olive oil

1 large onion, chopped

½ bag (16 ounces) baby carrots, coarsely chopped (about 1½ cups)

½ teaspoon ground cumin

6 cups low-sodium vegetable broth

1 package (1 pound) red lentils, picked over and rinsed

1 bunch fresh kale (about ¾ pound), rinsed, tough stems removed and leaves coarsely chopped (about 8 cups)

½ teaspoon salt

¼ teaspoon chipotle-flavored hot pepper sauce

① Heat oil in a large, deep pot over medium-high heat. Add onion, carrots and cumin; cook 5 minutes or until softened.

② Add broth and bring to a simmer. Add lentils. Cover, reduce heat to medium-low and cook 10 minutes.

③ Uncover pot. Raise heat to high; stir in kale and salt. Cook uncovered, stirring occasionally, 5 minutes or until kale is tender. Remove from heat; stir in hot sauce.

PER SERVING 375 calories; 7 g fat (0 g sat.); 23 g protein; 58 g carbohydrate; 15 g fiber; 387 mg sodium; 0 mg cholesterol

NUTRITION NOTE
Considered by many experts as one of the 5 healthiest foods, lentils have a high level of protein and contain dietary fiber, folate, vitamin B and minerals. Lentils are often mixed with grains, such as rice, which results in a complete protein dish.

Pizza is a fun and nutritious family meal that can be flavored in a variety of ways. This refreshing version tops the pizza with a crisp salad. Feel free to improvise—instead of salad, try sliced mushrooms, cooked spinach or chopped broccoli.

salad pizza

MAKES 4 servings **PREP** 5 minutes **BAKE** at 450°F for 13 minutes

2 plum tomatoes, cored and thinly sliced

1 whole-wheat or regular pre-baked pizza shell (10 ounces)

¼ teaspoon black pepper

¾ cup shredded part-skim mozzarella cheese

3 tablespoons grated Parmesan cheese

4 cups baby salad greens

3 tablespoons light balsamic vinaigrette

① Heat oven to 450°F. Spread tomato slices onto paper towels. Let sit 5 minutes.

② Place pizza shell on a large baking sheet. Top with tomatoes; sprinkle with pepper. Bake at 450°F for 8 minutes. Top with mozzarella and Parmesan cheeses and continue to bake an additional 5 minutes.

③ Meanwhile, in a large bowl, toss salad greens with dressing. Remove pizza from oven; top with salad. Cut into wedges.

PER SERVING 296 calories; 10 g fat (3 g sat.); 16 g protein; 40 g carbohydrate; 7 g fiber; 745 mg sodium; 17 mg cholesterol

3-bean caprese salad

MAKES 6 servings **PREP** 20 minutes **COOK** 4 minutes

Dressing:

- ⅓ cup balsamic vinegar
- 1 tablespoon honey Dijon mustard
- ¼ teaspoon salt
- ¼ teaspoon pepper
- 3 tablespoons extra-virgin olive oil

Salad:

- ½ pound green beans, trimmed and cut into 1-inch pieces
- 1 cup loosely packed basil leaves
- 1¼ pounds tomatoes, cored and chopped
- ½ pound fresh mozzarella cheese, cut into ½-inch cubes
- 1 can (15 ounces) red kidney beans, drained and rinsed
- 1 can (15 ounces) small white beans, drained and rinsed

① Dressing: In a medium-size bowl or measuring cup, whisk together vinegar, mustard, salt and pepper. While whisking, add oil in a thin stream until blended. Set aside.

② Salad: Heat a medium-size pot of water to boiling. Add green beans and cook 4 minutes or until crisp-tender. Drain and rinse with cold water.

③ Tear basil into bite-size pieces. In a large bowl, toss basil, green beans, tomatoes, mozzarella cheese and kidney and white beans. Whisk dressing, then drizzle over salad. Toss gently to coat, and serve.

PER SERVING 350 calories; 17 g fat (7 g sat.); 18 g protein; 35 g carbohydrate; 11 g fiber; 650 mg sodium; 27 mg cholesterol

TEST KITCHEN TIP

Make Ahead This salad improves with age. Make it a day ahead and store in the refrigerator, covered with plastic.

fresh 2-bean & corn salad

MAKES 6 servings **PREP** 10 minutes **BAKE** at 400°F for 10 minutes **COOK** 8 minutes

Dressing:

- 1 tablespoon cider vinegar
- 1 teaspoon Dijon mustard
- ¼ teaspoon salt
- ¼ teaspoon black pepper
- 2 tablespoons olive oil

Salad:

- 1 package (8.5 ounces) corn muffin mix (such as Jiffy)
- 2 ears corn, shucked
- 4 ounces fresh green beans, trimmed and cut into 1-inch lengths
- 4 ounces fresh yellow wax beans, trimmed and cut into 1-inch lengths
- ½ cup shredded reduced-fat sharp cheddar cheese (6 ounces)
- 1 large tomato, chopped
- 1 small sweet red pepper, cut into 1-inch strips
- 3 scallions, including green tops, thinly sliced
- ½ cup chopped fresh basil

① Dressing: Whisk vinegar, mustard, salt and pepper in a large bowl; slowly whisk in oil. Let stand.

② Salad: Prepare corn muffin mix in 8-inch square baking dish according to package directions. Cool completely, then cut into 1-inch cubes (5 cups). Heat oven to 400°F. Place cornbread cubes in a single layer on a baking sheet and bake, stirring once, 8 to 10 minutes or until lightly toasted. Cool.

③ Bring a large pot of salted water to a boil. Add corn and cook 5 minutes. Add green and wax beans and cook 3 minutes longer or until beans are crisp-tender. Using tongs, remove corn and rinse under cold running water. Drain beans and rinse under cold running water. Cut corn off cob (1½ cups kernels).

④ In serving bowl combine beans, corn, cheddar cheese, tomato, red pepper, scallions, basil and dressing; toss to combine. Add cornbread and toss gently. Serve immediately.

PER SERVING 311 calories; 15 g fat (6 g sat.); 16 g protein; 34 g carbohydrate; 5 g fiber; 410 mg sodium; 38 mg cholesterol

TEST KITCHEN TIP

Green beans are the most common of the string beans, but yellow wax and purple varieties are usually available in summer and can be used interchangeably in recipes.

greek-style veggie burgers

MAKES 4 servings   **PREP** 10 minutes   **COOK OR GRILL** 8 minutes

1½   cups loosely packed baby spinach

½   cucumber, peeled, seeded and diced

2   scallions, chopped

1   plum tomato, cored and diced

¼   cup crumbled reduced-fat feta cheese

1½   tablespoons bottled light vinaigrette

4   veggie burger patties

4   whole-wheat mini pitas

¼   cup light mayonnaise

① Stack baby spinach leaves and cut into thin strips, discarding stems. Place in a large bowl and combine with cucumber, scallions, tomato and feta cheese. Toss gently to combine, then add dressing and toss. Set aside.

② Heat veggie burgers for 8 minutes or as per package directions (either on grill or in skillet). Warm pitas in a toaster oven or toaster. Spread each pita with 1 tablespoon of light mayonnaise. Top each with a veggie burger, then with ¼ of salad topping (½ cup per burger). Serve immediately.

PER SERVING 282 calories; 11 g fat (3 g sat.); 17 g protein; 30 g carbohydrate; 6 g fiber; 794 mg sodium; 15 mg cholesterol

TEST KITCHEN TIP
Veggie burger patties are a must-have freezer item. Paired with a fresh vegetable salad and whole-wheat bread or grain, they form a quick weeknight meal that is both nutritious and delicious.

gazpacho pasta salad

MAKES 4 servings **PREP** 10 minutes **COOK** 8 minutes

8 ounces pipette or cavatappi pasta

3 tablespoons olive oil

2 tablespoons red wine vinegar

3 cloves garlic, finely chopped

½ teaspoon paprika

½ teaspoon salt

1 can (14.5 ounces) diced tomatoes with jalapeño chiles

1 large sweet green pepper, cored, seeded and cut into ½-inch pieces (about 1 cup)

2 medium-size celery ribs, cut into ½-inch pieces (about 1 cup)

½ seedless cucumber, peeled, quartered lengthwise and sliced crosswise into ½-inch-thick pieces (about 1¼ cups)

1 can (15 ounces) black beans, drained and rinsed

Chopped fresh parsley (optional)

① Cook pasta in large, deep pot of lightly salted water until al dente, firm yet tender, following package directions, about 8 minutes. Drain; rinse with cold water; drain.

② Meanwhile, in a large bowl, whisk oil, vinegar, garlic, paprika and salt. Add tomatoes with their juice, green pepper, celery, cucumber and beans; toss to mix. Add pasta; toss to coat.

③ Garnish with parsley, if desired. Serve immediately or refrigerate, covered, 30 minutes to chill.

PER SERVING 282 calories; 11 g fat (2 g sat.); 9 g protein; 41 g carbohydrate; 8 g fiber; 790 mg sodium; 0 mg cholesterol

eggplant & tomato gratin

MAKES 4 servings **PREP** 20 minutes **BROIL** 10 minutes **BAKE** at 350°F for 55 minutes

2 **large ripe tomatoes, cut into ½-inch-thick slices**

½ **teaspoon salt**

2 **eggplants (2 pounds total), cut into ½-inch-thick slices**

¼ **cup dry unseasoned bread crumbs**

¾ **teaspoon dried oregano**

¾ **teaspoon dried basil**

2 **cloves garlic, finely chopped**

½ **cup fat-free half-and-half**

1½ **cups shredded reduced-fat mozzarella cheese**

¼ **cup grated Parmesan cheese**

① Place tomato slices on paper towels; sprinkle with ¼ teaspoon of salt. Place more paper towels on top. Let stand 30 minutes. Pat top of tomatoes to remove as much liquid as possible.

② Coat both sides of eggplant slices with nonstick cooking spray. Heat broiler.

③ Broil eggplant slices on baking sheet coated with nonstick cooking spray for 5 minutes on each side or until tender.

④ Reduce oven heat to 350°F. Coat a 2½-quart baking dish with nonstick spray. Sprinkle bread crumbs over bottom. Arrange eggplant and tomato slices, alternating, around baking dish and down center, in a single layer if possible.

⑤ Sprinkle casserole with oregano, basil, garlic and remaining ¼ teaspoon salt. Drizzle with half-and-half. Top with both kinds of cheese. Cover with foil.

⑥ Bake at 350°F for 45 minutes. Remove foil; bake 10 minutes or until cheese is golden. Cool 10 minutes, then serve.

PER SERVING 282 calories; 6 g fat (5 g sat.); 8 g protein; 39 g carbohydrate; 9 g fiber; 800 mg sodium; 9 mg cholesterol

HOW-TO

Rinse whole eggplant in water. Trim off stem, then slice crosswise into ½-inch-thick rounds.

eggplant rollatini

MAKES 6 servings **PREP** 25 minutes **GRILL** eggplant slices for 8 minutes per batch **BAKE** at 350°F for 25 minutes

2 eggplants (about 2¼ pounds total)

½ teaspoon salt

1½ cups shredded reduced-sodium part-skim mozzarella cheese

1 cup part-skim ricotta cheese

1 egg yolk

⅛ teaspoon dried Italian seasoning

⅛ teaspoon black pepper

1 jar (12 ounces) roasted red peppers, drained, or homemade fresh-roasted peppers, if desired

1½ cups prepared low-fat marinara sauce

2 tablespoons grated Parmesan cheese

① Trim tops and bottoms from eggplants. Cut each into 6 lengthwise slices, about ½ inch thick. Spread slices onto 2 large cookie sheets lined with paper towels. Sprinkle slices with ¼ teaspoon of salt, then turn slices over and sprinkle with remaining ¼ teaspoon salt. Let stand 15 minutes, flipping slices halfway.

② Heat grill or grill pan to medium-high heat. Quickly rinse eggplant slices under running water; pat dry. Spray both sides with nonstick cooking spray. Grill slices until softened and nicely marked, about 4 minutes per side. Return slices (do not overlap) to large cookie sheets (without paper towels).

③ Heat oven to 350°F and coat a 13 x 9 x 2-inch baking dish with nonstick cooking spray. In a small bowl, stir together ¾ cup of mozzarella cheese, ricotta cheese, egg yolk, Italian seasoning and pepper. Stir until well combined.

④ Divide red pepper pieces evenly among eggplant slices, placing them on wider end of each slice. Top each pepper with a heaping tablespoon of cheese filling. Place ½ cup of marinara sauce on bottom of prepared dish. Roll up eggplant slices, starting at wide end and enclosing filling. Place in dish. Top with remaining 1 cup marinara sauce, remaining ¾ cup mozzarella cheese and grated Parmesan cheese.

⑤ Bake at 350°F for 25 minutes. Remove to wire rack and cool at least 10 minutes before serving.

PER SERVING 237 calories; 12 g fat (6 g sat.); 16 g protein; 22 g carbohydrate; 6 g fiber; 710 mg sodium; 63 mg cholesterol

TEST KITCHEN TIP

This dish may be assembled a day ahead. Store in the fridge, covered with plastic.

harvest chili

MAKES 12 cups **PREP** 20 minutes **COOK** 36 minutes

2 tablespoons olive oil

1 large onion, peeled and chopped

1½ teaspoons ground cumin

1 teaspoon chipotle chile powder (or more if desired)

2 cans (28 ounces each) whole tomatoes in puree

1 medium-size cauliflower, cut into florets (about 4 cups)

2 medium-size sweet potatoes (about 1 pound), peeled and cut into ½-inch cubes

4 large carrots, peeled and cut into ¼-inch coins

1 large green bell pepper, cored, seeded and cut into ½-inch dice

½ teaspoon salt

1 can (15 ounces) Mexican chili beans or red kidney beans

Sliced scallions

Cooked brown rice (optional)

① Heat olive oil in a large pot over medium-high heat. Add onion and cook for 5 minutes, stirring occasionally. Stir in cumin and chile powder; cook 1 minute. Stir in tomatoes, breaking up with a spoon.

② Stir in cauliflower, sweet potatoes, carrots, green pepper and salt. Cover and bring to a boil. Reduce heat and simmer, covered, for 25 minutes. Stir occasionally. Add chili beans and simmer for 5 minutes or until vegetables are fork-tender.

③ Garnish with scallions and serve with brown rice, if desired.

PER CUP 123 calories; 3 g fat (0 g sat.); 4 g protein; 20 g carbohydrate; 5 g fiber; 502 mg sodium; 0 mg cholesterol

COOKING IN COLOR

To improve your family's diet effortlessly, focus on brightly hued fruits and vegetables (plus grains) and offer 5 servings a day from the rainbow. In return you'll get vitamins, minerals, fiber and more.

RED

Benefits Improves heart health and memory; lowers risk of some cancers; promotes urinary tract health

Best Picks Tomatoes, sweet red peppers, radishes, beets, raspberries, apples, guavas, strawberries, watermelons

YELLOW & ORANGE

Benefits Boosts heart and vision health plus immune system; helps lower risk of prostate cancer

Best Picks Corn, squashes, sweet yellow peppers, oranges, mangoes, peaches, lemons, pineapples, bananas

GREEN

Benefits Improves eye health; promotes strong bones and teeth; helps cut risk of colon and breast cancers

Best Picks Asparagus, cabbages, broccoli, celery, spinach, zucchinis, Brussels sprouts, kiwis, honeydew melons

PURPLE & BLUE

Benefits Lowers risk of heart disease; promotes urinary tract health; helps improve memory

Best Picks Purple onions, eggplants, blueberries, grapes, plums

WHITE & TAN

Benefits Slows cholesterol absorption; boosts ability to fight infections; lowers blood pressure

Best Picks Cauliflower, onions, parsnips, turnips, jicama, garlic

baked potatoes florentine

MAKES 4 servings **PREP** 5 minutes **MICROWAVE** 16 minutes **COOK** 8 minutes
BAKE at 400°F for 10 minutes **BROIL** 2 minutes

- 4 **Idaho baking potatoes (about 8 ounces each), scrubbed**
- 1 **tablespoon olive oil**
- 1 **large onion, chopped**
- 1 **bag (9 ounces) baby spinach, coarsely chopped**
- ½ **teaspoon salt**
- ⅛ **teaspoon black pepper**
- 1 **large egg, separated**
- 1 **package (4 ounces) crumbled feta cheese**

① Heat oven to 400°F. Pierce potatoes with a fork. Place on paper towels in microwave. Microwave for 16 minutes, turning over halfway through.

② Meanwhile, heat oil in a large nonstick skillet over medium heat. Add onion and cook 5 minutes. Stir in half of spinach and cook down slightly. Add remaining spinach and cook until all is wilted, about 3 minutes. Season with ¼ teaspoon of salt and pepper. Remove skillet from heat; transfer spinach mixture to a large bowl and cool slightly.

③ Line a small baking sheet with aluminum foil; place potatoes on foil. Carefully cut open potatoes; sprinkle with remaining ¼ teaspoon salt.

④ Beat egg white to stiff peaks. Once spinach mixture has cooled slightly, stir in egg yolk and all but 2 tablespoons of feta cheese. Fold egg white into spinach mixture. Divide spinach mixture evenly among potatoes (about ½ cup in each). Sprinkle all with remaining cheese.

⑤ Bake at 400°F for 10 minutes. Increase heat to broil. Run potatoes under broiler for 2 minutes.

PER POTATO 345 calories; 11 g fat (5 g sat.); 12 g protein; 53 g carbohydrate; 7 g fiber; 739 mg sodium; 78 mg cholesterol

POTATO PRIMER

clockwise, starting top left

1. Idaho Russet: Ideal for baking; also good for potato skins or skin-on steak fries.

2. Yukon Gold: Named for its golden-colored flesh; best served mashed or roasted. Avoid whipping, as its waxy texture can get gluey.

3. All-Purpose White: The go-to potato for scalloped or au gratin dishes. Skin can be left on; perfect for potato salads or shredded into hash browns.

4. Red Bliss New: Small globes—1 to 2 inches—shine when roasted or boiled and tossed with butter and parsley.

edamame & mushroom risotto

MAKES 8 servings **PREP** 15 minutes **COOK** 47 minutes

2 tablespoons olive oil

8 ounces white button mushrooms, trimmed and sliced

1 pound frozen edamame

3 cups low-sodium vegetable broth mixed with 1½ cups water

1 small onion, peeled and finely chopped

1⅓ cups arborio rice

¼ cup white wine

⅛ teaspoon black pepper

⅓ cup shredded Parmesan cheese

① Heat 1 tablespoon of olive oil in a large nonstick skillet over medium-high heat. Add mushrooms and cook for 5 minutes, stirring occasionally. Set aside.

② Cook edamame, about 5 minutes, following package directions. Drain, cool and remove beans from shells. Add beans to mushrooms in skillet. Discard shells.

③ Place broth and water in a medium-size saucepan and bring to a simmer.

④ Heat remaining tablespoon oil in a large saucepan over medium heat. Add onion and cook 5 minutes, stirring occasionally. Add rice and stir until rice is coated with oil. Cook for 1 minute, stirring. Add wine and cook until wine is absorbed, about 1 minute.

⑤ Add ½ cup of simmering broth mixture. Cook over medium-low heat, stirring, until broth is absorbed. Add remaining broth mixture, ½ cup at a time, cooking in same manner. This should take about 30 minutes.

⑥ Gently heat mushrooms and edamame. Stir into rice and remove from heat. Stir in pepper and ¼ cup of Parmesan cheese.

⑦ Divide among 8 bowls and sprinkle with remaining Parmesan cheese.

PER SERVING 495 calories; 18 g fat (4 g sat.); 24 g protein; 60 g carbohydrate; 6 g fiber; 378 mg sodium; 15 mg cholesterol

NUTRITION NOTE

Edamame are a delicious source of complete protein. Their nutty flavor and creamy texture make them popular snacks.

asian-style grilled tofu

MAKES 6 servings   **PREP** 10 minutes   **MARINATE** 30 minutes   **COOK** 11 minutes   **GRILL** 4 minutes

⅓ cup teriyaki sauce

2 tablespoons rice vinegar

2 tablespoons fresh lime juice

1 tablespoon bottled oyster sauce

1 teaspoon ground ginger

½ teaspoon sugar

½ teaspoon red pepper flakes

½ teaspoon garlic powder

1 package (14 ounces drained weight) extra-firm tofu

2 teaspoons peanut or canola oil

1 package (12 ounces) fettuccine

8 ounces snow peas, strings removed

1 red pepper, cored, seeded and thinly sliced

1 medium onion, halved and cut into half-moons

½ cup vegetable broth

2 teaspoons cornstarch

1 teaspoon toasted sesame seeds

① In a small bowl, combine teriyaki, vinegar, lime juice, oyster sauce, ginger, sugar, red pepper flakes and garlic powder.

② Open package of tofu and drain. Slice tofu diagonally in half to form 2 triangular-shaped pieces. Turn triangle onto long flat cut side, with point facing up. Cut into 3 triangular slices, each about ½ inch thick. Repeat with second triangle to form six ½-inch-thick triangular slices.

③ Spread tofu onto a paper-towel-lined tray. Top with more paper towels, and cover with a sheet pan. Evenly weigh down sheet pan with soup cans. Let stand 10 minutes. Change paper towels and repeat.

④ Transfer tofu to a shallow glass dish and add marinade. Let marinate, at room temperature, 30 minutes, turning slices over after 15 minutes.

⑤ Drain marinade into a small saucepan. Bring a large pot of water to a boil. Heat a ridged grill pan over medium-high heat. Brush with 2 teaspoons oil.

⑥ Cook fettuccine in boiling water, according to package directions, 11 minutes, adding snow peas, red pepper and onion during last 4 minutes of cooking.

⑦ Grill tofu, about 2 minutes per side, until nicely marked and hot.

⑧ Stir broth and cornstarch into marinade and bring to a boil; boil until thickened, about 2 minutes.

⑨ Drain noodles and vegetables. Toss together with thickened marinade and sprinkle with sesame seeds. Top with grilled tofu.

PER SERVING 264 calories; 4 g fat (0 g sat.); 13 g protein; 44 g carbohydrate; 4 g fiber; 591 mg sodium; 0 mg cholesterol

HOW-TO

Sesame Savvy Toast sesame seeds in a dry, heavy skillet over medium heat until light brown, 2 to 3 minutes.

skillet summer squash parmesan

MAKES 6 servings **PREP** 15 minutes **BAKE** at 400°F for 20 minutes **COOK** 25 minutes

3	large summer squash (about 2 pounds)
½	teaspoon garlic salt
½	teaspoon black pepper
4	plum tomatoes, thinly sliced
1	can (14.5 ounces) Italian-flavored diced tomatoes
1½	cups reduced-fat shredded Italian cheese blend
¼	cup grated Parmesan cheese
½	pound whole-wheat spaghetti

① Heat oven to 400°F. Cut squash on the diagonal into ¼-inch slices. Season with ¼ teaspoon *each* garlic salt and pepper. Coat 2 baking sheets with cooking spray and place squash slices on pans. Bake at 400°F for 20 minutes.

② Season tomato slices with remaining ¼ teaspoon *each* garlic salt and pepper. Spoon ⅓ of diced tomatoes into bottom of a large nonstick skillet. Layer half of squash slices, half of tomato slices, ⅓ of diced tomatoes and half of Parmesan cheese. Repeat layering. Top with remaining Parmesan cheese.

③ Cover and simmer for 25 minutes over low heat.

④ Meanwhile, prepare pasta following package directions. Divide cooked pasta between plates. Top with squash mixture.

PER SERVING 458 calories; 11 g fat (7 g sat.); 30 g protein; 60 g carbohydrate; 13 g fiber; 776 mg sodium; 34 mg cholesterol

TEST KITCHEN TIP

When buying summer squash, be sure they are firm and smooth with glossy skin. Squash will keep in the refrigerator for up to 1 week.

This casserole of cauliflower layered with polenta, tomato sauce and cheese is a delectable way to serve cauliflower to your family. Even picky eaters will be back for seconds.

polenta with cauliflower & marinara

MAKES 6 servings **PREP** 10 minutes **COOK** 5 minutes **BAKE** at 375°F for 40 minutes **LET REST** 15 minutes

1⅓   **cups instant polenta**

2   **tablespoons grated Parmesan cheese**

¼   **teaspoon salt**

¼   **teaspoon pepper**

1   **head cauliflower (2 pounds)**

1   **jar (28 ounces) marinara sauce**

¼   **cup dry bread crumbs**

1¾   **cups shredded part-skim mozzarella cheese**

① Heat oven to 375°F. Coat a 13 x 9 x 2-inch baking dish with nonstick cooking spray. Set aside.

② Bring **2 cups water** to a boil in a medium-size saucepan. In a small bowl, combine polenta and **2 cups cool water**. Stir in Parmesan cheese, salt and pepper. Stir polenta into boiling water. Reduce heat to medium-high; cook 5 minutes, stirring. Spread into prepared dish.

③ Cut cauliflower into equal-size florets. Spread half over polenta. Top with 1½ cups marinara sauce. Sprinkle with half of bread crumbs and half of mozzarella cheese. Repeat layering, ending with mozzarella. Cover with foil. Bake at 375°F for 40 minutes. Let rest 15 minutes.

PER SERVING 348 calories; 9 g fat (4 g sat.); 17 g protein; 51 g carbohydrate; 8 g fiber; 748 mg sodium; 23 mg cholesterol

TEST KITCHEN TIP

Equally delicious boiled, steamed or roasted, cauliflower is a very versatile vegetable. Look for compact clusters, with bright-green, firmly attached leaves and no brown spots. Place in a plastic bag and refrigerate in crisper drawer for up to 1 week.

zucchini & chickpea ratatouille

MAKES 4 servings **PREP** 10 minutes **BAKE** at 425°F for 30 minutes **COOK** 11 minutes

2 medium-size zucchini (about 1¼ pounds), quartered lengthwise and cut into ½-inch pieces

1 large red pepper, cored, seeded and cut into ½-inch pieces

2 tablespoons olive oil

4 cloves garlic, finely chopped

2 cans (14.5 ounces) Italian-seasoned diced tomatoes

1 can (15.5 ounces) chickpeas, drained and rinsed

⅛ teaspoon black pepper

⅛ teaspoon red pepper flakes

3 cups cooked brown rice

① Heat oven to 425°F.

② Coat a baking sheet with nonstick cooking spray. Add zucchini and red pepper; toss with 1 tablespoon olive oil. Bake at 425°F for 30 minutes or until tender.

③ Heat remaining 1 tablespoon oil in a large nonstick skillet over medium-high heat. Add garlic, cook 30 seconds to 1 minute. Stir in tomatoes and cook for 5 minutes, stirring occasionally. Add zucchini, peppers, chickpeas, pepper and red pepper flakes. Cook an additional 5 minutes, stirring occasionally. Serve with cooked brown rice.

PER SERVING 402 calories; 9 g fat (1 g sat.); 16 g protein; 67 g carbohydrate; 10 g fiber; 710 mg sodium; 9 mg cholesterol

rainbow chard & white bean casserole

MAKES 8 servings **PREP** 20 minutes **COOK** 15 minutes **BAKE** at 350°F for 15 minutes

Polenta and Onions:

- **4** cups fat-free milk
- **1** teaspoon garlic powder
- **¾** teaspoon salt
- **¼** teaspoon black pepper
- **1½** cups instant polenta
- **¾** cup shaved Asiago cheese
- **½** cup basil, shredded
- **1** tablespoon extra-virgin olive oil
- **2** onions, peeled, halved and thinly sliced

Chard and Beans:

- **2** tablespoons extra-virgin olive oil
- **2** bunches rainbow chard, trimmed and cut across leaves and 2 inches of stem into 1-inch pieces
- **4** cloves garlic, peeled and coarsely chopped
- **½** teaspoon dried Italian seasoning
- **¼** teaspoon salt
- **¼** teaspoon black pepper
- **2** cans (15 ounces each) cannellini beans, drained and rinsed
- **¾** cup shaved Asiago cheese

① Polenta and Onions: Lightly coat a 13 x 9 x 2-inch baking dish with nonstick cooking spray. In a large saucepan, combine milk, **1 cup water**, garlic powder, salt and pepper. Bring to a simmer over medium-high heat. Gradually whisk in polenta. Cook, whisking continuously, for about 2 minutes, until thick. Add a little hot water if mixture becomes too thick. Stir in ¾ cup of Asiago cheese and fresh basil. Spread polenta in prepared baking dish and allow to set up at room temperature.

② Heat 1 tablespoon olive oil in a large nonstick skillet over medium to medium-high heat. Add onions and cook 8 minutes, stirring occasionally, until nicely browned. Remove onions to a plate and wipe out skillet.

③ Chard and Beans: Heat 2 tablespoons olive oil in same skillet over medium heat. Add chard (in batches) and garlic and cook 5 minutes, stirring occasionally. Season with Italian seasoning, salt and pepper. Stir in beans and heat through.

④ Assemble casserole. Heat oven to 350°F. Spoon chard and beans evenly over polenta. Sprinkle ½ cup Asiago cheese over chard and beans. Scatter onions and remaining cheese over top. Bake, uncovered, for 15 minutes.

⑤ Allow to cool slightly before slicing. May also be served at room temperature.

PER SERVING 383 calories; 12 g fat (5 g sat.); 16 g protein; 51 g carbohydrate; 6 g fiber; 681 mg sodium; 21 mg cholesterol

garam masala lentils & potatoes

MAKES 6 servings (12 cups) **PREP** 15 minutes **COOK** 40 minutes

1   pound brown lentils, rinsed and picked over

1½   pounds all-purpose potatoes, peeled and cut into ¾-inch pieces

2   onions, peeled and chopped

1   can (14.5 ounces) no-salt-added diced tomatoes

2   teaspoons salt

1½   teaspoons Garam Masala seasoning

½   teaspoon ground cumin

½   teaspoon black pepper

2   yellow or red peppers, cored, seeded and cut into 1-inch pieces

½   cup cilantro leaves, chopped

¾   cup toasted slivered almonds

① In a large saucepan, combine **4 cups water**, lentils, potatoes, onions, diced tomatoes, salt, Garam Masala, cumin and pepper. Cover and bring to a boil over high heat. Reduce heat to medium-low and simmer, covered, for 35 minutes. Stir occasionally. Add yellow peppers and simmer an additional 5 minutes.

② Stir in cilantro and sprinkle almonds over top.

PER SERVING 475 calories; 10 g fat (1 g sat.); 27 g protein; 75 g carbohydrate; 22 g fiber; 786 mg sodium; 0 mg cholesterol

Curry powders can be hot or very mild. Check the labels when purchasing and be sure to taste the curry powder before cooking with it. When used with discretion, its distinct flavor enhances the taste of sauces, stews and vegetable dishes.

vegetable curry

MAKES 6 servings **PREP** 15 minutes **COOK** 33 minutes

- 2 tablespoons vegetable oil
- 1 large onion, sliced
- 1 small butternut squash (about 8 ounces), peeled, seeded and cut into 1-inch pieces (6 cups)
- 1 small head cauliflower, trimmed and cut into florets (6 cups)
- 4 teaspoons curry powder
- 1 teaspoon salt
- 1 teaspoon ground ginger
- 1 teaspoon sugar
- ⅓ teaspoon cayenne pepper
- 2 cups vegetable broth
- 2 tablespoons cornstarch
- 1 can (19 ounces) chickpeas, drained
- 1 can (14.5 ounces) diced tomatoes (not drained)
- 1 bag (6 ounces) fresh baby spinach
- ¼ cup shelled pistachios

① Heat oil in a large pot over medium-high heat. Add onion and sauté about 7 to 8 minutes, stirring often, or until lightly browned.

② Add butternut squash and cauliflower; cook about 12 minutes, stirring occasionally, until softened and lightly browned. Add curry powder, salt, ginger, sugar and cayenne, and cook, stirring, for 1 minute.

③ Place ¼ cup of vegetable broth in a small measuring cup and stir in cornstarch. Set aside.

④ Stir remaining broth, chickpeas and tomatoes into pot; bring to a boil over high heat. Cover and reduce heat to medium-low. Simmer 12 minutes, stirring occasionally, or until vegetables are tender.

⑤ Stir in reserved cornstarch mixture and spinach. Stir until spinach is wilted and mixture has thickened. Add pistachios. Serve warm.

PER SERVING 290 calories; 16 g fat (2 g sat.); 8 g protein; 33 g carbohydrate; 9 g fiber; 794 mg sodium; 0 mg cholesterol

TEST KITCHEN TIP

Currying Flavor Cook curry powder in a little oil over low heat until its aroma is released.

Roasted, baked, grilled or poached, chicken is a nutritious alternative to red meat—and it tastes great, too. Its versatility makes it a star in the kitchen: The protein pairs well with a long list of ingredients, or it's perfect alone. No surprise—chicken dinners are among *Family Circle* readers' most requested recipes.

Aside from its many uses, chicken is easy to prepare and cooks quickly. This low-fat meat is packed with protein, iron, zinc and B vitamins, making it a popular choice for those looking to cut calories without sacrificing nutrition. The leanest part is the breast (without skin), which has less than half the fat of a T-bone steak. A 3-ounce cooked serving contains only 140 calories with 3 grams of fat.

But don't ignore the benefits of dark meat chicken. Drumstick and thigh meat is a bit higher in fat than breast meat, but 60% of that fat is the healthier mono- and

⋯➤ chicken & turkey

polyunsaturated kind. Leg meat delivers double the zinc of breast meat, satisfying 20% of your daily RDA. Dark meat chicken has a more intense flavor and remains moist during cooking; it's perfect roasted or placed in casseroles, stews and heavily spiced global dishes. Plus, it's much less expensive than chicken breast.

While chicken holds the top spot for poultry popularity, people are discovering that turkey isn't just a holiday bird. Like dark meat chicken, turkey packs a ton of flavor. Not only that, turkey actually contains fewer calories per ounce than chicken (117 for 3 ounces). Oftentimes, turkey can be substituted for chicken in recipes as its ease and time of preparation is virtually identical. Considering its size, turkey is ideal for leftovers—toss it in casseroles, soups, sandwiches or pastas for a quick protein addition.

roast chicken & veggies

MAKES 4 servings **PREP** 15 minutes **ROAST** at 400°F for 1 hour, 10 minutes **LET REST** 10 minutes

1 lemon

1 whole chicken (about 3¼ pounds)

2 cloves garlic, minced

6 sprigs fresh tarragon

1 teaspoon salt

½ teaspoon black pepper

12 ounces baby potatoes, quartered

2 teaspoons olive oil

1 pound asparagus, ends trimmed and cut into 2-inch lengths

3 leeks, cleaned and sliced

① Heat oven to 400°F.

② Grate lemon peel and set zest aside; cut lemon into quarters. Separate skin from breasts of chicken. Under skin, spread lemon zest, garlic and 2 tarragon sprigs. Season outside and cavity of chicken with ½ teaspoon of salt and ¼ teaspoon of pepper. Place lemon quarters and remaining 4 tarragon sprigs in cavity. Place chicken in center of a large roasting pan. Roast on lower shelf at 400°F for 30 minutes.

③ In a medium-size bowl, toss potatoes, 1 teaspoon of olive oil, ¼ teaspoon of salt and ⅛ teaspoon of pepper. Coat second large roasting pan with nonstick spray; add potatoes. After chicken has roasted for 30 minutes, add potatoes to top shelf; roast both 15 minutes longer.

④ In a medium-size bowl, combine asparagus, leeks, remaining 1 teaspoon oil, remaining ¼ teaspoon salt and remaining ⅛ teaspoon pepper; toss to coat.

⑤ After potatoes have roasted for 15 minutes, add asparagus mixture to pan; roast chicken and vegetables 25 minutes longer, stirring once. Chicken is done when internal temperature registers 165°F on an instant-read thermometer inserted in thigh meat.

⑥ Let rest 10 minutes before carving. Remove and discard skin before serving.

PER SERVING 404 calories; 13 g fat (3 g sat.); 45 g protein; 28 g carbohydrate; 5 g fiber; 708 mg sodium; 117 mg cholesterol

Easy to prepare and store (the recipe makes a double batch; freeze half for another meal), this soup forms the base for countless variations. Add vegetables in season and your favorite pasta and spices to make it your own.

chicken noodle soup

MAKES 2 batches, 6 servings each **PREP** 25 minutes **COOK** 1 hour, 40 minutes

1 **roaster chicken (about 6 pounds), giblets removed**

6 **carrots**

4 **celery ribs**

2 **medium onions**

6 **cloves garlic**

1 **tablespoon salt**

1½ **teaspoons dried dill**

1 **tablespoon olive oil**

1 **can (14 ounces) diced tomatoes, drained**

½ **teaspoon black pepper**

1 **bag (12 ounces) wide egg noodles**

① Place chicken in a large stock pot (8 quarts). Peel 3 carrots and cut each into 3 pieces. Trim 2 celery ribs and cut each into 3 pieces. Peel and quarter 1 onion. Peel garlic; cut 3 cloves in half. Add prepped carrots, celery, onion and garlic to pot with chicken. Add enough cold water to cover, about 2½ quarts. Stir in 1 teaspoon *each* of salt and dill. Bring to a boil over high heat and then reduce heat to medium. Simmer for 1½ hours, occasionally skimming any foam from top.

② Meanwhile, peel and slice remaining 3 carrots and slice 2 ribs celery. Chop remaining onion and slice remaining 3 cloves garlic.

③ Carefully remove chicken from pot to a large bowl and let rest until cool enough to handle. Strain broth into a large bowl; discard soggy vegetables. Remove fat from top of broth. Once chicken has cooled, remove meat from bones and discard skin and bones. Chop meat into bite-size pieces.

④ Heat olive oil in soup pot over medium heat. Add sliced carrots, celery and onion. Cook 3 minutes. Add sliced garlic; cook an additional minute. Stir in remaining 2 teaspoons salt, remaining ½ teaspoon dried dill, tomatoes and pepper. Add defatted broth back to pot and bring to a simmer. Simmer 6 minutes, until vegetables are tender.

⑤ Meanwhile, bring a large pot of salted water to a boil. Add noodles to boiling water and cook 6 minutes.

⑥ Once vegetables are tender, add chicken back to pot. Remove half of soup (8 cups) and transfer to a freezer-safe container. Save for another meal. Drain and freeze half of noodles along with soup (in a separate container). Stir remaining noodles into soup in pot and serve immediately.

PER SERVING 274 calories; 6 g fat (1 g sat.); 28 g protein; 24 g carbohydrate; 1 g fiber; 787 mg sodium; 109 mg cholesterol

TEST KITCHEN TIP

Make Ahead Prepare soup through step 3 one day ahead. Add chicken to strained broth, let cool and refrigerate, covered. When ready to complete recipe, bring chicken and broth to a simmer.

tex-mex chicken cutlets

MAKES 4 servings **PREP** 5 minutes **COOK** 10 minutes **STAND** 8 to 10 minutes

1 tablespoon olive oil

1 small red onion, chopped

2 cloves garlic, minced

2 tablespoons all-purpose flour

4 boneless, skinless chicken breasts (about 1½ pounds total)

½ teaspoon ground cumin

1 cup chicken broth

1 teaspoon red wine vinegar

1 cup medium-hot salsa

1 package (10 ounces) frozen corn, thawed

1 cup instant rice

① Heat oil in a large nonstick skillet over medium-high heat. Add onion and garlic; sauté, stirring occasionally, for 2 minutes or until softened.

② Meanwhile, place flour on a plate. Place chicken in flour to coat each side, patting off excess. Add to skillet; sauté for 2 minutes per side or until lightly golden. Add cumin, chicken broth, vinegar, salsa and corn. Cook about 4 minutes.

③ Remove from heat. Stir rice into liquid. Cover, let stand 8 to 10 minutes or until rice is tender. Serve with extra salsa, if desired.

PER SERVING 455 calories; 11 g fat (2 g sat.); 46 g protein; 44 g carbohydrate; 5 g fiber; 766 mg sodium; 100 mg cholesterol

TEST KITCHEN TIP

Tight on time? Chicken cutlets are the way to get dinner on the table ASAP, so be sure to keep a stash in your freezer at all times.

Selection: Avoid packages with a lot of blood or juice in them; it could mean the chicken was frozen, then thawed and held too long. Make sure there is no smell or, at most, just a faint pleasant aroma.

Storage: Refrigerate as soon as you get home. If you plan to use within 2 days, keep in original wrapping and set over a plate to catch drippings. Otherwise, wrap individual cutlets in plastic, then place in resealable plastic freezer bag. They keep frozen for up to 1 year.

Cooking Know-How: Don't eyeball to gauge doneness; always use an instant-read thermometer. Cook to 165°F; juices will run clear and a fork can be easily inserted. Use leftover cooked chicken within 2 to 3 days.

chicken scaloppine al marsala

MAKES 6 servings **PREP** 15 minutes **COOK** 27 minutes

¼ **cup rice flour**

6 **thin-cut boneless, skinless chicken breasts (about 4 ounces each)**

3 **tablespoons olive oil**

1 **package (8 ounces) sliced brown mushrooms**

½ **cup marsala wine**

½ **cup low-sodium beef broth**

¼ **teaspoon salt**

⅛ **teaspoon black pepper**

1 **package (10 ounces) brown rice couscous (such as Lundberg)**

1 **tablespoon unsalted butter**

1 **tablespoon chopped parsley**

① Place rice flour on a large plate. Coat chicken in flour. Heat a large nonstick skillet over medium-high heat. Add 1 tablespoon of oil and sauté half of chicken for 1 to 2 minutes per side until lightly browned. Remove to a plate and keep warm. Repeat with a second tablespoon of oil and remaining chicken.

② Add remaining tablespoon oil to skillet and stir in mushrooms. Cook for 2 to 3 minutes, until tender. Off heat, add in marsala and cook for 1 minute, scraping any browned bits from skillet. Add broth, salt and pepper. Bring to a simmer and return chicken and any accumulated juices to skillet. Gently simmer, covered, for 15 minutes.

③ Meanwhile, prepare couscous following package directions, about 15 minutes.

④ Stir butter and parsley into sauce and serve with cooked couscous.

PER SERVING 429 calories; 14 g fat (3 g sat.); 32 g protein; 35 g carbohydrate; 4 g fiber; 410 mg sodium; 8 mg cholesterol

NUTRITION NOTE

Brown rice couscous is a wheat-free alternative to traditional couscous. It's gluten-free, made with 100% brown rice and high in fiber.

chicken with balsamic succotash

MAKES 4 servings   **PREP** 10 minutes   **COOK** 30 minutes

1   tablespoon plus 1 teaspoon chili powder

½   teaspoon salt

¼   teaspoon black pepper

4   boneless, skinless chicken breasts (1½ pounds total)

2   tablespoons olive oil

2   cloves garlic, minced

1   cup chopped sweet onion (such as Vidalia)

1   sweet red pepper, cut into ½-inch pieces

2   cups frozen corn, thawed

2   cups frozen lima beans, thawed

3   tablespoons balsamic vinegar

¼   cup chicken broth or water

1   tablespoon chopped parsley

① In a small bowl, mix together 1 tablespoon of chili powder, salt and pepper. Sprinkle chicken with chili powder mixture and set aside.

② Heat 1 tablespoon of oil in a large nonstick skillet over medium heat. Add chicken and cook for 7 to 8 minutes per side until browned and internal temperature registers 165°F on an instant-read thermometer. Remove chicken from skillet and tent loosely with foil.

③ In same skillet, heat remaining 1 tablespoon oil and garlic over low heat; cook for 3 to 4 minutes or until garlic is softened. Increase heat to medium and add onions and red pepper; cook for 5 minutes. Add corn, lima beans, remaining 1 teaspoon chili powder and vinegar and cook for 5 minutes. Add broth and parsley; heat through.

④ Place a bed of succotash on plate or platter and top with sliced or whole chicken breasts.

PER SERVING 446 calories; 10 g fat (2 g sat.); 47 g protein; 42 g carbohydrate; 8 g fiber; 627 mg sodium; 99 mg cholesterol

HOW-TO

Sauté Secrets This classic chef's technique seals in moisture and flavor. Master it and you can turn chicken cutlets into supper in no time:

Make sure the pan is hot (you have to pull your hand away after a few seconds). Add oil, butter or spray.

Pat cutlets dry. Coat in seasoned all-purpose flour, shaking off excess. Add to pan in single layer; do not crowd.

Do not move cutlets—let them cook until edges begin to turn golden-brown. Use tongs to flip. If pan was heated correctly, cutlets will easily release from pan.

lemony chicken & orzo

MAKES 4 servings **PREP** 5 minutes **COOK** 24 minutes

4 boneless, skinless chicken breasts (1½ pounds)

½ teaspoon salt

½ teaspoon black pepper

1 can (14.5 ounces) low-sodium chicken broth

⅓ cup lemon juice

2 teaspoons honey

2½ tablespoons low-fat sour cream

¾ cup orzo

8 ounces green beans, cut into 1-inch pieces

① Cut chicken into 1-inch cubes. Sprinkle with ¼ teaspoon *each* of salt and pepper.

② Pour broth and lemon juice into a Dutch oven; bring to a boil and add chicken. Cover and reduce heat to medium. Cook for 9 minutes or until chicken is cooked through.

③ Remove chicken from pot; set aside. Increase heat to high and cook sauce for 5 minutes. Stir in remaining ¼ teaspoon *each* salt and pepper; whisk in honey and sour cream.

④ Add **2 cups water** to pot and bring to a boil; add orzo and cook for 10 minutes or until pasta is tender and most of liquid has been absorbed. Add green beans to pot for final 4 minutes of cook time. Stir chicken back into pot and serve.

PER SERVING 384 calories; 4 g fat (1 g sat.); 47 g protein; 39 g carbohydrate; 3 g fiber; 685 mg sodium; 106 mg cholesterol

NUTRITION NOTE

Meat and poultry portions have grown in recent decades, like most dishes in our supersize-me nation. If your chicken breasts are too thick, carefully slice in half horizontally to yield 2 thinner pieces. The average cutlet should weigh 4 to 5 ounces.

chicken & soba noodles

MAKES 6 servings **PREP** 10 minutes **COOK** 8 minutes

3   tablespoons low-sodium soy sauce

2   tablespoons rice vinegar

1   tablespoon sesame oil

2   teaspoons grated fresh ginger

2   teaspoons sugar

1   teaspoon lime juice

¼   teaspoon hot sauce (such as Tabasco)

1   pound boneless, skinless, thinly sliced chicken breasts

1   package (8.8 ounces) soba noodles

3   cups broccoli florets

1   small sweet red pepper, thinly sliced

1   tablespoon sesame seeds (optional)

① In a small bowl, whisk together soy sauce, rice vinegar, sesame oil, ginger, sugar, lime juice and hot sauce.

② Fill a large skillet halfway with water and bring to a boil over medium-high heat. Add chicken and cook 4 minutes or until cooked through; set aside. When cool enough to handle, shred chicken using 2 forks and place pieces in a large serving bowl.

③ Bring a large pot of lightly salted water to a boil. Cook noodles following package directions. Add broccoli florets to pot for final 4 minutes of cooking time. Drain noodles and rinse with cold water.

④ Place noodle mixture and red pepper in serving bowl with chicken. Drizzle soy sauce mixture on top and toss well to coat. Sprinkle sesame seeds on top, if desired, and serve at room temperature or cold.

PER SERVING 267 calories; 4 g fat (1 g sat.); 25 g protein; 36 g carbohydrate; 1 g fiber; 585 mg sodium; 44 mg cholesterol

SWITCH IT UP

Not a fan of soba? Sub Chinese noodles or lo mein.

thai peanut chicken

MAKES 4 servings   **PREP** 15 minutes   **COOK** 2 minutes   **BROIL** 6 minutes

Sauce:

- 2 tablespoons reduced-sodium soy sauce
- 1 tablespoon lemon juice
- 1 teaspoon cornstarch
- ½ teaspoon garlic powder
- ¼ to ½ teaspoon red pepper flakes
- ¼ cup smooth peanut butter

Chicken:

- 2 large boneless, skinless chicken breasts (about 10 ounces each), cut in half lengthwise
- ⅛ teaspoon salt
- ⅛ teaspoon black pepper
- 2 cups cooked white rice
- 1 small sweet red pepper, cored, seeded and thinly sliced
- 2 scallions, trimmed and thinly sliced
- ½ pound steamed snow peas

① Sauce: In a small bowl, whisk together soy sauce, lemon juice, cornstarch, garlic powder and red pepper flakes. In a small saucepan, whisk together peanut butter with **½ cup hot water**. Stir in soy sauce mixture and bring to a simmer over medium heat until mixture thickens, about 2 minutes. Reserve.

② Chicken: Heat broiler and coat broiler pan with nonstick cooking spray. Season chicken with salt and pepper. Broil for 3 minutes per side or until internal temperature registers 165°F on an instant-read thermometer.

③ Slice chicken and serve with rice and peanut sauce. Garnish with red pepper and scallions. Serve with snow peas.

PER SERVING 415 calories; 10 g fat (2 g sat.); 42 g protein; 38 g carbohydrate; 4 g fiber; 547 mg sodium; 82 mg cholesterol

NUTRITION NOTE

Breast meat is the leanest part of the chicken with 120 calories and 1.5 fat grams in a 3-ounce cooked serving. As for removing the skin to cut calories and fat, it makes no difference whether you do so before or after cooking.

jerk chicken & rice

MAKES 4 servings **PREP** 15 minutes **BAKE** at 450°F for 15 minutes **COOK** 25 minutes

1 cup long-grain, parboiled rice

2 cups reduced-sodium chicken broth

4 teaspoons jerk seasoning

1 can (15 ounces) red kidney beans, drained and rinsed

1½ pounds boneless, skinless chicken breasts

Chopped parsley, to garnish (optional)

① Heat oven to 450°F. Coat a baking dish with nonstick cooking spray.

② Cook rice following package directions, about 25 minutes, replacing water with broth and adding 1 teaspoon of jerk seasoning. Gently stir in kidney beans during last 5 minutes of cooking.

③ Meanwhile, cut chicken into 1-inch pieces and toss with remaining 3 teaspoons of jerk seasoning. Place in prepared pan and bake at 450°F for 15 minutes or until internal temperature registers 165°F on an instant-read thermometer, turning once halfway through.

④ Serve chicken with rice and beans on the side, garnished with parsley, if desired.

PER SERVING 487 calories; 4 g fat (1 g sat.); 52 g protein; 59 g carbohydrate; 12 g fiber; 623 mg sodium; 99 mg cholesterol

TEST KITCHEN TIP

Better than Store-Bought It's a cinch to make your own jerk seasoning: combine 2 tablespoons onion powder, 2 teaspoons *each* sugar and dried thyme, 1 teaspoon *each* salt, red pepper flakes, black pepper and allspice and ¼ teaspoon ground cinnamon.

stuffed chicken breasts & cherry tomato salad

MAKES 4 servings **PREP** 15 minutes **BAKE** at 425°F for 30 minutes **COOK** 13 minutes

Chicken:

- ⅔ cup part-skim ricotta cheese
- ¼ cup chopped fresh basil
- 4 sun-dried tomatoes (not oil packed), finely chopped
- 1 clove garlic, finely chopped
- 4 chicken breasts, each trimmed to weigh about 6½ ounces

  Wooden toothpicks
- ¾ teaspoon salt-free Onion & Herb seasoning blend (such as Mrs. Dash)

Salad:

- 8 ounces sugar snap peas, trimmed
- 2 cups cherry tomatoes, halved
- 1 clove garlic, minced
- ¾ teaspoon sugar
- ½ teaspoon salt-free Onion & Herb seasoning blend
- 1 tablespoon lemon juice

① Chicken: Heat oven to 425°F. In a small bowl, stir together ricotta cheese, basil, sun-dried tomatoes and garlic until well combined; set aside.

② Using a paring knife, cut deep pockets in thickest part of breasts, about 2 inches wide. Spoon about 2 tablespoons of cheese mixture into each pocket. Seal closed with 3 wooden toothpicks.

③ Place chicken in a 13 x 9 x 2-inch baking dish and sprinkle with salt-free seasoning. Bake at 425°F for 25 to 30 minutes or until chicken registers 165°F on an instant-read thermometer.

④ Salad: Meanwhile, heat a large nonstick skillet over medium heat for 5 minutes. Add snap peas and **2 tablespoons water** to skillet and cover; cook 3 minutes or until bright green and tender. Remove cover and cook until water has evaporated, about 2 minutes. Add tomatoes, garlic, sugar and salt-free seasoning to skillet and cook 3 minutes. Stir in lemon juice and serve with chicken.

PER SERVING 333 calories; 6 g fat (3 g sat.); 51 g protein; 16 g carbohydrate; 4 g fiber; 217 mg sodium; 20 mg cholesterol

SWITCH IT UP

Check your grocery store for ingredients that spice things up with no effort on your part as we did here with sun-dried tomatoes. Sub marinated artichoke hearts or roasted red peppers for the tomatoes.

chicken cacciatore

MAKES 8 servings **PREP** 5 minutes **COOK** 35 minutes

1 broiler/fryer chicken (about 5 pounds), giblets removed, cut into 8 pieces (save wings for another use)

¼ teaspoon salt

2 tablespoons olive oil

1 package (10 ounces) white mushrooms, cleaned and quartered

2 small green bell peppers, seeded and diced

1 medium-size onion, chopped

2 cloves garlic, sliced

2 cans (14 ounces each) diced tomatoes with basil, garlic and oregano

½ cup red wine or water

1 teaspoon fresh rosemary, chopped

¼ teaspoon red pepper flakes

1 pound whole-wheat spaghetti, cooked

① Remove skin from chicken and discard. Season chicken with salt.

② Heat 1 tablespoon of oil in a large, deep covered sauté pan over medium-high heat. Add chicken and brown, meaty-side down, 3 minutes. Turn chicken over and continue to cook 1 minute. Remove to plate.

③ Reduce heat to medium. Add remaining tablespoon of oil to pan and add mushrooms, green peppers and onion. Cook, stirring occasionally, 5 minutes until softened. Add garlic and cook 1 more minute. Stir in tomatoes, wine or water, rosemary and red pepper flakes. Bring to a simmer. Add chicken, cover and simmer 15 minutes. Uncover and continue to cook 10 minutes, until chicken is cooked through and tender. Serve over whole-wheat spaghetti.

PER SERVING 437 calories; 9 g fat (2 g sat.); 39 g protein; 50 g carbohydrate; 9 g fiber; 418 mg sodium; 95 mg cholesterol

Szechuan peppercorn seasoning adds a distinctive flavor to this dish and transforms it from simple roast chicken to an exotic entrée. The peppercorns have an earthy taste with a hint of clove and are great for picking up the flavor in rubs and marinades.

szechuan roasted chicken

MAKES 4 servings **PREP** 15 minutes **COOK** 3 minutes **ROAST** at 425°F for 40 minutes **BROIL** 5 minutes

1 cup orange juice

3 tablespoons light soy sauce

1 tablespoon minced garlic

1 tablespoon Szechuan seasoning (such as Spice Islands)

1 teaspoon vegetable oil

4 chicken quarters (3 pounds total), skin and excess fat removed

1 large sweet potato (about 1 pound), cut into 1-inch pieces

2 medium-size white potatoes (about 1 pound total), cut into 1-inch pieces

1 tablespoon olive oil

1½ teaspoons cornstarch

1 bunch scallions, trimmed

① Heat oven to 425°F. Coat a rack with nonstick cooking spray, place in a roasting pan and set aside. In a medium-size bowl, combine juice, soy sauce, garlic, seasoning and oil.

② Place chicken quarters and ¼ cup of orange juice mixture in a bowl; toss to coat. Remove leg pieces; place on rack in roasting pan, leaving breasts in marinade. Roast at 425°F for 10 minutes.

③ Meanwhile, add potatoes to a second roasting pan. Drizzle with olive oil and 2 tablespoons of orange juice mixture; stir to coat.

④ After legs have roasted for 10 minutes, add breast pieces to rack with legs, discarding marinade. Place potatoes in oven on lower rack. Roast 30 minutes.

⑤ Meanwhile, whisk cornstarch into remaining orange juice mixture; place in a saucepan. Bring to a boil and cook for 3 minutes or until thickened. Set aside.

⑥ Add scallions to potatoes when there are 5 minutes of cooking time left.

⑦ When chicken is done (instant-read thermometer inserted in thigh without touching bone registers 160°F) and potatoes are tender, remove from oven and turn on broiler. Brush chicken, potatoes and scallions generously with thickened sauce. Broil chicken for 3 minutes and potatoes for 2 minutes to crisp. Serve chicken and potatoes warm, topped with scallions.

PER SERVING 490 calories; 10 g fat (2 g sat.); 44 g protein; 59 g carbohydrate; 6 g fiber; 567 mg sodium; 122 mg cholesterol

arroz con pollo

MAKES 8 servings **PREP** 15 minutes **COOK** 35 minutes

1 **broiler/fryer chicken (about 5 pounds), giblets removed, cut into 8 pieces (save wings for another use)**

¾ **teaspoon salt**

¼ **teaspoon black pepper**

¼ **cup all-purpose flour**

3 **tablespoons vegetable oil**

1 **small onion, diced**

3 **cloves garlic, sliced**

1 **cup white rice, uncooked**

1 **can (14.5 ounces) reduced-sodium chicken broth**

1 **packet (from 1.41-ounce box) Goya Sazón with Azafrán seasoning**

1 **box (10 ounces) frozen green peas, thawed**

① Remove skin from chicken and discard. Season pieces with ¼ teaspoon of salt and ⅛ teaspoon of pepper. Toss in flour to coat.

② Heat 1 tablespoon of oil in a large covered sauté pan over medium-high heat. Brown half of chicken pieces, about 3 minutes. Transfer to a plate. Add another tablespoon of oil and repeat with remaining chicken.

③ Reduce heat to medium and add remaining tablespoon of oil and onion to pan. Cook 3 minutes. Add garlic; cook 1 minute. Stir in rice. Add broth, seasoning packet, remaining ½ teaspoon salt and remaining ⅛ teaspoon pepper. Increase heat to high and bring to a boil.

④ Stir in peas and return chicken to pan along with any accumulated juices. Cover and reduce heat to medium-low. Cook 20 to 25 minutes or until rice is tender. Let stand 5 minutes, covered, before serving.

PER SERVING 351 calories; 10 g fat (2 g sat.); 34 g protein; 30 g carbohydrate; 2 g fiber; 576 mg sodium; 95 mg cholesterol

TEST KITCHEN TIP

Food Safety Savvy Don't cross-contaminate; separate raw chicken from other foods. Wash hands with soap and hot water after handling raw chicken and clean anything that came in contact with your hands or the chicken.

HOW TO CUT UP A CHICKEN

For a meal with lots of flavor that only costs a little dough, buy a whole bird and bone up on your knife skills—it's way more cost-effective than paying for pricey pre-cut pieces. Here's how to cut up a chicken:

Rinse chicken; pat dry. Place on cutting board with wings away from you. Pull leg away from side of breast and slice through skin and meat.

Bend leg away from body. Cut down through joint in one motion, separating leg from body. Turn leg skin-side down and slice along fat line between thigh and drumstick. Cut cleanly through leg joint.

Repeat with opposite leg and wings. Starting at pointed end of breast, slice down through cavity toward thickest part of breast, separating from backbone.

Turn breast skin-side down and split in half along breastbone (this will take firm pressure).

Turn over breast pieces and cut each in half.

chicken curry & brown basmati rice

MAKES 6 servings **PREP** 15 minutes **BAKE** at 350°F for 45 minutes **COOK** 10 minutes

1 tablespoon vegetable oil

1½ pounds boneless, skinless chicken thighs, cut into 1-inch pieces

¼ teaspoon salt

1 medium-size onion, chopped

1 tablespoon chopped fresh gingerroot

2 teaspoons curry powder

1½ cups reduced-sodium chicken broth

1 can (15 ounces) chickpeas, drained and rinsed

½ cup golden raisins

3 cups cooked brown basmati rice

2 small sweet red peppers, seeded and sliced

¼ cup sliced almonds

① Heat oven to 350°F. Coat a 13 x 9 x 2-inch baking dish with nonstick cooking spray.

② Heat oil in a large nonstick skillet over medium-high heat. Add chicken and sauté for 5 minutes, turning after 3 minutes. Season with ⅛ teaspoon of salt. Remove from skillet and keep warm.

③ Add onion and ginger to skillet and cook for 3 minutes, stirring occasionally. Add curry and cook 1 minute. Add broth and remaining ⅛ teaspoon salt to skillet. Bring to a simmer and add chickpeas, raisins and chicken. Simmer for 1 minute.

④ Evenly spoon cooked rice into prepared dish. Spoon chicken curry mixture over top. Scatter red peppers over curry. Cover with foil. Bake, covered, at 350°F for 30 minutes. Uncover and scatter almonds over peppers. Bake, uncovered, for 15 additional minutes. Cool slightly before serving.

PER SERVING 297 calories; 7 g fat (1 g sat.); 10 g protein; 51 g carbohydrate; 7 g fiber; 353 mg sodium; 7 mg cholesterol

TEST KITCHEN TIP

Gingerroot Known for its stomach-soothing power, this go-to ingredient in Asian cooking lends any dish light spiciness and lemony tang. Fresh gingerroot packs way more flavor than ground and will keep in the fridge—stored in a paper bag—for up to 3 weeks.

baked greek chicken

MAKES 6 servings **PREP** 10 minutes **BAKE** at 425°F for 40 minutes **COOK** 9 minutes

1 whole broiler/fryer chicken (about 5 pounds), giblets removed, cut into 6 pieces

¾ teaspoon salt

2 lemons

3 cloves garlic, minced

1 tablespoon fresh oregano, chopped

⅛ teaspoon black pepper

1 tablespoon olive oil

1 fennel bulb (about 1¼ pounds), trimmed, cored and sliced

1 cup dry orzo

⅓ cup pitted kalamata olives, halved

⅓ cup crumbled feta cheese

① Heat oven to 425°F. Pat chicken pieces dry. Loosen skin and sprinkle ¼ teaspoon of salt under skin. Grate zest of 1 lemon, then cut lemon in half and juice. In a small bowl, stir together 2 teaspoons of zest, 2 tablespoons of lemon juice, remaining ½ teaspoon salt, garlic, oregano and pepper. Tuck half of this mixture under skin of chicken. Cut peel off second lemon; chop fruit into pieces.

② Add olive oil to remaining herb mixture in bowl. Toss with sliced fennel and chopped lemon. Transfer to a large baking dish. Top with chicken pieces and bake at 425°F for 40 minutes or until instant-read thermometer inserted in thickest part of breast registers 160°F.

③ Meanwhile, cook orzo following package directions, about 9 minutes. Drain and transfer to a bowl. Transfer chicken and fennel to a platter and spoon 1 tablespoon of pan drippings in with orzo. Add olives and feta to orzo and stir to combine. Serve warm.

PER SERVING 416 calories; 12 g fat (3 g sat.); 45 g protein; 32 g carbohydrate; 5 g fiber; 684 mg sodium; 134 mg cholesterol

HOW-TO

Pitting Olives Here's an annoying task made easy. To pit olives roll them inside a clean dish cloth under the palm of your hand; this will loosen the pit, and you will be able to pop it right out.

chicken in soft tacos

MAKES 12 tacos **PREP** 10 minutes **COOK** 11 minutes

1 tablespoon extra-virgin olive oil

2 chorizo sausages, cut into ½-inch pieces

1 pound ground chicken

2 small zucchini, chopped

1 small yellow squash, chopped

1 tablespoon hot chili powder

½ teaspoon salt

⅛ teaspoon cayenne pepper

½ cup sour cream

1 ripe avocado

3 tablespoons bottled salsa

1 tablespoon lime juice

1 package (9 ounces) white corn tortillas (12 total)

Lime wedges for garnish (optional)

① Heat oil in a large nonstick skillet over medium-high heat. Add chorizo and chicken; cook for 3 minutes. Add zucchini, squash, chili powder, salt and cayenne; stir to combine. Add sour cream and reduce heat to medium; cook for 5 to 8 minutes longer or until zucchini is tender and sauce has reduced.

② Peel and remove pit from avocado. In a bowl, mash avocado with fork. Stir in salsa and lime juice. Heat tortillas according to package directions. Serve chicken mixture wrapped in tortillas with avocado salsa on the side. If desired, garnish with lime wedges.

PER SERVING 227 calories; 14 g fat (5 g sat.); 11 g protein; 14 g carbohydrate; 2 g fiber; 300 mg sodium; 63 mg cholesterol

SWITCH IT UP

Sub ground turkey for the chicken.

chicken meatballs with spaghetti

MAKES 6 servings **PREP** 15 minutes **BAKE** at 375°F for 24 minutes **COOK** 14 minutes

2 slices whole-grain white bread, torn into pieces

¼ cup fat-free milk

1 pound ground chicken

2 tablespoons grated Parmesan cheese

4 tablespoons chopped parsley

½ teaspoon plus ⅛ teaspoon salt

1 tablespoon canola oil

2 cloves garlic, minced

2 pounds plum tomatoes, cored, seeded and cut into ½-inch pieces

2 tablespoons balsamic vinegar

½ teaspoon Italian seasoning

⅛ teaspoon black pepper

1 box (14.5 ounces) fiber- and calcium-enriched spaghetti (such as Ronzoni Smart Taste)

① Heat oven to 375°F. Line a rimmed baking sheet with foil and place a baking rack over it; coat rack with nonstick cooking spray and set aside.

② In a large bowl, combine bread pieces and milk and let stand for 5 minutes or until bread softens. Mash with fork until a paste forms. Add chicken, Parmesan cheese, 2 tablespoons of parsley and ½ teaspoon of salt, and stir until evenly mixed.

③ With clean hands kept wet with water, shape mixture into thirty 1½-inch meatballs. Place meatballs on prepared rack and bake at 375°F for 24 minutes.

④ While meatballs are cooking, make sauce. Heat oil in a nonstick medium-size skillet over medium heat. Add garlic and cook for 1 minute. Add tomatoes, balsamic vinegar, Italian seasoning and black pepper and increase heat to medium-high. Cook for about 13 minutes. Stir in remaining ⅛ teaspoon salt and 2 tablespoons parsley.

⑤ Cook pasta according to package directions. Drain, reserving ½ cup pasta water. Transfer pasta to a large serving bowl and top with meatballs. Stir pasta water into sauce and spoon sauce on top of pasta and meatballs.

PER SERVING 432 calories; 13 g fat (3 g sat.); 24 g protein; 65 g carbohydrate; 10 g fiber; 394 mg sodium; 93 mg cholesterol

TEST KITCHEN TIP

To help meatballs retain a uniform shape, refrigerate for 15 minutes before baking.

sausage & lentil salad

MAKES 4 servings **PREP** 15 minutes **COOK** 25 minutes

1¼ cups lentils, rinsed

1 package (12 ounces) roasted red pepper and Asiago or Italian-flavored chicken sausage (such as Al Fresco)

1 box (9 ounces) frozen artichoke hearts, thawed and quartered

4 scallions, trimmed and thinly sliced

1 small sweet red pepper, finely chopped

1 large carrot, grated

¼ cup reduced-fat balsamic vinaigrette

1. Cook lentils according to package directions, 20 to 25 minutes or until tender; drain.

2. While lentils are cooking, cut sausages into ½-inch-thick half-moons and cook in a medium-size nonstick skillet over medium-high heat for 7 minutes or until lightly browned; remove from skillet and set aside.

3. Stir together lentils, sausages, artichokes, scallions, red pepper and carrot in a medium-size bowl. Drizzle vinaigrette over top and stir until well blended. Serve immediately.

PER SERVING 419 calories; 10 g fat (3 g sat.); 35 g protein; 54 g carbohydrate; 14 g fiber; 796 mg sodium; 70 mg cholesterol

chicken tortilla soup

MAKES 6 servings **PREP** 15 minutes **COOK** 23 minutes

1 tablespoon olive oil

1 medium green pepper, seeded and finely chopped

1 small onion, finely chopped

1 jalapeño pepper, seeded and finely chopped

1 tablespoon chili powder

5 cups low-sodium chicken broth

3 cups cooked, shredded chicken (from a rotisserie chicken)

1 can (14.5 ounces) no-salt-added diced tomatoes

1 can (14.5 ounces) black beans, drained and rinsed

2 tablespoons lime juice

¾ teaspoon salt

½ of a firm, ripe avocado, cut into chunks

1 cup crumbed baked tortilla chips (optional)

① Heat oil in a large saucepan over medium-high heat. Add green pepper, onion and jalapeño to saucepan and cook, stirring often, for 7 minutes. Stir chili powder into pot and cook, stirring occasionally, for 1 minute.

② Pour broth and **1 cup water** into saucepan. Bring to a boil and reduce heat to medium; simmer for 10 minutes. Stir in chicken, tomatoes, beans, lime juice and salt; cook for 5 minutes or until warmed through.

③ Ladle 1½ cups soup into 6 bowls; divide avocado chunks among bowls. Serve with chips on top, if desired.

PER SERVING 165 calories; 4 g fat (0 g sat.); 15 g protein; 16 g carbohydrate; 5 g fiber; 983 mg sodium; 26 mg cholesterol

NUTRITION NOTE

Avocados have lots of healthy fats and over a dozen vitamins and minerals. Ripe avocados will appear purplish-black and yield to gentle squeezing. Choose softer ones to make guacamole, firmer ones to slice and add to sandwiches as an alternative to mayo.

This dish will remind you of the salads your mom used to make. What could be more delicious than diced turkey, crisp bacon, red onion and raisins tossed in a light mayo dressing. We've made it more nutritious by adding crisp-tender broccoli.

turkey & broccoli salad

MAKES 6 servings **PREP** 20 minutes **COOK** 4 minutes **MICROWAVE** 7 minutes

⅔ cup light mayonnaise

2 tablespoons red wine vinegar

2 teaspoons sugar

¼ teaspoon salt

¼ teaspoon black pepper

1 large head broccoli (1½ pounds), cut into florets, or 6 cups broccoli florets

1 package turkey breast cutlets (about ¾ to 1 pound)

1 package (6 ounces) turkey bacon

½ small red onion, chopped

½ cup golden raisins

① In a small bowl, whisk together mayonnaise, red wine vinegar, sugar, salt and pepper. Set aside.

② Heat a medium-size pot of water to boiling and a large skillet of water to simmering. Add broccoli to boiling water and cook 3 minutes, until tender but still crisp. Drain. Meanwhile, add turkey to skillet of simmering water and poach for 3 to 4 minutes or until cooked through. Remove to a cutting board and cool.

③ While broccoli and turkey cool, stack bacon slices on a paper-towel-lined plate (about 5 slices per layer; paper towels between each layer). Microwave on HIGH for 7 minutes, checking and removing any crisp slices after 5 minutes. Cool slightly, then crumble.

④ Cut turkey into bite-size pieces, then transfer to a large bowl. Add broccoli, bacon, red onion and raisins. Toss with mayonnaise mixture until combined. Serve or refrigerate until serving.

PER SERVING 283 calories; 15 g fat (3 g sat.); 20 g protein; 18 g carbohydrate; 3 g fiber; 693 mg sodium; 71 mg cholesterol

turkey tetrazzini

MAKES 6 servings **PREP** 15 minutes **COOK** 20 minutes

1 teaspoon olive oil

10 ounces white mushrooms, sliced

1 small onion, chopped

½ teaspoon salt

½ teaspoon black pepper

2 tablespoons all-purpose flour

6 ounces egg noodles

1 can (14.5 ounces) low-sodium chicken broth

¾ cup light cream

1 package cooked turkey breast strips (such as Perdue Short Cuts)

1 package (10 ounces) frozen peas, thawed

① Heat olive oil in a Dutch oven over medium heat. Add mushrooms and onion to pot. Sprinkle with ¼ teaspoon *each* salt and pepper. Cook, stirring, for 7 minutes or until tender.

② Stir in flour and cook 1 minute. Remove mushroom mixture from pot and set aside.

③ Return pot to medium-high heat and add noodles, broth, light cream and **2¼ cups water**. Cover and cook, stirring occasionally, for 12 minutes or until tender.

④ Stir in mushroom mixture, remaining ¼ teaspoon *each* salt and pepper, turkey and peas. Heat through; serve.

PER SERVING 339 calories; 10 g fat (10 g sat.); 28 g protein; 33 g carbohydrate; 4 g fiber; 497 mg sodium; 84 mg cholesterol

turkey florentine

MAKES 4 servings **PREP** 15 minutes **COOK** 18 minutes

- **4** turkey breast cutlets (about 1 pound total), cut into 1-inch pieces
- **⅛** teaspoon plus ¼ teaspoon salt
- **1** large onion, chopped
- **½** pound mushrooms, sliced
- **2** tablespoons all-purpose flour
- **1** cup fat-free half-and-half
- **¼** teaspoon ground nutmeg
- **¼** teaspoon hot pepper sauce
- **1** bag (6 ounces) fresh baby spinach
- **2** tablespoons grainy mustard
- **½** cup shredded reduced-fat Swiss cheese (such as Alpine Lace)
- **2** cups cooked egg noodles

① Coat a large nonstick skillet with nonstick spray. Add turkey pieces, season with ⅛ teaspoon salt and cook over medium-high heat for 5 minutes, turning halfway through cooking. Remove to a plate and reserve.

② Coat skillet with more spray; add onion. Cook on medium-low for 5 minutes, stirring occasionally; add **2 tablespoons of water** to prevent sticking if needed. Add mushrooms; cook for 5 more minutes, stirring occasionally. Sprinkle flour over top and stir. Cook for 1 minute.

③ Stir in half-and-half, nutmeg, hot pepper sauce and remaining ¼ teaspoon salt. Bring to a boil. Lower heat and simmer 1 minute. Gradually stir in spinach and cook until wilted. Add turkey and mustard and heat through. Stir in Swiss cheese until just melted. Serve immediately with cooked noodles.

PER SERVING 397 calories; 6 g fat (3 g sat.); 43 g protein; 39 g carbohydrate; 4 g fiber; 517 mg sodium; 119 mg cholesterol

TEST KITCHEN TIP

Look for mushrooms that are firm, plump and free of bruises, with no visible moisture on the outside. Keep unwashed in the refrigerator for up to 2 days, either in a paper bag or in original packaging. To clean, wipe mushrooms with damp paper towel or lightly rinse and dry.

The microwave oven is one of the most useful and versatile tools of the kitchen. It concentrates the flavors of food, saves time and generally requires little cleanup.

turkey & spinach manicotti

MAKES 14 pieces **PREP** 20 minutes **MICROWAVE** 28 minutes **STAND** 10 minutes

1¼ **pounds ground turkey**

1 **package (10 ounces) frozen chopped spinach, excess liquid squeezed out**

¼ **cup pine nuts**

1 **teaspoon Italian seasoning**

½ **teaspoon salt**

¼ **teaspoon black pepper**

1 **jar (36 ounces) chunky pasta sauce**

14 **manicotti shells**

1 **can (14.5 ounces) chicken broth**

1 **cup shredded reduced-fat mozzarella cheese**

Grated Parmesan cheese (optional)

① In a large bowl, mix together ground turkey, spinach, pine nuts, Italian seasoning, salt and pepper. Spread ½ cup of pasta sauce in bottom of a 10-inch square microwave-safe dish. Fill uncooked manicotti shells with meat mixture and place in dish. (It will be tight but all 14 filled shells will fit.)

② Pour broth and remaining pasta sauce evenly over manicotti. Gently press shells into liquid. Cover with microwave-safe plastic wrap; vent one corner. Microwave on HIGH for 25 minutes.

③ Sprinkle with mozzarella cheese and microwave for 3 minutes, uncovered. Allow to stand for 10 minutes before serving. Garnish with grated Parmesan cheese, if desired.

PER SERVING 236 calories; 9 g fat (2 g sat.); 14 g protein; 24 g carbohydrate; 2 g fiber; 579 mg sodium; 37 mg cholesterol

TEST KITCHEN TIP

Make Ahead Prepare recipe through Step 1. Refrigerate, covered with plastic, overnight.

harvest pot pie

MAKES 6 servings **PREP** 15 minutes **COOK** 21 minutes **BAKE** at 400°F for 25 minutes

- 2 bunches Swiss chard (red is okay)
- 2 tablespoons olive oil
- 1 small onion, diced
- 2 medium-size carrots, sliced
- 1 package (20 ounces) ground turkey
- ½ teaspoon dried thyme
- 1 can (14.5 ounces) low-sodium chicken broth
- 2 tablespoons cornstarch
- 2 tablespoons Dijon mustard
- ½ teaspoon salt
- ¼ teaspoon ground black pepper
- 1 sheet frozen puff pastry (from a 17.3-ounce box), thawed

① Heat oven to 400°F. Coat a 2-quart baking dish with nonstick cooking spray. Rinse chard well; trim stems, then separate at base of leaves. Cut into ½-inch pieces; set aside. Chop leaves.

② Place half of leaves in a large nonstick skillet. Cover and cook over medium heat for 3 minutes, until wilted. Transfer to a bowl. Repeat with remaining chard leaves.

③ Add oil to same skillet; stir in onion, chard stems and carrots; cook 5 minutes. Stir in turkey and thyme, breaking turkey apart with a spoon. Cook 7 minutes, until carrots are tender. Stir in wilted chard; increase heat to medium-high.

④ In bowl, blend broth, cornstarch, mustard, salt and pepper. Add to skillet; bring to a simmer. Simmer 3 minutes, until thickened and clear. Transfer to prepared dish; top with puff pastry. Cut a few holes to vent.

⑤ Bake at 400°F for 25 minutes, until browned. Cool 15 minutes before serving.

PER SERVING 377 calories; 17 g fat (4 g sat.); 31 g protein; 26 g carbohydrate; 4 g fiber; 800 mg sodium; 39 mg cholesterol

TEST KITCHEN TIP

When choosing Swiss chard, look for crisp stalks and vivid green leaves with no tiny holes. Store unwashed chard in the refrigerator for several days in a plastic bag. To clean: immerse greens in a large bowl of cold water and wash thoroughly.

ultimate turkey burger with caramelized onions

MAKES 4 servings **PREP** 15 minutes **COOK** 30 minutes

- 1 tablespoon unsalted butter
- 1 large Vidalia onion, thinly sliced
- 1 package (20.8 ounces) ground turkey
- ½ cup part-skim ricotta cheese
- 1¾ teaspoons Worcestershire sauce
- 1¾ teaspoons Dijon mustard
- ¼ teaspoon salt
- ¼ teaspoon black pepper
- 1 tablespoon vegetable oil
- ¼ cup crumbled blue cheese
- 2 tablespoons light mayonnaise
- 4 whole-grain white hamburger buns
- 4 romaine lettuce leaves

① Melt butter in a large skillet over medium-high heat. Add onion and cook for 15 minutes or until well browned; set aside.

② In a large bowl, combine turkey, ricotta cheese, Worcestershire sauce, mustard, salt and pepper. Stir until well combined. Form into 4 equal-size patties and flatten.

③ Heat oil in a large nonstick skillet over medium heat. Cook burgers about 5 minutes per side, then partially cover, reduce heat to medium and cook another 5 minutes or until instant-read thermometer registers 160°F in burger centers.

④ While burgers are cooking, stir together blue cheese and mayonnaise in a small bowl. Place burgers on buns and top each with some onions, 1 tablespoon blue cheese sauce and a lettuce leaf.

PER SERVING 425 calories; 16 g fat (6 g sat.); 46 g protein; 28 g carbohydrate; 4 g fiber; 716 mg sodium; 85 mg cholesterol

sausage bolognese with linguine

MAKES 8 servings **PREP** 15 minutes **COOK** 57 minutes

3 medium carrots, peeled and coarsely chopped

2 ribs celery, coarsely chopped

1 large onion, coarsely chopped

1 tablespoon vegetable oil

1 package (20 ounces) sweet Italian turkey sausage, casings removed

¾ cup dry white wine

1 can (28 ounces) whole tomatoes

¾ cup milk

1 box (13.25 ounces) low-carb linguine (such as Dreamfields)

Grated Parmesan cheese (optional)

① Pulse carrots, celery and onion in a food processor until finely chopped.

② Heat oil in a large nonstick skillet over medium-high heat. Add vegetable mixture and cook, stirring, 6 minutes. Rinse food processor bowl; set aside. Crumble sausage into skillet and cook for 3 minutes.

③ Add wine to skillet; bring to a simmer over medium-low heat. Simmer for 10 minutes.

④ Drain tomatoes and save liquid. Add tomatoes to food processor bowl; pulse until finely chopped. Add tomatoes and their liquid to skillet; bring to a simmer. Reduce heat to medium; cook for 30 minutes or until most of liquid has been absorbed. Stir in milk and cook another 8 minutes.

⑤ Meanwhile, cook pasta according to package directions in salted boiling water, about 12 minutes. Serve pasta with sauce, and Parmesan cheese, if desired.

PER SERVING 289 calories; 6 g fat (1 g sat.); 17 g protein; 39 g carbohydrate; 3 g fiber; 536 mg sodium; 38 mg cholesterol

NUTRITION NOTE

What's so good about low-carb pasta? A typical 2-ounce serving of regular pasta has 42 grams of carbs. Low-carb pasta has only 5 grams of digestible carbs. The main benefit is for diabetics who need to count carbs.

sausage & cornbread stuffed peppers

MAKES 8 servings **PREP** 15 minutes **MICROWAVE** 4 minutes **COOK** 9 minutes **BAKE** at 350°F for 18 to 20 minutes

4 large sweet red peppers

2 tablespoons unsalted butter

1 medium onion, chopped

2 ears of corn, kernels removed (about 1⅓ cups)

4 links hot Italian turkey sausage (¾ pound total), casings removed

1 box (6 ounces) cornbread stuffing mix

2 tablespoons chopped fresh parsley

1 cup shredded Pepper Jack cheese (about 4 ounces)

① Heat oven to 350°F. Slice peppers in half from stems to bottoms. Remove seeds and membranes. Place pepper halves, cut-side down, in 13 x 9 x 2-inch baking dish (overlapping, if needed) and add ½ **cup warm water** to dish. Cover dish with plastic wrap and microwave on HIGH for 4 minutes. Remove dish from microwave, carefully remove plastic and drain off water.

② Melt butter in medium-size pot over medium to medium-high heat. Add onion and corn and cook for 4 minutes. Add sausage, breaking apart with a wooden spoon. Cook 5 minutes, or until meat is no longer pink. Add **1 cup warm water** and bring to a simmer. Add stuffing mix and stir once or twice. Remove from heat and cover. Let stand 5 minutes. Uncover; gently stir in parsley.

③ Flip peppers over. Divide filling among peppers, mounding mixture slightly, about ¾ cup for each. Top peppers with grated Pepper Jack cheese, about 2 tablespoons for each stuffed pepper.

④ Bake peppers at 350°F for 18 to 20 minutes, or until cheese is melted and peppers are tender. Serve warm.

PER SERVING 291 calories; 12 g fat (5 g sat.); 16 g protein; 35 g carbohydrate; 5 g fiber; 768 mg sodium; 52 mg cholesterol

TEST KITCHEN TIP
Choose red peppers that are firm, smooth and glossy without dings or cracks; stems should be green and not too dried out. Store unwashed in a plastic bag in refrigerator for a few days.

sausage & peppers

MAKES 6 servings **PREP** 10 minutes **BAKE** at 250°F for 18 minutes **COOK** 18 minutes

1½   cups 2% reduced-fat milk

3¼   cups low-sodium chicken broth

1¼   cups instant polenta

½   teaspoon salt

2   tablespoons grated Parmesan cheese

⅓   cup balsamic vinegar

2   tablespoons cornstarch

1   tablespoon sugar

6   links sweet Italian turkey sausage

1   teaspoon canola oil

1   large onion, cut into ½-inch slices

1   medium-size sweet red pepper, cut into 2 x ½-inch slices

1   medium-size green pepper, cut into 2 x ½-inch slices

2   cloves garlic, minced

① Coat 13 x 9 x 2-inch baking dish with nonstick spray; set aside.

② Heat oven to 250°F. In a small bowl, stir together 1 cup of milk, 1 cup of broth, polenta and salt. In a medium-size saucepan, bring remaining ½ cup milk and 1¼ cups of chicken broth to a boil. Pour polenta mixture into saucepan of boiling milk mixture and whisk to combine. Cook for 2 minutes, stirring, or until thickened. Stir in Parmesan cheese; spread into prepared dish. Cover and place in oven, for about 18 minutes while preparing sausage and peppers.

③ In a small bowl, stir remaining 1 cup chicken broth, vinegar, cornstarch and sugar. Set aside.

④ Pierce sausages with a fork. Place in a large, deep skillet and cook over medium-high heat about 10 minutes, turning occasionally, until browned.

⑤ Add oil and onion to sausages, and cook 2 minutes, stirring occasionally.

⑥ Add peppers and cook for 4 minutes. Add garlic and cook for 30 seconds. Stir in vinegar mixture and bring to a boil. Cook for 1 minute, adding a little water if mixture appears too thick. Remove sausages and cut into ½-inch slices on the diagonal; return to pan.

⑦ Remove polenta from oven and spoon sausage mixture on top. Cut into squares and serve immediately.

PER SERVING 377 calories; 10 g fat (3 g sat.); 26 g protein; 46 g carbohydrate; 3 g fiber; 798 mg sodium; 75 mg cholesterol

sausage, spinach & swiss strata

MAKES 8 servings   **PREP** 15 minutes   **BAKE** at 375°F for 40 minutes   **COOK** 8 minutes

2 cups 1% low-fat milk

4 large eggs

4 large egg whites

¾ teaspoon salt

¼ teaspoon cayenne pepper

¼ teaspoon nutmeg

12 slices day-old whole-grain white bread, cut into ½-inch cubes (about 9 cups)

6 ounces turkey breakfast sausage, crumbled

1 medium-size onion, chopped

1 medium-size sweet red bell pepper, chopped

2 cloves garlic, minced

1 package (10 ounces) frozen chopped spinach, thawed and squeezed dry

4 ounces (1 cup) reduced-fat Swiss cheese, shredded and divided

① Heat oven to 375°F. Coat an 11 x 7-inch baking dish with cooking spray and set aside.

② In a large bowl, whisk together milk, eggs, egg whites, salt, cayenne and nutmeg. Add bread and toss to combine. Let stand 5 minutes or until most of liquid is absorbed.

③ Meanwhile, coat a large nonstick skillet with cooking spray. Cook sausage, onion, red pepper and garlic in skillet over medium-high heat, stirring often, for 6 to 8 minutes or until sausage is cooked and vegetables are softened.

④ Stir sausage mixture, spinach and ½ cup of Swiss cheese into bread mixture. Spoon into prepared baking dish. Bake at 375°F for 30 minutes. Remove from oven and top with remaining ½ cup of cheese. Bake an additional 10 minutes or until cheese melts.

PER SERVING 299 calories; 11 g fat (4 g sat.); 21 g protein; 32 g carbohydrate; 4 g fiber; 588 mg sodium; 36 mg cholesterol

TEST KITCHEN TIP

Make Ahead Strata may be prepared up to the point where it is baked. Refrigerate, covered with plastic, overnight. Bring to room temp before baking or add 10 minutes to baking time.

Meat used to be the star of a family meal with vegetable side dishes as the supporting players. Roles have now been reversed—today meat takes a back seat to vegetables and grains.

Lean cuts of meat like filet mignon, sirloin, strip steak and flank have far fewer calories than their rib-eye cousins; their low fat content means care should be taken in the way they are cooked. Invest in an instant-read thermometer and begin testing the meat five minutes before the end of cooking time to make sure

meat

it doesn't overcook. Allow large pieces of meat to rest 10 minutes before carving to ensure juiciness. The way you carve will also affect its tenderness—cut the meat into thin slices across the grain.

A healthy serving of meat is 3 ounces cooked, which means starting with 4 ounces raw. The trick to making the most of meat is to play up its flavor and surround it with bold ingredients as in Asian cuisines. One taste of our Beef Kabobs over Couscous (page 198) and you'll understand why meat can still be the star.

Remember those Sunday suppers when the aromas of mom's pot roast filled the house and everyone couldn't wait to sit down at the table? Create your own memories with this delicious dish. Succulent and tender, it is sure to become a family tradition.

mom's pot roast

MAKES 6 servings **PREP** 15 minutes **COOK** 2 hours, 45 minutes

Pot Roast:

- 1 tablespoon olive oil
- 1 piece bottom-round pot roast (about 2 to 2½ pounds)
- ½ teaspoon salt
- ½ teaspoon garlic pepper (such as McCormick)
- 1 large onion, peeled and cut into 8 wedges
- ½ cup dry red wine
- 2 cups reduced-sodium beef broth
- 1 can (8 ounces) no-salt-added tomato sauce
- 2 carrots, peeled and cut into 1-inch pieces
- 2 ribs celery, cut into 1-inch pieces
- 3 tablespoons all-purpose flour

Potato-Cauliflower Mash:

- 1½ pounds all-purpose potatoes, peeled and cut into 1-inch pieces
- 1 medium-size cauliflower, trimmed and cut into 1-inch pieces
- ¼ cup fat-free milk
- ½ teaspoon salt
- ¼ teaspoon garlic pepper
- ⅛ teaspoon ground nutmeg
- 2 tablespoons extra-virgin olive oil
- 2 tablespoons chopped parsley
- Prepared red cabbage (optional)

① Pot Roast: Heat oil in a large heavy-bottomed pot over medium-high heat. Season roast with salt and garlic pepper. Add roast and onion to pot and brown meat on all sides, about 15 minutes total. Remove meat to a plate and stir in wine; cook 2 minutes, scraping up browned bits on bottom of pan.

② Add 1½ cups of beef broth, tomato sauce, carrots and celery. Place meat back into pot and bring to a boil. Lower heat to medium-low and simmer, covered, for 2 hours, 30 minutes, turning every ½ hour.

③ Remove roast from pot and allow to rest in a warm place, reserving cooking liquid. Whisk together remaining ½ cup beef broth and flour. Add to liquid in pot and simmer for 2 minutes, until thickened. Strain and reserve.

④ Potato-Cauliflower Mash: Meanwhile, place potatoes and cauliflower in a large pot and cover with water. Salt lightly. Bring to a boil; reduce heat to medium and cook for 20 to 25 minutes until potatoes and cauliflower are tender. Drain completely. Place back into pot and add milk, salt, garlic pepper, nutmeg and olive oil. Beat on medium-high speed until smooth. Stir in parsley.

⑤ Thinly slice pot roast against grain and serve with gravy and potato-cauliflower mash. Accompany with prepared red cabbage, if desired.

PER SERVING 489 calories; 16 g fat (4 g sat.); 43 g protein; 37 g carbohydrate; 5 g fiber; 758 mg sodium; 104 mg cholesterol

jerk rubbed london broil

MAKES 6 servings **PREP** 15 minutes **REFRIGERATE** 4 hours or overnight **COOK** 25 minutes **BROIL** 12 minutes

Rub:

1 teaspoon garlic powder

1 teaspoon onion powder

1 teaspoon sugar

1 teaspoon dried thyme

1 teaspoon ground allspice

1 teaspoon black pepper

½ teaspoon cayenne pepper

½ teaspoon salt

¼ teaspoon ground clove

1½ pounds top round for London broil

Potato Salad:

1½ pounds fingerling potatoes

1 green pepper, seeded and thinly sliced

1 yellow pepper, seeded and thinly sliced

½ red onion, thinly sliced

½ cup light mayonnaise

¼ cup reduced-fat sour cream

¼ cup fat-free milk

½ teaspoon salt

① Rub: In a small bowl, mix together garlic powder, onion powder, sugar, thyme, allspice, black pepper, cayenne, salt and clove. Reserve 1 teaspoon of mixture for potato salad. Press rub evenly over both sides of London Broil and place in a resealable plastic food-storage bag. Refrigerate 4 hours or overnight.

② Potato Salad: Place potatoes in a medium-size saucepan and cover with lightly salted water. Simmer for 20 to 25 minutes until fork tender. Drain and cut into bite-size pieces.

③ Place peppers and onion in a large bowl. Add potatoes on top. Cover with plastic wrap and let cool on counter 15 to 30 minutes.

④ Meanwhile, in a small bowl, whisk together mayonnaise, sour cream, milk, salt and reserved teaspoon of rub. Fold into potatoes and peppers. Cover and refrigerate for at least 4 hours.

⑤ Steak: Heat broiler and coat a broiler pan with nonstick cooking spray. Broil steak 6 minutes. Turn and broil 5 to 6 minutes more or until internal temperature registers 135°F on an instant-read thermometer for medium-rare. Allow to rest 5 minutes before slicing.

PER SERVING 388 calories; 17 g fat (6 g sat.); 29 g protein; 29 g carbohydrate; 3 g fiber; 639 mg sodium; 57 mg cholesterol

KNIFE PRIMER

Every good cook needs a few quality knives on hand for peeling, slicing and dicing. Here are four that we can't live without—whether at home in our own kitchens or at work in our test kitchens.

Chef's Knife Available in 7-, 8- or 10-inch options, this will be your go-to knife for chopping fruit and vegetables, and for dicing pieces of meat and poultry. Hold firmly with your thumb running parallel to the handle for control. Rock knife up and down, keeping the tip on your work surface and using your opposite hand to guide the motion.

Utility Knife With a length of 5 to 8 inches, it is more thin and flexible than a chef's knife. Best for small, precise jobs, such as slicing steak and trimming fat from chicken thighs.

Serrated Knife Usually 10 inches long (sometimes offset for ease), this knife is handy for cutting through crusty bread or slicing soft-fleshed fruit and vegetables—such as tomatoes—without bruising. Look for one with evenly spaced pointed teeth. Run knife back and forth, using a sawing motion.

Paring Knife A small, multi-purpose knife whose size can vary from 3 to 4½ inches long. Perfect for peeling apples or slicing garlic and other small foods.

stuffed flank steak

MAKES 6 servings **PREP** 20 minutes **ROAST** at 425°F for 35 minutes **BROIL** 10 minutes

1 flank steak (1½ to 2 pounds)

1 package frozen chopped spinach, thawed

½ cup crumbled blue cheese

1 jar (7 ounces) roasted red peppers, drained and chopped

2 tablespoons seasoned dry bread crumbs

1 egg yolk

¾ teaspoon garlic salt

¾ teaspoon ground black pepper

1 tablespoon olive oil

① Heat oven to 425°F.

② Lay steak on work surface. Holding sharp knife parallel to work surface and starting at a long side, slice flank steak in half to opposite long side, without cutting all the way through; open up steak like a book. Flatten slightly to an even thickness.

③ Squeeze liquid from spinach; discard liquid. In medium-size bowl, combine spinach, blue cheese, peppers, bread crumbs, egg yolk and ¼ teaspoon *each* of garlic salt and pepper.

④ Season steak with an additional ¼ teaspoon *each* of garlic salt and pepper. Press filling onto steak, leaving a 1-inch border on all sides.

Roll up steak to enclose filling, beginning on a short side; grain of meat will be running from left to right. Tuck any loose filling back into ends.

⑤ Tie steak with cotton twine at 2-inch intervals to secure. Rub outside with oil, then sprinkle with remaining ¼ teaspoon *each* garlic salt and pepper.

⑥ Roast at 425°F for 35 minutes, then increase heat to broil and cook for 10 minutes, turning once. Let meat rest 15 minutes. Remove twine, slice and serve.

PER SERVING 305 calories; 15 g fat (6 g sat.); 36 g protein; 7 g carbohydrate; 2 g fiber; 588 mg sodium; 92 mg cholesterol

HOW TO STUFF A FLANK STEAK

1. Starting on a long side, split steak in half (not all the way through), and open like a book.

2. Spread spinach filling over flattened meat, leaving a 1-inch border around all edges.

3. Roll up meat, starting at a short end, until you enclose all of the spinach filling.

4. Tie steak with cotton twine at 2-inch intervals to secure.

filet with mushroom sauce

MAKES 4 servings **PREP** 5 minutes **COOK** 8 minutes **BROIL** 8 minutes

4   filet mignon steaks (5 to 6 ounces each)

¼   teaspoon salt

¼   teaspoon black pepper

1   tablespoon olive oil

8   ounces pre-sliced mixed mushrooms

3   cloves garlic, chopped

¼   cup steak sauce (such as A-1)

1   tablespoon onion flakes

2   teaspoons brown sugar

   Green salad and asparagus (optional)

① Heat broiler. Coat a broiler pan with nonstick spray.

② Season steaks with salt and pepper. Place on prepared pan and broil for 3 to 4 minutes per side for medium-rare or until internal temperature registers 135°F on an instant-read thermometer. Keep warm and allow to rest for 5 minutes.

③ Meanwhile, heat a large nonstick skillet over medium-high heat. Add olive oil, mushrooms and garlic and cook, stirring occasionally, for 5 minutes. Stir in steak sauce, onion flakes, brown sugar and ¼ **cup water**. Cook, stirring occasionally, for about 3 minutes, until thickened.

④ Serve with salad and asparagus, if desired.

PER SERVING 364 calories; 15 g fat (5 g sat.); 43 g protein; 14 g carbohydrate; 1 g fiber; 474 mg sodium; 112 mg cholesterol

NUTRITION NOTE

Filet mignon is one of the most tender cuts of meat. Because it is so lean, it is relatively low in calories. Lean beef is a good source of protein, providing 64.1% of the daily value for protein in just 4 ounces. An easier-to-find 5-ounce serving has 310 calories and 15 grams of fat.

A CUT ABOVE

Protein-packed beef provides vitamin B, iron and zinc, but to steer clear of too much fat and cholesterol, opt for these leaner, healthier cuts.

BOTTOM ROUND ROAST & STEAK

Calories & fat*: 139/4.9 g
Prime tip: It's easy for holiday gatherings. Braise or roast to medium rare.

95% LEAN GROUND BEEF

Calories & fat: 139/5.1 g
Prime tip: This versatile family favorite works best in chili or meat sauce.

EYE ROUND ROAST & STEAK

Calories & fat: 144/4 g
Prime tip: Wallet-friendly and great even as leftovers if you cook to medium-rare and carve into thin slices.

TOP SIRLOIN

Calories & fat: 156/4.9 g
Prime tip: Cook this tender cut as is or with a rub. Ideal for kabobs.

FLANK STEAK

Calories & fat: 158/6.3 g
Prime tip: Try strips in your next stir-fry or fajita recipe. Use a tenderizing marinade before grilling or broiling.

*per 3 ounces

cube steak & onion gravy

MAKES 6 servings **PREP** 10 minutes **COOK** 19 minutes

Cube Steaks:

2 tablespoons canola oil

6 cube steaks (about 4 ounces each)

¼ teaspoon salt

¼ teaspoon black pepper

3 tablespoons all-purpose flour

Onion Gravy:

2 large onions, thinly sliced

1 can (14.5 ounces) low-sodium beef broth

4 teaspoons all-purpose flour

½ teaspoon salt

⅛ teaspoon black pepper

⅛ teaspoon ground nutmeg

1½ teaspoons chopped tarragon

12 ounces egg noodles, cooked

2 tablespoons chopped flat-leaf parsley

Steamed green vegetable (optional)

① Cube Steaks: Heat oil in a large nonstick skillet over medium-high heat. Season meat with salt and pepper and lightly coat with flour. Sauté in batches 2 minutes per side. Place on a plate and keep warm.

② Onion Gravy: Add onions to skillet and cook for 6 to 8 minutes, until softened. If mixture becomes too dry add **1 or 2 tablespoons of water**. Stir occasionally. Add ¼ cup of broth to skillet and scrape up any browned bits from bottom of pan. Sprinkle flour over onions and cook, stirring, for 1 minute. Gradually stir in remaining beef broth. Add salt, pepper and nutmeg; cook for 2 minutes stirring continuously. Add tarragon, cube steaks and any accumulated liquid.

③ Serve steaks and gravy on top of cooked egg noodles and garnish with parsley. Accompany with steamed green vegetable, if desired.

PER SERVING 462 calories; 12 g fat (2 g sat.); 36 g protein; 48 g carbohydrate; 2 g fiber; 473 mg sodium; 125 mg cholesterol

TEST KITCHEN TIP

Perfect Portion A 3- to 4-ounce serving of beef is slightly larger than a deck of cards.

beef with garlic potatoes

MAKES 4 servings **PREP** 15 minutes **BAKE** at 400°F for 20 minutes **COOK** 10 minutes

1 cup beef broth

2 tablespoons ketchup

1 tablespoon Dijon mustard

1 tablespoon cornstarch

¾ pound small Yukon Gold potatoes

½ teaspoon garlic salt

¼ teaspoon black pepper

½ pound green beans

1½ cups baby carrots

1 cup frozen pearl onions, thawed

1 tablespoon canola oil

1 pound sirloin tip (about 1 inch thick), cut into 2-inch pieces

① Heat oven to 400°F. Coat a baking sheet with nonstick cooking spray; set aside. In a medium-size bowl, whisk broth, ketchup, mustard and cornstarch; set aside. Cut potatoes into ½-inch wedges; place on prepared baking sheet and sprinkle with ¼ teaspoon of garlic salt and ⅛ teaspoon of pepper. Bake at 400°F for 20 minutes or until tender. Remove from oven and set aside.

② Trim beans and cut into 2-inch pieces; cut carrots in quarters lengthwise. Place in a large skillet; add onions and ¼ **cup water.** Cover; cook on medium-high heat for 5 minutes. Remove lid and cook until water is gone. Remove vegetables and keep warm.

③ Add oil to skillet and heat over medium-high heat. Sprinkle sirloin with remaining ¼ teaspoon garlic salt and ⅛ teaspoon pepper and add to skillet. Cook for 3 to 4 minutes. Pour broth mixture into skillet; boil for 1 minute or until thickened. Stir in vegetables. Add potatoes to skillet and gently toss to coat.

PER SERVING 335 calories; 9 g fat (2 g sat.); 29 g protein; 35 g carbohydrate; 5 g fiber; 762 mg sodium; 68 mg cholesterol

TEST KITCHEN TIP

Named for its golden-colored flesh, Yukon Gold potatoes are best served roasted or mashed.

beef kabobs over couscous

MAKES 4 servings **PREP** 10 minutes **BROIL** 8 minutes

1   pound sirloin steak (about 1½ inches thick), trimmed

1   sweet red pepper, cored and cut into 1-inch pieces

¼   teaspoon curry powder

¼   teaspoon plus ⅛ teaspoon salt

⅛   teaspoon pumpkin pie spice

⅛   teaspoon black pepper

1   large chicken bouillon cube

1   box (7.6 ounces) whole-wheat couscous

3   scallions, chopped

⅓   cup apricots, chopped

⅓   cup pistachios, chopped

① Heat broiler. Cut steak into 1-inch cubes. Thread onto 4 metal skewers, dividing equally and alternating with pepper pieces. Stir together curry powder, ¼ teaspoon of salt, pumpkin pie spice and pepper. Sprinkle over skewers (all sides). Place on a broiler pan and set aside.

② Bring 1½ **cups water**, bouillon and remaining ⅛ teaspoon salt to a boil in a saucepan. Stir in couscous, scallions and apricots. Turn off heat and cover. Let stand 5 minutes.

③ Broil skewers, 2 inches from heat, 8 minutes. Turn once.

④ Fluff couscous and stir in pistachios. Spoon onto platter; top with skewers and serve.

PER SERVING 430 calories; 10 g fat (2 g sat.); 33 g protein; 54 g carbohydrate; 9 g fiber; 268 mg sodium; 42 mg cholesterol

CHOICE CUTS

These new picks taste like our old favorites but cost less.

DELMONICO
Flavor is similar to rib eye, but priced like beef chuck

How to cook: Pan-broil or grill using medium, direct heat

RANCH
Lean like top sirloin

How to cook: Grilled to medium-rare or medium

PETITE TENDER
Texture close to tenderloin

How to cook: Grill whole or slice into medallions and pan-broil

FLAT IRON
Well marbled like rib eye

How to cook: Grill or pan-broil

southwest meatloaf

MAKES 6 servings **PREP** 15 minutes **BAKE** at 375°F for 60 minutes

Meatloaf:

1½ pounds lean ground beef

½ cup unseasoned bread crumbs, mixed with ½ cup fat-free milk

½ large onion, chopped

½ large green pepper, chopped

2 eggs, lightly beaten

1 teaspoon ancho chile powder

1 teaspoon dried oregano

¾ teaspoon ground cumin

¾ teaspoon salt

½ cup cilantro leaves, chopped

1 can (14.5 ounces) no-salt-added diced tomatoes, drained

Cauliflower:

1 medium-size head cauliflower, trimmed and cut into florets

1 pound carrots, peeled and cut into 1-inch pieces

6 teaspoons olive oil

¼ teaspoon salt

¼ teaspoon ancho chile powder

¼ teaspoon ground cumin

¼ cup unseasoned bread crumbs

① Meatloaf: Heat oven to 375°F. Coat a 13 x 9 x 2-inch baking pan with nonstick cooking spray.

② In a large bowl, mix together ground beef, soaked bread crumbs, onion, green pepper, eggs, chile powder, oregano, cumin, salt and cilantro. Form into a loaf, approximately 9 x 5 inches and place into prepared pan. Evenly spoon drained tomatoes over top.

③ Bake at 375°F for 1 hour or until internal temperature registers 160°F on an instant-read thermometer. Allow to cool 10 minutes before slicing.

④ Cauliflower: While meatloaf is baking, coat another 13 x 9 x 2-inch baking dish with nonstick cooking spray. In a large bowl, mix together cauliflower, carrots, 4 teaspoons of olive oil, salt, chile powder and cumin. Spoon evenly into prepared baking dish. Mix remaining 2 teaspoons of olive oil with bread crumbs and evenly sprinkle over vegetables. Bake at 375°F for about 40 minutes or until vegetables are tender.

PER SERVING 368 calories; 13 g fat (4 g sat.); 33 g protein; 29 g carbohydrate; 6 g fiber; 714 mg sodium; 141 mg cholesterol

sloppy joes (+ 3 variations)

MAKES 6 servings **PREP** 5 minutes **COOK** 18 minutes

1½   pounds lean ground beef

1   can (8 ounces) tomato sauce

⅓   cup ketchup

2   tablespoons white wine vinegar

1   tablespoon Worcestershire sauce

2   teaspoons sugar

6   hamburger buns

① Coat a large nonstick skillet with nonstick cooking spray; heat over medium-high heat. Crumble in ground beef and cook, stirring occasionally, for 8 minutes.

② Stir in tomato sauce, ketchup, vinegar, Worcestershire sauce and sugar. Simmer on medium-low for 10 minutes, stirring occasionally.

③ Spoon about ½ cup of mixture on each hamburger bun. Serve with pickles and coleslaw, if desired.

PER SERVING 304 calories; 7 g fat (7 g sat.); 28 g protein; 29 g carbohydrate; 1 g fiber; 717 mg sodium; 70 mg cholesterol

SWITCH IT UP

Asian: Add 2 cloves chopped garlic, ½ teaspoon ground ginger and substitute 2 tablespoons light soy sauce for Worcestershire. Serve over white rice or on hamburger buns.

Italian: Add 1 teaspoon dried oregano and ½ teaspoon dried Italian seasoning. Stir in marinara sauce instead of ketchup. Substitute pre-baked pizza crust for hamburger buns and garnish with shredded mozzarella.

Mexican: Add 1 tablespoon chili powder and substitute prepared salsa for ketchup. Serve in taco shells.

GROUND BEEF: SAFETY FIRST

1. When shopping, pick up ground beef last and make sure it's cold.

2. Once home, refrigerate beef immediately. Place in plastic bag to avoid leakage and keep on plate in coldest part of refrigerator; use within 2 days.

3. Thaw frozen ground beef in refrigerator—never on the counter.

4. Cook meat to 160°F, checking temp with a meat thermometer.

5. Wash hands, utensils and work surfaces with soap and hot water to avoid cross-contamination.

6. After meat is cooked, don't return it to raw meat platter.

Storage: 1 to 2 days in the refrigerator and 3 to 4 months in the freezer

cheeseburger-zucchini pie

MAKES 6 servings **PREP** 10 minutes **BAKE** at 400°F for 25 minutes **COOK** 6 minutes

¾ pound lean ground beef

1 medium onion, peeled and chopped

1 medium zucchini (about 6 ounces), shredded

½ teaspoon salt

¼ teaspoon black pepper

1 cup shredded Italian cheese blend

½ cup heart-healthy reduced-fat biscuit mix (such as Bisquick)

1 cup milk

2 eggs

① Heat oven to 400°F. Spray a 9-inch pie plate with nonstick cooking spray.

② Spray a large nonstick skillet with nonstick cooking spray; heat over medium-high heat. Crumble in ground beef. Stir in onion and zucchini and cook for 6 minutes, stirring occasionally. Season with salt and pepper.

③ Spread beef mixture into prepared 9-inch pie plate. Sprinkle cheese over top.

④ In a medium-size bowl, whisk together biscuit mix, milk and eggs until smooth. Pour over beef mixture.

⑤ Bake at 400°F for 25 minutes or until a knife inserted in center comes out clean. Allow to cool for 5 to 10 minutes. Cut into 6 wedges and serve with a green salad, if desired.

PER SERVING 239 calories; 11 g fat (5 g sat.); 21 g protein; 13 g carbohydrate; 1 g fiber; 441 mg sodium; 123 mg cholesterol

TEST KITCHEN TIP

If you have mozzarella, Parmesan and smoked provolone in your fridge, you can make your own Italian blend.

asian beef & noodles

MAKES 4 servings   **PREP** 15 minutes   **COOK** 11 minutes

1 tablespoon vegetable oil

1 pound lean ground beef

1 small green bell pepper, seeded and thinly sliced

4 scallions, trimmed and thinly sliced

2 tablespoons ginger, finely chopped

1 clove garlic, finely chopped

¼ teaspoon red pepper flakes

1 teaspoon sugar

3 tablespoons stir-fry sauce

3 tablespoons lime juice

8 ounces fiber- and calcium-enriched thin spaghetti (such as Ronzoni Smart Taste)

1. Bring a large pot of lightly salted water to a boil.

2. Heat oil in a large skillet over medium-high heat. Add beef to skillet and cook for 6 minutes or until no longer pink.

3. Add green pepper, scallions, ginger, garlic, red pepper flakes and sugar to skillet; cook for 5 minutes, stirring occasionally. Turn off heat and stir in stir-fry sauce and lime juice.

4. While beef is cooking, prepare spaghetti following package directions. Drain and add to skillet with beef mixture. Toss to combine.

PER SERVING 404 calories; 10 g fat (3 g sat.); 32 g protein; 52 g carbohydrate; 7 g fiber; 481 mg sodium; 70 mg cholesterol

NUTRITION NOTE

Look for calcium-enriched pasta—it's the first white pasta to be enriched with fiber, calcium and vitamin D. It's also lower in calories and fat than traditional pasta.

maple-glazed pork with mashed sweet potatoes & parsnips

MAKES 4 servings **PREP** 10 minutes **COOK** 41 minutes **ROAST** at 400°F for 20 minutes

1   pork tenderloin (about 1¼ pounds)

1¼   teaspoons smoked black pepper blend (such as McCormick)

3   tablespoons maple syrup

8   ounces parsnips, trimmed, peeled and cut into ¼-inch-thick half-moons

½   cup low-sodium chicken broth

1½   pounds sweet potatoes, peeled and cut into ¼-inch-thick half-moons

① Heat oven to 400°F. Heat a large oven-safe nonstick skillet over medium-high heat.

② Pat pork dry with paper towels and rub with ¾ teaspoon of black pepper blend. Place pork in skillet and cook for 2 minutes per side or until browned. Transfer pork to oven and roast at 400°F for about 20 minutes or until internal temperature registers 145°F on an instant-read thermometer. Let rest 3 minutes. Use 1 tablespoon of maple syrup to twice brush pork during last 10 minutes of cook time.

③ While pork is cooking, heat a medium-size saucepan over medium heat. Add parsnips to saucepan; coat generously with nonstick cooking spray. Cover and cook, stirring occasionally, for 10 minutes or until browned.

④ Add broth, sweet potatoes and ¼ **cup water** to saucepan and cook, covered, for about 23 minutes, stirring occasionally, or until liquid has been absorbed. Gently mash. Stir in remaining 2 tablespoons maple syrup and ½ teaspoon black pepper blend and serve with pork.

PER SERVING 400 calories; 5 g fat (2 g sat.); 33 g protein; 55 g carbohydrate; 8 g fiber; 246 mg sodium; 93 mg cholesterol

TEST KITCHEN TIP

Parsnips taste nutty and sweet, without being high in calories, yet this cousin of the carrot is often ignored in the produce aisle.

mexican-style pork roast

MAKES 6 servings **PREP** 10 minutes **ROAST** at 350°F for 1 hour

1 boneless pork loin roast (about 2 pounds)

1 teaspoon ancho chile powder

¼ teaspoon salt

¼ teaspoon black pepper

1½ pounds small red potatoes, cut into bite-size pieces

2 pounds small zucchini, cut into 1-inch chunks

1 can (14.5 ounces) jalapeño-flavored diced tomatoes, not drained

① Heat oven to 350°F. Sprinkle pork with ½ teaspoon of chile powder, salt and pepper. Place in a roasting pan.

② In a large bowl, stir together potatoes, zucchini, tomatoes and remaining chile powder. Spoon around pork.

③ Roast at 350°F for 1 hour or until pork registers 145°F on an instant-read thermometer. Let rest 3 minutes. Remove from oven and cover loosely with foil for 10 minutes before serving.

PER SERVING 349 calories; 11 g fat (4 g sat.); 36 g protein; 24 g carbohydrate; 3 g fiber; 374 mg sodium; 92 mg cholesterol

Don't be discouraged by the length of the ingredient list. The first set is for the mole sauce, one of the most versatile sauces used in Mexican cooking. Double the recipe and freeze half for future use—it's excellent with chicken and meat as well as pork.

pork tenderloin & green mole sauce

MAKES 4 servings **PREP** 15 minutes **COOK** 31 minutes **ROAST** at 425°F for 15 minutes

Mole Sauce:

- 1 small onion, chopped
- 1 clove garlic, chopped
- ½ cup chicken broth
- 1 can (4.25 ounces) green chiles, drained
- ¼ cup fresh cilantro leaves
- ¼ cup fresh parsley leaves
- 2 tablespoons shelled sunflower seeds
- ⅛ teaspoon ground cumin
- ⅛ teaspoon salt
  Pinch cayenne pepper
- 2 teaspoons lime juice

Pork:

- 2 teaspoons olive oil
- 1 green pepper, thinly sliced
- 1 sweet red pepper, thinly sliced
- 1 sweet onion, thinly sliced
- 1 pork tenderloin (about ¾ pound)
- ½ teaspoon dried oregano
- ¼ teaspoon salt
- ⅛ teaspoon black pepper
- 2 cups cooked white rice

① Mole Sauce: In a medium-size nonstick skillet, cook onion and garlic over medium heat for 5 minutes, stirring occasionally. Place in a food processor with broth, ¼ **cup water**, chiles, cilantro, parsley, sunflower seeds, cumin, salt and cayenne. Process until smooth. Return mixture to skillet; simmer on medium-low heat for 15 minutes, stirring occasionally. Stir in lime juice. Keep warm.

② Pork: Heat oven to 425°F. Heat oil in a large ovenproof skillet over medium-high heat. Add peppers and onion and sauté for 4 to 5 minutes until softened. Remove from pan and keep warm.

③ Wipe out skillet and coat with nonstick cooking spray. Season pork with oregano, salt and black pepper. Cook over medium-high heat for 3 minutes per side. Roast at 425°F for 15 minutes or until internal temperature registers 145°F on an instant-read thermometer. Let rest 3 minutes. Remove from oven; let stand 5 minutes before serving.

④ Slice meat and serve with rice, peppers and sauce.

PER SERVING 350 calories; 10 g fat (2 g sat.); 23 g protein; 42 g carbohydrate; 4 g fiber; 583 mg sodium; 57 mg cholesterol

NUTRITION NOTE

Recent studies have shown that pork tenderloin is just as lean as skinless, boneless chicken breast. The U.S. Department of Agriculture (USDA) analysis found that pork tenderloin contains only 2.98 grams of fat per 3-ounce serving compared to 3.03 grams of fat in a 3-ounce serving of skinless chicken breast. Pork is also rich in many essential vitamins and minerals, such as B6, B12, niacin, thiamine, riboflavin, iron, magnesium, potassium and zinc.

quick pork schnitzel

MAKES 6 servings **PREP** 10 minutes **COOK** 8 minutes

6   thin boneless center-cut pork chops (about 1¼ pounds total)

½   teaspoon salt

¼   teaspoon black pepper

⅓   cup all-purpose flour

1   egg, beaten with ¼ cup water

⅔   cup plain dry bread crumbs

½   package medium egg noodles

4   tablespoons unsalted butter

Chopped fresh parsley

① Place 1 pork chop between 2 sheets of waxed paper and pound to ⅛-inch thickness. Repeat with all chops.

② Bring a large pot of lightly salted water to boiling. Season pork chops on both sides with salt and pepper. Spread flour on a dinner plate. Place egg mixture in a shallow dish or pie plate. Place bread crumbs on a third plate.

③ Add noodles to boiling water and cook 7 minutes. Meanwhile, melt 2 tablespoons of butter in a large nonstick skillet over medium heat. Coat a pork chop with flour, dip in egg mixture, then coat with bread crumbs. Repeat with all chops.

④ Cook 3 pork chops in skillet for 2 minutes. Flip and cook an additional 1 to 2 minutes. Transfer to a platter; add remaining 2 tablespoons butter to skillet. Repeat cooking with remaining 3 chops.

⑤ Drain noodles; place on platter with cutlets and sprinkle with parsley. Serve immediately.

PER SERVING 412 calories; 13 g fat (6 g sat.); 30 g protein; 39 g carbohydrate; 1 g fiber; 480 mg sodium; 151 mg cholesterol

SWITCH IT UP

Like extra crunch? Sub Japanese panko for bread crumbs.

pork & sweet potato stir-fry

MAKES 4 servings   **PREP** 15 minutes   **COOK** 17 minutes

½   cup beef broth

2   tablespoons reduced-sodium soy sauce

1   tablespoon ketchup

1   tablespoon rice vinegar

2   teaspoons cornstarch

¼   teaspoon red pepper flakes

2   tablespoons olive oil

1   pound thin boneless pork chops, cut, across grain, ¼ inch thick

⅛   teaspoon salt

1½   pounds sweet potatoes (about 2 large), peeled, quartered lengthwise and sliced crosswise ¼ inch thick

2   green peppers, cored, seeded and cut into ½-inch-thick strips

① In small bowl, mix broth, soy sauce, ketchup, vinegar, cornstarch and red pepper flakes until smooth. Set aside.

② Heat 1 tablespoon of oil in a large nonstick skillet over medium-high heat. Add pork and stir-fry for 2 minutes. Season with salt. Remove to plate and keep warm.

③ Add remaining 1 tablespoon oil to skillet; sauté sweet potatoes and peppers over medium-high heat for 8 minutes. Add **1 cup water** and simmer, covered, on medium-low for 6 minutes, until sweet potato is tender, stirring occasionally.

④ Stir in broth mixture and cooked pork and bring to a boil. Reduce heat and simmer for 1 minute, until sauce is thickened and meat is heated through. Serve immediately.

PER SERVING 355 calories; 10 g fat (2 g sat.); 30 g protein; 37 g carbohydrate; 6 g fiber; 787 mg sodium; 62 mg cholesterol

HOW-TO

Cutting Sweet Potatoes Cutting vegetables into equal-size pieces allows for more even cooking.

tacos al pastor

MAKES 6 servings   **PREP** 35 minutes   **REFRIGERATE** at least 1 hour or overnight   **COOK** 4 minutes

1   **can (20 ounces) pineapple chunks in juice**

2   **dried guajillo or ancho chiles (about 1 ounce from a 2-ounce package)**

3   **cloves garlic, peeled**

1   **teaspoon dried oregano**

¼   **teaspoon ground cumin**

¼   **teaspoon salt**

2   **tablespoons cider vinegar**

1   **pound boneless center-cut pork loin chops, trimmed of any fat**

1   **tablespoon vegetable oil**

2   **teaspoons cornstarch blended with 1 tablespoon water**

1   **package (7.5 ounces) soft corn tortillas (12 per package), heated**

1   **small red onion, finely chopped**

¼   **cup loosely packed cilantro leaves**

½   **cup reduced-fat sour cream, thinned with 2 tablespoons milk**

① Drain pineapple, reserving juice. Place juice in a small saucepan with ½ **cup water**. Bring to a boil; add chiles. Let soak 30 minutes.

② Remove stems from softened chiles, then pour chiles and liquid into a blender or food processor. Add ¾ cup of pineapple chunks, garlic, oregano, cumin, salt and vinegar. Puree until smooth.

③ Slice pork in half horizontally, then chop into small pieces. Place in a shallow glass dish or resealable plastic food-storage bag and add chile-pineapple mixture. Cover with plastic wrap or seal bag and marinate in refrigerator at least 1 hour or overnight. Meanwhile, dice remaining pineapple pieces. Refrigerate for later.

④ Heat oil in a large nonstick skillet over high heat. Scoop pork pieces from marinade with a slotted spoon and add to pan. Discard marinade. Cook pork for 3 minutes. Add reserved pineapple pieces and cornstarch-water mixture. Cook 1 minute, until pork is cooked through and sauce is thick. Serve mixture in warm corn tortillas, topped with onion, cilantro and sour cream.

PER SERVING 321 calories; 9 g fat (3 g sat.); 20 g protein; 38 g carbohydrate; 3 g fiber; 399 mg sodium; 55 mg cholesterol

TEST KITCHEN TIP

Ancho chiles are large and triangular in shape. The dried version of the poblano chile, the ancho is sweeter than the ripe chile. Use in salsas, sauces, soups and stews.

sausage jambalaya

MAKES 4 servings **PREP** 10 minutes **COOK** 26 minutes

1   tablespoon olive oil

½   pound Cajun sausage (or kielbasa), sliced into coins

1   onion, chopped

1   small green pepper, seeded and chopped

1   rib celery, chopped

1   teaspoon Cajun or Creole seasoning

1   bay leaf

1   can (14.5 ounces) no-salt-added stewed tomatoes, Cajun style, or diced tomatoes with mild green chiles

2   cups low-sodium chicken broth

1½ cups long-grain rice

① Heat large nonstick skillet over medium heat. Add olive oil, then sausage, onion, pepper and celery. Cook, stirring, for 5 minutes or until onion is soft. Stir in seasoning and bay leaf; cook 1 more minute.

② Add tomatoes, broth, **1½ cups water** and rice; bring to a boil, then cover, reduce heat to medium-low and simmer 20 minutes or until rice is tender and liquid is absorbed. Remove bay leaf.

Parent-Pleasing Alternative for each portion: In nonstick skillet, heat 1 teaspoon olive oil. Add ¼ pound cleaned shrimp, ⅛ teaspoon Cajun seasoning and a pinch of cayenne. Cook 2 minutes until shrimp turns pink. Stir into jambalaya.

PER SERVING 476 calories; 13 g fat (4 g sat.); 19 g protein; 76 g carbohydrate; 4 g fiber; 792 mg sodium; 40 mg cholesterol

There are many reasons to get hooked on fish—it can be tasty, nutritious, and so simple to prepare.

It's also an excellent source of high-quality protein—just as high as beef or pork but with healthier fats. Choosing fish just two times a week can have a significant impact on your health, lowering your risk of heart disease, stroke, and high blood pressure. But not all fish are created equal.

White fish, such as cod, tilapia and flounder are lean, contain healthy fats and are low in calories and carbohydrates. A 3-ounce serving is fewer than 125 calories with only 3 grams of fat.

fish

Oily fish, such as salmon, trout, sardines, black cod (sablefish), and herring, are higher in calories and fat (184 calories per 3-ounce serving), but offer high amounts of Omega-3 fatty acids. This has been shown to reduce the risk of heart disease and may even counter depression and early dementia.

Although high in cholesterol, shellfish are low in saturated fat which has a much greater impact on blood cholesterol levels. So go ahead and enjoy that lobster roll—just keep portions moderate.

Our favorite techniques for cooking fish are sautéing, broiling and roasting. Thin fish fillets are ideal for sautéing. Use a non-stick skillet to reduce the amount of fat needed.

Tilapia, a mild-tasting lean white fish, is widely available and relatively inexpensive, making it easily adaptable and a perfect family choice. This light refreshing dish is sure to please the entire family—even those non–fish lovers.

tilapia with lemony herb salad

MAKES 4 servings **PREP** 15 minutes **COOK** 8 minutes

1 clove garlic, minced

1 teaspoon lemon zest plus 1 tablespoon lemon juice

¼ teaspoon Dijon mustard

1 tablespoon chopped fresh parsley

1 tablespoon olive oil

4 tilapia fillets, trimmed to 6 ounces each

1 teaspoon lemon-herb seasoning (such as McCormick)

6 cups arugula

2 cups parsley leaves

Lemon wedges (optional)

① In a small bowl, stir together garlic, lemon zest and juice, Dijon and chopped parsley. Slowly whisk in olive oil; set aside.

② Sprinkle tilapia with lemon-herb seasoning. Heat large nonstick skillet over medium-high heat. Spritz both sides of tilapia with nonstick cooking spray and place in skillet. Cook 3 to 4 minutes per side or until fish flakes easily with a fork. Remove fish from skillet to a serving platter.

③ In a large bowl, toss together arugula and parsley leaves; drizzle with prepared dressing and serve with tilapia and lemon wedges, if desired.

PER SERVING 215 calories; 7 g fat (2 g sat.); 36 g protein; 4 g carbohydrate; 2 g fiber; 190 mg sodium; 85 mg cholesterol

TEST KITCHEN TIP

Flat-leaf parsley, also called Italian parsley, lends fabulous fresh flavor to any dish. Use it in salads, sauces and for cooking. Save curly parsley for garnishing. To store, shake off excess water from leaves, loosely wrap in damp paper towels and place in a plastic bag. Change the paper towels every few days. Keep in the warmest part of the refrigerator for up to 1 week.

red snapper with gazpacho salsa

MAKES 4 servings **PREP** 15 minutes **COOK** 7 minutes

3   plum tomatoes, seeded and cut into ¼-inch pieces

1   yellow pepper, seeded and cut into ¼-inch pieces

1   small rib celery, cut into ¼-inch pieces

½   cucumber, seeded and cut into ¼-inch pieces

½   small red onion, minced

½   teaspoon salt

½   teaspoon black pepper

1½   tablespoons extra-virgin olive oil

1   tablespoon white wine vinegar

2   red snapper fillets (about 9 ounces each), cut in half on the diagonal

2   tablespoons Wondra granulated flour

① In a medium-size bowl, stir together tomatoes, yellow pepper, celery, cucumber, onion, ¼ teaspoon *each* of salt and pepper, olive oil and vinegar; set aside.

② Sprinkle fish with remaining ¼ teaspoon *each* salt and pepper. Place Wondra on plate. Dip flesh side of fish (not skin) in Wondra, shaking off excess. Heat a large nonstick skillet over medium-high heat. Coat pan generously with nonstick cooking spray. Add fish to pan, flesh-side down, and cook 3 minutes. Flip and cook an additional 4 minutes or until fish flakes easily. Remove fish to serving platter and keep warm.

③ Meanwhile, heat a medium-size skillet over medium-high heat and add tomato mixture to pan. Cook 4 minutes, stirring often. Serve salsa with fish immediately.

PER SERVING 218 calories; 7 g fat (1 g sat.); 28 g protein; 10 g carbohydrate; 2 g fiber; 385 mg sodium; 47 mg cholesterol

TEST KITCHEN TIP

Because they are relatively meaty, plum tomatoes are perfect for sauces and condiments.

Choose unblemished tomatoes with smooth skins. Store on a counter or place in a brown paper bag with an apple to ripen. Only cut tomatoes should be placed in the fridge.

The addition of fresh ginger picks up the flavor of any dish. It works particularly well in this quick sauté of fish and greens. Since this recipe easily adapts to variations, let your family decide on the fish and leafy green to be used.

gingered tilapia & swiss chard

MAKES 4 servings **PREP** 10 minutes **COOK** 10 minutes

4 tilapia fillets (about 6 ounces each)

1½ tablespoons grated fresh ginger

½ teaspoon salt

½ teaspoon black pepper

1½ tablespoons olive oil

1 small onion, chopped

2 bunches Swiss chard, stems removed and leaves roughly chopped (about 6 cups)

¼ cup low-sodium chicken broth

¼ cup white wine

① Sprinkle tilapia with ¾ tablespoon of ginger and ¼ teaspoon *each* of salt and pepper. Heat 1 tablespoon of oil in a large nonstick skillet over medium-high heat. Cook tilapia 2 to 3 minutes per side or until fish flakes easily. Remove from skillet and keep warm.

② Heat remaining ½ tablespoon oil in skillet; cook onion and remaining ¾ tablespoon ginger for 1 minute.

③ Increase heat to high. Add Swiss chard, remaining ¼ teaspoon *each* salt and pepper, chicken broth and wine to skillet. Cook 3 minutes, stirring, until chard is wilted.

PER SERVING 233 calories; 8 g fat (2 g sat.); 35 g protein; 3 g carbohydrate; 1 g fiber; 533 mg sodium; 85 mg cholesterol

FISH BUYING GUIDELINES

Head to a store with a lot of turnover that smells clean with no strong "fishy" aroma.

• If possible, purchase fish that is not already wrapped; it might be good, but it's difficult to evaluate.

• The surface of fillets and steaks should be bright, clear and reflective—almost translucent.

• The color should be consistent with the type of fish; for example, pearly white fish should not have spots of pink (which indicates spoilage). Ivory-colored fish should have no areas of deep red or brown.

• Sniff fish for freshness: Ocean fish smells pleasantly briny like fresh, clean seawater.

• Whole fish should have red gills, firm flesh, an undamaged layer of scales and no browning.

• If buying frozen fish, look for packages that are intact and frozen solid.

• If there's a clear window, check to see that it has no ice crystals or discoloration.

catfish & corn salsa

MAKES 4 servings **PREP** 15 minutes **COOK** 12 minutes

4 teaspoons olive oil

3 ears corn, kernels cut off cob

3 scallions, thinly sliced

1 jalapeño, seeded and minced

1 clove garlic, minced

¾ teaspoon ground cumin

1 large tomato, chopped

2 tablespoons chopped fresh cilantro

2 teaspoons fresh lime juice

¾ teaspoon salt

½ teaspoon black pepper

4 catfish fillets (6 ounces each)

Cornmeal (about ¼ cup)

Lime wedges

① Heat 1 teaspoon of oil in a large nonstick skillet over medium-high heat. Add corn, scallions, jalapeño, garlic and ¼ teaspoon of cumin. Cook 3 minutes, stirring often, or until corn is crisp-tender. Stir in tomato and cook, 1 minute, stirring constantly. Stir in cilantro, lime juice, ¼ teaspoon *each* of salt and pepper. Remove; set aside.

② Sprinkle catfish with remaining cumin, salt and pepper. Coat fillets in cornmeal. Wipe out skillet; add remaining oil. Cook on medium-high heat 3 to 4 minutes on each side or until fish flakes when tested with a fork. Serve topped with salsa and lime wedges.

PER SERVING 412 calories; 8 g fat (1 g sat.); 38 g protein; 48 g carbohydrate; 5 g fiber; 596 mg sodium; 82 mg cholesterol

HOW-TO

Remove Corn Kernels Place a clean dish towel on your counter, stand the corn cob, stem side down, on the towel and with a sharp knife cut down the cob. Instead of scattering all over the counter, the kernels will land gently on the towel. Lift the towel and empty the kernels into a bowl. When choosing corn, look for ears with green husks and moist, golden silks. Refrigerate in their husks for no more than 2 days.

fish tacos

MAKES 4 servings **PREP** 10 minutes **COOK** 18 minutes

- ½ cup low-fat sour cream
- 3 tablespoons minced cilantro
- ¼ cup lime juice
- 1 green pepper, finely chopped
- 1 pound cod
- ½ teaspoon salt
- ½ teaspoon chili powder
- 4 corn tortillas

① In a small bowl, stir together sour cream, 2 tablespoons of cilantro and 1 tablespoon of lime juice; set aside.

② Coat an 8-inch nonstick skillet with nonstick spray; heat over medium heat. Add green pepper; cook 3 minutes. Add cod to pan and sprinkle with 2 tablespoons of lime juice, salt and ¼ teaspoon of chili powder. Cover; cook 15 minutes or until fish is cooked through.

③ In a medium-size bowl, flake fish; add skillet contents. Add remaining cilantro, lime juice and chili powder to bowl; stir gently. Heat tortillas. Divide fish among tortillas and serve with sauce.

PER SERVING 202 calories; 5 g fat (3 g sat.); 23 g protein; 15 g carbohydrate; 2 g fiber; 388 mg sodium; 64 mg cholesterol

TEST KITCHEN TIP

In the Limelight Store limes in the refrigerator, in a plastic bag, up to 10 days uncut, 5 days if sliced. They are best when firm, heavy for their size and deep green in color.

lemony flounder with roasted zucchini

MAKES 4 servings **PREP** 15 minutes **COOK** 14 minutes **ROAST** at 450°F for 20 minutes

4   small zucchini (about 1½ pounds), cut lengthwise into ¼-inch-thick slices

1   lemon, zest and juice

4   tablespoons chopped fresh parsley

1½ teaspoons dried oregano

1   medium-size onion, chopped

2   cloves garlic, chopped

½   cup white wine or water

1⅓ cups low-sodium vegetable broth

2   flounder fillets (about 1 pound), cut in half

1   cup orzo, prepared according to package directions (optional)

① Cover 2 large baking sheets with nonstick foil and place in oven. Heat oven to 450°F.

② Carefully spread zucchini slices in a single layer on prepared baking sheets. Drizzle with 2 tablespoons lemon juice and sprinkle with 1 tablespoon of parsley and ½ teaspoon of oregano. Roast at 450°F for 20 minutes or until tender, flipping slices halfway through.

③ Heat a large nonstick skillet over medium heat. Add onion, remaining 3 tablespoons parsley and remaining 1 teaspoon oregano to skillet and spritz with nonstick cooking spray. Cover and cook for 5 minutes or until softened. Uncover and add lemon zest and garlic to skillet; cook 1 minute.

④ Pour wine or water, vegetable broth and remaining lemon juice (about 2 tablespoons) into skillet. Bring to a simmer over medium heat. Add fish to skillet and cook, covered, for 5 to 8 minutes, until opaque, carefully flipping halfway through.

⑤ Remove fish from skillet and pour some of poaching liquid over orzo (if using). Serve orzo with fish and zucchini.

PER SERVING 188 calories; 2 g fat (0 g sat.); 24 g protein; 14 g carbohydrate; 3 g fiber; 311 mg sodium; 54 mg cholesterol

TEST KITCHEN TIP

Reasons to Roast To concentrate the flavor of vegetables and bring out their natural sweetness, try roasting them.

herb-crusted salmon & israeli couscous

MAKES 4 servings **PREP** 10 minutes **COOK** 8 minutes **BROIL** 7 minutes

¾ **teaspoon salt**

1 **cup Israeli couscous**

2½ **tablespoons panko bread crumbs**

2 **tablespoons chopped fresh dill**

4 **salmon fillets (about 4 ounces each)**

¼ **teaspoon black pepper**

2 **teaspoons Dijon mustard**

3 **cups baby spinach, roughly chopped**

¼ **cup low-sodium chicken broth**

① Heat oven to broil. Place nonstick foil on a rimmed baking sheet and set aside.

② Bring 1¼ **cups water** to a boil in a medium-size pot. Add ½ teaspoon of salt and couscous. Cover and cook 8 minutes, stirring occasionally; set aside.

③ Meanwhile, stir together bread crumbs and 1 tablespoon dill; set aside. Sprinkle salmon with remaining ¼ teaspoon salt and pepper and place on prepared baking sheet. Place directly under broiler and cook for 5 minutes.

④ Remove salmon from oven and lower rack so it's 6 inches from heating element. Brush salmon with mustard and sprinkle with bread crumb mixture, pressing to adhere. Generously spritz each fillet with nonstick cooking spray and return to oven; broil 2 minutes.

⑤ Stir remaining tablespoon dill, spinach and chicken broth into couscous; let sit 5 minutes. Serve with salmon.

PER SERVING 307 calories; 7 g fat (1 g sat.); 27 g protein; 31 g carbohydrate; 2 g fiber; 318 mg sodium; 63 mg cholesterol

TEST KITCHEN TIP

Don't let the name fool you! Israeli couscous is a small, round semolina pasta. Don't confuse it with the tiny, yellow North African couscous most commonly used in this country. It's sometimes called pearl couscous and resembles barley.

teriyaki salmon with glazed broccoli salad

MAKES 4 servings **PREP** 15 minutes **COOK** 18 minutes **BROIL** 8 minutes

- 2 tablespoons honey
- 2 tablespoons low-sodium teriyaki sauce
- 1 tablespoon rice wine vinegar
- 4 scallions, trimmed and thinly sliced
- 2 cloves garlic, minced
- ½ cup sliced almonds
- 1 bunch (1½ pounds) broccoli cut into florets; stalks peeled and cut in ¼-inch coins
- 4 salmon fillets (about 4 ounces each)
- 2 teaspoons cornstarch

① In a small bowl, blend honey, teriyaki, vinegar, scallions and garlic; divide in half and set aside.

② Adjust top oven rack so that it is 6 inches from heating element and heat broiler. Line a rimmed baking sheet with aluminum foil.

③ Heat a large nonstick skillet over medium-high heat; toast almonds for 6 minutes. Remove almonds; carefully wipe out skillet.

④ Place ¼ **cup water** in skillet; reduce heat to medium-low. Add broccoli and cook, covered, for 7 to 8 minutes or until bright green and tender.

⑤ Place salmon on prepared baking sheet; brush with half of reserved teriyaki mixture. Broil salmon 5 to 8 minutes or until top is browned and interior temperature registers 120°F on an instant-read thermometer.

⑥ Stir cornstarch into remaining reserved teriyaki mixture and pour into skillet. Bring to a simmer and cook, stirring, for 4 minutes or until sauce has reduced to a thick glaze. Stir in almonds and serve alongside salmon.

PER SERVING 332 calories; 14 g fat (2 g sat.); 30 g protein; 25 g carbohydrate; 6 g fiber; 239 mg sodium; 62 mg cholesterol

TEST KITCHEN TIP
Safety Questions

Oily fish like salmon and mackerel are rich sources of heart-healthy Omega-3 fatty acids. However, concerns over mercury contamination can make buying decisions difficult. Go to the Monterey Bay Aquarium Seafood Watch's site to find regional guides to sustainable seafood choices as well as an overview of health issues; seafoodwatch.org.

swordfish with gremolata

MAKES 4 servings **PREP** 15 minutes **BAKE** at 450°F for 15 minutes

Gremolata:

- 1½ cups packed flat-leaf parsley
- 1 lemon
- 2 tablespoons chopped dill
- 3 cloves garlic, chopped
- 1 teaspoon lemon pepper

Swordfish and Rice:

- 4 swordfish steaks (about 6 ounces each, ¾ inch thick)
- 2 cups raw quick-cook brown rice
- 1 can (14.5 ounces) chicken broth
- 1 cup mixed sweet red and orange peppers, diced

  Lemon slices

① Heat oven to 450°F. Coat a glass baking dish with nonstick spray.

② Gremolata: Chop parsley; you will need ¾ cup. Grate lemon; you will need 1 tablespoon zest. Juice lemon; you will need 2 tablespoons; set aside. In a bowl, mix parsley, grated lemon peel, dill, garlic and ¾ teaspoon of lemon pepper. Set gremolata aside.

③ Swordfish: Place swordfish in prepared baking dish and drizzle with reserved lemon juice. Season with remaining ¼ teaspoon lemon pepper.

④ Bake at 450°F for 15 minutes or until fish flakes easily.

⑤ Meanwhile, prepare rice following package directions, substituting chicken broth for water. Stir in peppers and 2 tablespoons of gremolata; cover and let stand for 5 minutes.

⑥ Sprinkle remaining gremolata over swordfish and serve with rice. Garnish with lemon.

PER SERVING 407 calories; 8 g fat (2 g sat.); 29 g protein; 53 g carbohydrate; 4 g fiber; 680 mg sodium; 48 mg cholesterol

TEST KITCHEN TIP

Gremolata is the traditional garnish for osso buco, the classic Italian dish of braised veal shanks. But this zesty condiment is equally good on fish, chicken and vegetables. Keep it on hand to enliven the flavor of a dish and to add an elegant garnish. Store gremolata in the fridge, covered with plastic, up to 3 days.

oven-roasted cod with tomato relish

MAKES 4 servings **PREP** 10 minutes **COOK** 1 minute **BROIL** 1 minute **BAKE** at 450°F for 15 to 18 minutes

4   cod fillets (about 1½ pounds total)

2   tablespoons extra-virgin olive oil

¼   teaspoon salt

¼   teaspoon black pepper

2   cups grape tomatoes, quartered

¼   cup pitted kalamata olives, coarsely chopped

½   cup fresh basil, chopped

1   to 2 teaspoons balsamic vinegar

2   cups low-sodium chicken broth

1   cup shredded carrots

1   cup uncooked couscous

① Heat oven to 450°F. Coat a 13 x 9 x 2-inch baking dish with nonstick cooking spray.

② Place cod in prepared baking dish, skin-side down. Brush with 1 tablespoon of oil and ⅛ teaspoon *each* of salt and pepper. Bake at 450°F for 15 to 18 minutes or until fish flakes easily with a fork. Run under broiler for a minute, if desired, to lightly brown.

③ Meanwhile, in a small bowl, mix together tomatoes, olives, basil, remaining 1 tablespoon olive oil, vinegar, remaining ⅛ teaspoon *each* salt and pepper. Cover and set aside.

④ While cod is cooking, bring chicken broth to a simmer and stir in carrots. Simmer for 1 minute. Stir in couscous and take off heat. Cover and allow to sit 5 minutes.

⑤ Serve cod with tomato relish and couscous on the side.

PER SERVING 390 calories; 9 g fat (2 g sat.); 34 g protein; 41 g carbohydrate; 5 g fiber; 510 mg sodium; 65 mg cholesterol

TEST KITCHEN TIP

For a burst of juice in salads, reach for grape tomatoes. These little gems pack intense flavor and sweetness. Perfect as a garnish or quickly sautéed with fresh herbs.

This delicious all-purpose glaze of brown sugar and mustard will tempt even the most skeptical fish lover in your family and have them coming back for seconds.

brown sugar–glazed salmon

MAKES 4 servings   **PREP** 5 minutes   **BAKE** at 325°F for 25 minutes

4   **2-inch wide salmon fillets (about 1½ pounds total)**

¼   **cup packed dark-brown sugar**

2   **teaspoons unsalted butter**

2   **teaspoons Dijon mustard**

¼   **teaspoon salt**

¼   **teaspoon black pepper**

8   **ounces steamed snow peas**

2   **cups heat-and-serve brown rice**

① Heat oven to 325°F. Line a small baking sheet with nonstick aluminum foil. Place salmon on prepared sheet.

② In a small bowl, stir together brown sugar, butter, mustard, salt and pepper. Carefully spread over salmon pieces, dividing equally.

③ Transfer salmon to 325°F oven and bake for 25 minutes, or until fish flakes easily with a fork. Serve with snow peas and rice on the side.

PER SERVING 478 calories; 15 g fat (3 g sat.); 43 g protein; 41 g carbohydrate; 3 g fiber; 303 mg sodium; 112 mg cholesterol

TEST KITCHEN TIP

Brown Sugar Fix What do you do when your brown sugar has turned as hard as a rock? Place it in a microwave-safe bowl and microwave at 10-second intervals until it is soft.

gingered carrots & cod

MAKES 4 servings **PREP** 15 minutes **COOK** 12 minutes **MICROWAVE** 1½ minutes **BAKE** at 400°F for 23 minutes

4   **cod or scrod fillets (about 5 ounces each)**

¼   **cup honey**

1   **tablespoon chopped fresh ginger**

2   **tablespoons balsamic vinegar**

2   **tablespoons low-sodium soy sauce**

⅛   **plus ¼ teaspoon salt**

    Pinch ground black pepper

3   **tablespoons unsalted butter**

1   **large bunch carrots, peeled and cut on the diagonal into ½-inch slices**

1   **sweet yellow pepper, cored and cut into 1-inch pieces**

    Mashed potatoes (optional)

① Heat oven to 400°F. Coat a baking dish with nonstick cooking spray. Place cod in dish, spacing fillets at least ½ inch apart.

② In a 2-cup measuring cup, combine honey, ginger, vinegar, soy sauce, ⅛ teaspoon of salt and pepper. Cover with plastic wrap and microwave on HIGH for 1½ minutes (mixture will bubble up). Remove from microwave and whisk in 1 tablespoon butter. Spoon 1 tablespoon sauce over each cod fillet. Sprinkle cod with remaining ¼ teaspoon salt. Cover dish with foil and bake at 400°F for 20 to 23 minutes, until fish is opaque and flakes easily with a fork.

③ Meanwhile, melt remaining 2 tablespoons butter in a large nonstick skillet over medium-high heat. Add carrots; sauté 3 minutes. Add yellow pepper and sauté 2 minutes. Reduce heat to medium; add ¼ **cup water** and cover. Cook 5 minutes, until tender.

④ Uncover skillet; stir in remaining sauce from measuring cup. Raise heat to medium-high and cook 2 minutes.

⑤ Divide carrot mixture evenly among 4 plates. Top each with a piece of cod. Serve with mashed potatoes, if desired.

PER SERVING 293 calories; 10 g fat (6 g sat.); 22 g protein; 31 g carbohydrate; 3 g fiber; 645 mg sodium; 71 mg cholesterol

TEST KITCHEN TIP

How long will fish stay fresh? If recently caught, it will keep up to a week. Store-bought fish won't last that long nor will a piece of fish such as a fillet or a steak. Eat these within a few days of buying. If the fish is lean (bass or cod), add an extra day. If oily (salmon or trout), subtract a day. Enjoy really oily fish (mackerel or bluefish) on the day of purchase.

curried salmon & mint raita

MAKES 4 servings **PREP** 15 minutes **COOK** 15 minutes **BAKE** at 450°F for 15 minutes

½ cup reduced-fat plain yogurt

½ cucumber, peeled and seeds removed, diced

2 tablespoons chopped fresh mint

⅛ teaspoon salt

1 cup long-grain white rice

1 can (14.5 ounces) vegetable broth

4 Alaskan wild salmon fillets (about 5 ounces each)

1 tablespoon canola oil

1 teaspoon hot curry powder

¼ teaspoon cinnamon

¼ teaspoon ground ginger

⅛ teaspoon garlic powder

Pinch salt

① In a small bowl, mix together yogurt, cucumber, mint and salt. Cover and refrigerate until ready to serve.

② In a medium-size saucepan, cook rice following package directions, substituting vegetable broth for water.

③ Heat oven to 450°F. Coat a 13 x 9 x 2-inch glass baking dish with nonstick cooking spray. Place salmon fillets, skin-side down, in dish. In a small bowl, mix together oil, curry powder, cinnamon, ginger, garlic powder and salt. Spoon curry mixture over salmon. Bake at 450°F for 15 minutes or until fish flakes easily when tested with a fork.

④ Serve salmon with raita and rice.

PER SERVING 479 calories; 15 g fat (2 g sat.); 38 g protein; 45 g carbohydrate; 1 g fiber; 667 mg sodium; 91 mg cholesterol

NUTRITION NOTE

Choose yogurt with 4 or fewer grams of fat, the live and active cultures seal, and a daily calcium value of 20%.

panko-crusted tilapia & bow ties

MAKES 4 servings **PREP** 15 minutes **BAKE** at 450°F for 10 minutes **COOK** 9 minutes **BROIL** 2 minutes

- **4** **U.S. farm-raised tilapia fillets (about 5 ounces each)**
- **½** **teaspoon salt**
- **¼** **teaspoon black pepper**
- **½** **cup Italian-seasoned panko bread crumbs (such as Progresso)**
- **½** **pound bow tie pasta**
- **1** **container (10 ounces) Brussels sprouts, trimmed and halved**
- **3** **tablespoons olive oil**
- **4** **cloves garlic, peeled and chopped**
- **⅛** **teaspoon red pepper flakes**
- **¼** **cup grated Parmesan cheese**

① Heat oven to 450°F. Bring a large pot of water to a boil. Coat a broiler-safe baking pan with nonstick cooking spray. Place tilapia fillets in pan, skin-side down, and coat lightly with cooking spray. Season fish with ¼ teaspoon of the salt and the pepper. Sprinkle 2 tablespoons panko crumbs over each fillet. Bake at 450°F for 10 minutes.

② While fish is baking, boil bow ties for 4 minutes. Add Brussels sprouts and cook an additional 5 minutes. Drain, reserving ½ cup cooking liquid.

③ Heat olive oil in a large skillet over medium-high heat. Add garlic and red pepper flakes and cook 30 seconds. Add bow ties, Brussels sprouts, reserved cooking liquid and remaining ¼ teaspoon of the salt. Cook 1 minute until heated through. Stir in Parmesan cheese.

④ Turn oven up to broil. Run fillets under broiler for 1 to 2 minutes, until browned and crisp. Serve with bow ties on the side.

PER SERVING 497 calories; 16 g fat (4 g sat.); 40 g protein; 50 g carbohydrate; 3 g fiber; 587 mg sodium; 78 mg cholesterol

NUTRITION NOTE

A 3-ounce serving of tilapia on its own contains 80 calories, 16 grams of protein, and 1.5 grams of fat, with 0 grams of saturated and trans fats. It's an excellent source of healthy protein.

fish & zucchini chips

MAKES 4 servings **PREP** 15 minutes **BAKE** at 450°F for 18 minutes

½ cup all-purpose flour

4 egg whites

1¼ cups panko bread crumbs

2 tablespoons grated Parmesan cheese

1 tablespoon low-sodium Old Bay seasoning

2 small zucchini (about ½ pound total), cut into 2½ x ½-inch sticks

½ cup light mayonnaise

2 tablespoons malt vinegar

¼ teaspoon hot pepper sauce

4 tilapia fillets (1½ pounds total)

① Heat oven to 450°F. Place racks over 2 baking sheets; set aside.

② Place flour and egg whites in separate shallow glass dishes. Whisk whites until foamy.

③ Place panko, Parmesan cheese and Old Bay on a separate glass plate; stir to combine.

④ Coat zucchini in flour, dip into egg whites, then coat with panko mixture. Place on rack and coat lightly with nonstick cooking spray; set aside.

⑤ In a small bowl, whisk mayonnaise, vinegar and hot pepper sauce. Divide in half; set one half aside. Brush one side of tilapia fillets with mayonnaise mixture and place that side down in flour. Brush top side of fillets with mayonnaise mixture and carefully flip over into flour. Dip in egg whites; coat with panko mixture. Place fillets on second rack. Coat lightly with nonstick cooking spray.

⑥ Place zucchini in oven. Bake at 450°F for 3 minutes, then add fish and cook 15 more minutes or until fish flakes easily. Serve with reserved mayonnaise mixture.

PER SERVING 415 calories; 13 g fat (2 g sat.); 42 g protein; 31 g carbohydrate; 1 g fiber; 800 mg sodium; 94 mg cholesterol

TEST KITCHEN TIP
Japanese-style panko bread crumbs are coarser and fry up crispier than their American counterparts. Look for them in the Asian food aisle; store in the refrigerator.

mediterranean fish casserole

MAKES 4 servings **PREP** 10 minutes **BAKE** at 400°F for 1 hour

2 tablespoons olive oil

1 pound small white potatoes, cut into quarters

2 large Italian frying peppers, thinly sliced

¼ teaspoon salt

¼ teaspoon black pepper

3 cloves garlic, peeled and chopped

4 U.S. Pacific-caught cod or halibut fillets (about 5 ounces each, ¾ inch thick)

¼ cup pitted kalamata olives, chopped

2 plum tomatoes, seeded and cut into ¼-inch wedges

2 tablespoons lemon juice

¼ cup flat-leaf parsley, chopped

① Heat oven to 400°F. Grease an oval 2-quart casserole dish with 1 tablespoon of olive oil. Spread potatoes and peppers over bottom of dish. Season with ⅛ teaspoon *each* of salt and pepper. Bake at 400°F for 35 minutes or until potatoes are tender, stirring occasionally.

② Scatter garlic over potatoes and peppers. Season fish with remaining ⅛ teaspoon *each* salt and pepper and place on top of potatoes. Distribute olives and tomatoes over casserole. Drizzle with lemon juice and remaining 1 tablespoon olive oil. Sprinkle with parsley.

③ Bake at 400°F for 25 minutes or until fish flakes easily when tested with a fork.

PER SERVING 272 calories; 8 g fat (1 g sat.); 26 g protein; 26 g carbohydrate; 4 g fiber; 417 mg sodium; 54 mg cholesterol

The "reveal" of food cooked in a packet adds fun to any meal and the preparation makes the food so moist and flavorful. It's a simple, irresistible way to cook fish.

cod & ratatouille packets

MAKES 4 servings **PREP** 15 minutes **BAKE** at 450°F for 20 minutes

2 plum tomatoes, seeded and cut into ½-inch pieces

1 small zucchini (5 ounces), halved lengthwise and cut into ¼-inch-thick half-moons

1 small yellow squash (5 ounces), halved lengthwise and cut into ¼-inch-thick half-moons

½ of 1 large fennel bulb, trimmed, halved, cored and thinly sliced (about 2 cups)

½ small onion, thinly sliced

2 cloves garlic, minced

1 tablespoon chopped fresh thyme

¼ teaspoon salt

⅛ teaspoon black pepper

3 tablespoons low-sodium chicken broth

4 cod fillets (about 6 ounces each)

4 teaspoons unsalted butter

① Heat oven to 450°F.

② In a large bowl, stir together tomatoes, zucchini, squash, fennel, onion, garlic, ½ tablespoon of thyme, ⅛ teaspoon of salt, pepper and broth; set aside.

③ Lay 4 large pieces of foil or parchment paper (each 16 inches long) on work surface. Place 1½ heaping cups vegetable mixture on lower half of each piece. Place fish on top of vegetables and sprinkle with remaining ½ tablespoon thyme and ⅛ teaspoon salt. Place 1 teaspoon butter on top of each fillet. Fold foil or parchment over fish and fold edges to create a sealed packet. Place packets on a rimmed baking sheet, overlapping if necessary.

④ Bake at 450°F for 20 minutes or until fish is cooked through and veggies are tender. Carefully cut open packets and slide contents onto plates; serve immediately.

PER SERVING 230 calories; 4 g fat (1 g sat.); 37 g protein; 9 g carbohydrate; 3 g fiber; 300 mg sodium; 55 mg cholesterol

TEST KITCHEN TIP

Seal in moisture Cooking in foil or parchment keeps food moist and concentrates natural flavors. It also makes cleanup a snap.

baked flounder with crabmeat stuffing

MAKES 4 servings **PREP** 15 minutes **REFRIGERATE** 30 minutes **BAKE** at 400°F for 20 minutes **COOK** 5 minutes

½ small onion, minced

½ small red pepper, finely chopped

¾ teaspoon low-sodium Old Bay seasoning

¼ teaspoon salt

⅔ cup light cream

8 ounces imitation crabmeat, finely chopped

3 teaspoons chopped parsley

4 flounder fillets (about 4 ounces each)

¾ cup white wine or water

Cooked brown rice (optional)

① Heat a medium-size nonstick skillet over medium heat. Coat pan with nonstick cooking spray, then add onion and red pepper and coat generously with spray; cover and cook 4 minutes or until softened, stirring occasionally.

② Remove cover and stir in ½ teaspoon of Old Bay, ⅛ teaspoon of salt and the light cream. Increase heat to medium-high and bring to a boil; cook for 1 minute or until reduced and thickened. Gently fold in crabmeat and 2 teaspoons of parsley; refrigerate 30 minutes.

③ Heat oven to 400°F. Coat a 13 x 9 x 2-inch baking dish with nonstick cooking spray. Place 1 flounder fillet skinned-side up on work surface, then spoon ½ cup crab mixture onto end of fillet; roll up, creating a small bundle. Repeat using remaining fillets and crab. Transfer bundles to prepared baking dish, seam-side down, and sprinkle with remaining ¼ teaspoon Old Bay, ⅛ teaspoon salt and 1 teaspoon parsley. Add wine or water to pan; transfer to oven.

④ Bake at 400°F for 20 minutes or until fish is solid white and flakes easily with a fork. Remove to plates with a large spatula and serve with rice, if desired.

PER SERVING 281 calories; 9 g fat (5 g sat.); 27 g protein; 13 g carbohydrate; 1 g fiber; 800 mg sodium; 92 mg cholesterol

TEST KITCHEN TIP

Make Ahead Stuffed flounder rolls may be prepared through step 3 several hours ahead. Refrigerate, covered with plastic. When ready to cook, increase baking time by 5 minutes, or until fish flakes easily.

wild rice–stuffed flounder

MAKES 4 servings **PREP** 10 minutes **COOK** 55 minutes **BAKE** at 400°F for 20 minutes

½ cup wild rice

3 tablespoons mayonnaise

2 tablespoons Dijon mustard

1 egg yolk

1 cup small broccoli florets

1 small scallion, chopped

½ teaspoon dried tarragon

¾ cup grape tomatoes, halved

4 flounder fillets (about 6 ounces each)

¼ teaspoon regular or smoked paprika

⅛ teaspoon salt

⅛ teaspoon black pepper

1 lemon, thinly sliced

¾ cup white wine or water

① Bring **1½ cups water** to a boil in a medium-size saucepan. Add rice. Cover tightly, reduce heat to low; simmer 45 minutes.

② Meanwhile, in a medium-size bowl, stir together mayonnaise, mustard and egg yolk. Set aside.

③ Add broccoli florets, scallion and tarragon to wild rice and cook an additional 10 minutes or until rice is tender and water is absorbed. Remove from heat; cool about 10 minutes.

④ Transfer rice mixture along with grape tomatoes to bowl with mayonnaise mixture. Stir until evenly blended.

⑤ Heat oven to 400°F. Coat a 13 x 9 x 2-inch baking dish with nonstick cooking spray. Place 1 flounder fillet skin-side up in prepared dish. Spoon a scant ⅔ cup rice mixture onto half of fillet, then fold over other half to cover. Repeat using remaining flounder fillets and rice filling. Sprinkle with paprika, salt and pepper; top each with 2 slices of lemon. Add wine or water to pan; transfer to oven.

⑥ Bake at 400°F for 20 minutes or until fish is solid white and flakes easily with a fork (filling should register 160°F on an instant-read thermometer). Remove to plates with a large spatula; serve with baby carrots.

PER SERVING 317 calories; 12 g fat (2 g sat.); 29 g protein; 21 g carbohydrate; 2 g fiber; 433 mg sodium; 128 mg cholesterol

TEST KITCHEN TIP

Some Like It Wild Wild rice, that is. This appealing grain—it isn't a rice at all but the seeds of a marsh grass—adds a toasty flavor and slightly nutty texture to pilafs. It will keep indefinitely in a cool, dry place.

sautéed shrimp & red chard

MAKES 6 servings **PREP** 10 minutes **COOK** 10 minutes

4 tablespoons olive oil

6 cloves garlic, sliced

1¼ pounds medium-size shrimp, peeled and deveined

¾ teaspoon salt

¼ teaspoon black pepper

1 pound red chard, stems cut off and reserved (see Note); leaves cut into 1-inch slices

½ teaspoon dried oregano

1 package (17.5 ounces) whole-wheat spaghetti (such as De Cecco)

⅓ cup grated Parmesan cheese

① Heat 2 tablespoons of oil in a large nonstick skillet over medium-high heat. Add garlic and cook 30 seconds. Season shrimp with ¼ teaspoon of salt and ⅛ teaspoon of pepper. Add shrimp to skillet and cook 2 minutes per side. Remove to a plate and keep warm.

② Add chard leaves to skillet and season with remaining ½ teaspoon of salt, ⅛ teaspoon pepper and oregano. Reduce heat to medium-low. Cook 4 to 5 minutes until tender. Add shrimp back into skillet. Cover and set aside.

③ Meanwhile, cook pasta following package directions, about 10 minutes. Drain, reserving ½ cup cooking water. Toss pasta with shrimp mixture and remaining 2 tablespoons oil. Add enough of pasta water to create a sauce. Transfer to a large bowl and sprinkle with Parmesan cheese.

Note: If desired, rinse and dry stems. Toss with a little olive oil, salt and pepper. Roast at 350°F for 20 minutes or until tender. Cut into bite-size pieces and add to pasta.

PER SERVING 468 calories; 14 g fat (3 g sat.); 31 g protein; 61 g carbohydrate; 11 g fiber; 671 mg sodium; 122 mg cholesterol

TEST KITCHEN TIP

How many shrimp to a pound?

Jumbo: 21/25
Extra Large: 26/30
Large: 31/35
Medium: 41/50
Small: 51/60

mediterranean shrimp

MAKES 6 servings **PREP** 15 minutes **COOK** 12 minutes

12 ounces linguine

1 tablespoon olive oil

2 cloves garlic, minced

1 cup sliced fresh mushrooms

1 small zucchini, cut into ¼-inch pieces

1 small yellow squash, cut into ¼-inch pieces

¼ teaspoon red pepper flakes

1 pound large shrimp, peeled and deveined

2 small plum tomatoes

½ cup kalamata olives, coarsely chopped

1½ cups marinara sauce, heated

① Cook linguine in boiling salted water for 12 minutes. Drain and transfer to a large serving bowl.

② Meanwhile, heat oil in a large skillet over medium heat. Cook garlic for 1 minute. Add mushrooms and cook for 3 minutes. Increase heat to medium-high; add zucchini, squash and red pepper flakes. Cook, stirring occasionally, for 3 minutes.

③ Add shrimp to skillet and cook for 3 minutes or until uniformly pink. Coarsely chop tomatoes; add to skillet along with olives and marinara. Warm through. Toss shrimp mixture with pasta in serving bowl.

PER SERVING 323 calories; 7 g fat (1 g sat.); 23 g protein; 42 g carbohydrate; 4 g fiber; 573 mg sodium; 115 mg cholesterol

TEST KITCHEN TIPS

Choosing Shrimp

- 1½ pounds of shrimp with shells = 1 pound cleaned shrimp.

- Buy frozen shrimp with shells on to protect them from freezer burn.

- Thaw shrimp in refrigerator; use within 2 days and never refreeze.

HOW TO PEEL AND CLEAN SHRIMP

1. Gently remove shell with fingers.

2. With a small paring knife, cut along inside of shrimp to expose vein.

3. With small paring knife, cut along rounded part of shrimp to expose vein.

4. Run under cold water to rinse away veins.

tomatillo shrimp enchiladas

MAKES 8 enchiladas **PREP** 30 minutes **BAKE** at 375°F for 15 minutes **COOK** 6 minutes

2 tablespoons olive oil

½ medium-size red onion, peeled and thinly sliced

½ medium-size green bell pepper, seeded and thinly sliced

1¼ pounds medium-size shrimp, peeled, deveined and cut in half crossways

1 cup frozen corn, thawed

1 teaspoon chili powder

½ teaspoon ground cumin

8 corn tortillas

1 bottle (16 ounces) tomatillo salsa (such as La Victoria)

3 tablespoons half-and-half

1 cup shredded reduced-fat Monterey Jack cheese

① Heat oil in a large nonstick skillet over medium-high heat. Add onion and green pepper; cook 3 minutes, stirring occasionally. Add shrimp; cook an additional 3 minutes, until shrimp is opaque. Stir in corn, ¼ **cup water**, chili powder and cumin. Heat through.

② Heat oven to 375°F. Coat a 13 x 9 x 2-inch baking dish with nonstick cooking spray.

③ Wrap 4 tortillas in damp paper towels. Microwave 30 seconds. Brush one side of each tortilla with salsa. Spoon ½ cup shrimp mixture on each. Roll up and place seam-side down in prepared dish. Repeat with remaining tortillas and filling. Top with any extra filling.

④ Mix remaining salsa with half-and-half. Spoon over enchiladas. Sprinkle with Monterey Jack cheese. Bake at 375°F, uncovered, for 15 minutes or until bubbly.

PER SERVING 240 calories; 8 g fat (2 g sat.); 20 g protein; 20 g carbohydrate; 2 g fiber; 677 mg sodium; 15 mg cholesterol

TEST KITCHEN TIP

Make Ahead Enchiladas may be prepared through step 3 several hours ahead or overnight. Refrigerate, covered with plastic. When ready to cook, increase baking time by 5 minutes or until bubbly.

scallop & shrimp fettuccine

MAKES 6 servings **PREP** 25 minutes **BAKE** at 350°F for 20 minutes **COOK** 5 minutes

2 tablespoons olive oil

¾ pound scallops

¾ pound large shrimp, peeled and deveined

½ teaspoon salt

⅛ teaspoon black pepper

2 cups fat-free half-and-half

1 tablespoon cornstarch

1 can (6.5 ounces) chopped clams, undrained

½ cup plus 6 tablespoons shredded Swiss and Gruyère cheese blend

2 tablespoons chopped fresh tarragon

⅛ teaspoon cayenne pepper

1 box (12 ounces) spinach fettuccine, cooked following package directions

① Heat oven to 350°F. Coat a 3½-quart oval dish with nonstick cooking spray.

② Heat oil in a large nonstick skillet over medium-high heat. Add scallops, shrimp, ¼ teaspoon of salt and pepper. Cook for 2 minutes per side. Remove to a plate.

③ In a medium-size bowl, blend half-and-half and cornstarch. Add to skillet and bring to a simmer. Simmer 1 minute. Take off heat and stir in clams and juices, ½ cup of cheese, tarragon, cayenne and remaining ¼ teaspoon salt. Add cooked shellfish and toss with fettuccine.

④ Spoon into prepared dish. Sprinkle with remaining 6 tablespoons cheese. Bake at 350°F for 20 minutes. Serve warm.

PER SERVING 467 calories; 12 g fat (4 g sat.); 35 g protein; 53 g carbohydrate; 2 g fiber; 736 mg sodium; 127 mg cholesterol

TEST KITCHEN TIP

Choosing Scallops

- Look for fresh scallops that are cream-tan in color or slightly pinkish
- Although their aroma can be fairly strong, they should never smell fishy
- They should be moist but not oozy
- There should be little or no milky liquid in the tray
- The flesh should be tight, not loose or falling apart

lobster roll

MAKES 6 rolls **PREP** 15 minutes **REFRIGERATE** at least 1 hour

⅔ cup light mayonnaise

1 tablespoon lemon juice

1 tablespoon extra-virgin olive oil

2 teaspoons Dijon mustard

1 teaspoon chopped fresh tarragon

¼ teaspoon black pepper

¼ teaspoon hot sauce

⅛ teaspoon salt

2 lobster tails, cooked, shelled and meat coarsely chopped (about 2 cups)

1½ cups chopped celery

6 soft frankfurter rolls

① In a medium-size bowl, whisk together mayonnaise, lemon juice, olive oil, mustard, tarragon, pepper, hot sauce and salt.

② In a large bowl, mix together lobster meat and celery. Gently fold in mayonnaise mixture until lobster meat is evenly coated. Cover and refrigerate for at least 1 hour.

③ Fill each roll with a generous ½ cup of lobster mixture.

PER SERVING 323 calories; 16 g fat (3.5 g sat.); 15 g protein; 15 g carbohydrate; 1 g fiber; 785 mg sodium; 44 mg cholesterol

The unique flavor of foods cooked over charcoal or scented wood have made grilling America's favorite pastime. And there's another good reason why it's so popular: There's much less mess or cleanup than when you cook in the kitchen—a welcome bonus any day. In fact, you can cook your entire meal on the grill—protein, vegetables and dessert.

Grilling lends itself to healthy cooking. Cooking foods over direct heat not only results in a crisp, browned crust and a moist tender interior, it allows excess fat to drip away into the grill. Be sure to trim all fat first, which will cut down on saturated fat and help prevent flare-ups.

grilling

For successful grilling follow these simple steps: Begin by evenly spreading the coals across the bottom of your grill. Cook thin pieces of meat or poultry at a high temperature over direct heat, covered, turning only once. For thicker cuts of meat and poultry, begin over high heat for a short time to seal in flavor and then lower the heat to cook the food through.

Marinades, rubs and glazes provide extra flavor and can be used to baste during cooking. If you can't make your own, there are dozens of creative BBQ sauces and glazes available at supermarkets. Be sure to carefully read labels to make sure the sodium is within an acceptable range.

When the weather turns warm and you can't wait to get outside, this is a crowd-pleasing recipe to start the grilling season.

smoky bbq chicken with sweet potatoes

MAKES 6 servings **PREP** 15 minutes **COOK** 15 minutes **GRILL** 70 minutes

1   can (8 ounces) tomato sauce

½   cup chopped onion

3   tablespoons white vinegar

3   tablespoons honey

1   tablespoon Worcestershire sauce

2   cloves garlic, chopped

1   to 2 chipotle chiles in adobo, chopped

1   whole chicken, quartered (3½ to 4 pounds)

½   teaspoon salt

¼   teaspoon black pepper

2   pounds sweet potatoes, peeled and cut into ½-inch slices

① In a medium-size saucepan, combine tomato sauce, onion, vinegar, honey, Worcestershire, garlic and chipotle. Simmer, uncovered, for 15 minutes, stirring occasionally. Set aside.

② Heat half of a gas grill to medium-high or prepare a grill with medium-hot coals for indirect grilling.

③ Season chicken with ¼ teaspoon of salt and ⅛ teaspoon of pepper. Lightly grease grates and place chicken, bone-side down, on side of gas grill that is not on or side of grill opposite coals. Cover and grill for about 70 minutes. Rotate pieces after 35 minutes. Start to brush chicken with sauce during last 15 minutes of cooking time.

④ Place sweet potato slices on grill over direct heat after chicken has been grilling about 40 minutes. Brush liberally with sauce. Cook for about 20 minutes, turning every 5 minutes and brushing with more sauce, until tender.

⑤ Serve chicken with sweet potatoes and any remaining sauce on the side. Grill onion slices along with sweet potatoes, if desired.

PER SERVING 446 calories; 17 g fat (5 g sat.); 37 g protein; 35 g carbohydrate; 4 g fiber; 617 mg sodium; 111 mg cholesterol

vidalia chicken & potatoes

MAKES 4 servings **PREP** 8 minutes **MICROWAVE** 5 minutes **GRILL** 20 minutes

1½ **pounds small red potatoes**

4 **boneless, skinless chicken breasts (5 ounces each)**

1 **cup reduced-fat Vidalia onion dressing**

1 **small red onion, cut in half and thinly sliced**

½ **teaspoon salt**

½ **teaspoon black pepper**

Steamed sugar snap peas, if desired

① Prepare charcoal grill with hot coals or heat gas grill to high.

② Slice red potatoes crosswise into ⅛-inch-thick coins. Place in medium-size glass bowl, cover with plastic wrap and microwave on HIGH for 5 minutes. Meanwhile, place chicken breasts in ⅓ cup of dressing, turn to coat and let sit 15 minutes at room temperature.

③ Add onion slices to potatoes and toss with remaining ⅔ cup dressing. Sprinkle with ¼ teaspoon of salt and ¼ teaspoon of pepper. Cut four 10-inch-long pieces of heavy-duty foil. Generously coat centers of foil pieces with cooking

spray. Divide potato mixture among foil pieces. Create a packet, tightly sealing top edges. Place on grill; cook 10 minutes. Flip over packets; cook 10 minutes more.

④ Remove chicken from dressing, shaking off excess. Sprinkle with remaining salt and pepper. Grill on high heat about 3 to 5 minutes per side, turning once, or until done. Serve chicken and potatoes with sugar snap peas, if desired.

PER SERVING 433 calories; 11 g fat (0 g sat.); 37 g protein; 44 g carbohydrate; 3 g fiber; 609 mg sodium; 82 mg cholesterol

---

HOW-TO

Great Grilling Guidelines:

1. Clean the grill rack with a wire brush before heating.

2. If using a charcoal grill, spread out coals evenly across the bottom.

3. To prevent sticking, heat grill for about 15 minutes before starting to cook, and resist turning food until it is halfway done.

4. Determine if the charcoal or grill is ready by holding your palm about 6 inches above the coals and counting off until the warmth forces it away. Hot = 2 seconds; medium = 4 seconds; low = 5 seconds.

5. Never grill in an area that isn't well ventilated and never use gasoline or kerosene to start a fire.

mustard-basil chicken with grilled corn

MAKES 4 servings **PREP** 10 minutes **GRILL** 23 minutes

3 tablespoons grainy Dijon mustard

4 tablespoons basil-infused olive oil

1 tablespoon honey

½ teaspoon salt

½ teaspoon black pepper

4 boneless, skinless chicken breasts (about 1½ pounds)

4 ears corn

① Heat gas grill to medium-high or prepare a charcoal grill with medium-hot coals.

② Stir together mustard, 3 tablespoons oil, honey and ¼ teaspoon *each* salt and pepper.

③ Lightly coat grill with nonstick cooking spray or oil. Place chicken on grill and brush generously with mustard mixture; cover and grill for 5 minutes. Remove cover and flip breasts, baste generously with sauce and cover.

④ Continue flipping chicken every 5 minutes, basting each time, for about 18 minutes or until internal temperature registers 165°F on an instant-read thermometer.

⑤ Meanwhile, brush corn with remaining tablespoon oil; sprinkle with remaining ¼ teaspoon *each* salt and pepper. Wrap corn in aluminum foil. Grill corn, turning once, about 18 minutes or until tender. Serve alongside chicken.

Broiler method: Heat broiler. Coat a broiler pan with nonstick cooking spray. Coat chicken with sauce and broil for about 20 minutes, brushing occasionally with sauce. Meanwhile, broil corn for about 18 minutes or until tender.

PER SERVING 412 calories; 17 g fat (3 g sat.); 42 g protein; 24 g carbohydrate; 3 g fiber; 685 mg sodium; 98 mg cholesterol

TEST KITCHEN TIP

Unless corn is labeled "supersweet," the sugar in it will start to turn to starch the minute it is picked. Your best bet? Head to your farmers' market, buy early in the morning and use it quickly. Choose ears with fresh, firm, green husks. Do not strip ears; rather look for pale and silky tassels with only a little brown at the top. Corn can be refrigerated, with the husks on, for 1 day.

chicken with apricot bbq sauce

MAKES 4 servings **PREP** 5 minutes **GRILL** 30 minutes

Apricot BBQ Sauce:

- ⅔ **cup apricot preserves**
- 2 **tablespoons Dijon mustard**
- ½ **teaspoon garlic powder**
- 1 **teaspoon finely chopped fresh ginger**
- ¼ **cup ketchup**

Chicken:

- 4 **whole chicken legs (about 1¾ pounds total)**
- ½ **teaspoon salt**
- ¼ **teaspoon black pepper**

① Prepare grill with medium-hot coals or heat gas grill to medium-high.

② Apricot BBQ Sauce: In a small bowl, stir apricot preserves, mustard, garlic powder, ginger and ketchup until combined. Set aside.

③ Chicken: Remove skin from chicken legs. Season all over with salt and pepper. Grill 25 to 30 minutes, turning occasionally or until an instant-read thermometer registers 165°F. Brush chicken with half of sauce during last 5 minutes of cooking; serve remaining sauce on the side.

PER SERVING 316 calories; 5 g fat (1 g sat.); 28 g protein; 39 g carbohydrate; 1 g fiber; 791 mg sodium; 109 mg cholesterol

SWITCH IT UP

Substitute pineapple preserves or orange marmalade for the apricot preserves.

HOW-TO

Grilling Like the Pros

- For grilling thin pieces of meat or poultry, cook at a high temperature over direct heat with the cover on, flipping the meat only once.

- Sear meat and fish by using high heat for a short time to seal in the flavor, then lower heat to cook through.

- Create high and low zones by stacking briquettes on one side of the grill so you have room to move your food from one zone to another.

citrusy tequila chicken thighs with rice salad

MAKES 6 servings **PREP** 10 minutes **REFRIGERATE** 4 hours or overnight **COOK** 1 minute **GRILL** 30 minutes

Chicken and Marinade:

- ½ cup orange juice
- ¼ cup lime juice
- ¼ cup tequila
- 2 tablespoons canola oil
- 1 teaspoon salt
- ½ teaspoon McCormick Smokehouse pepper or ground black pepper
- 6 large skinless bone-in chicken thighs

Rice Salad:

- 3 tablespoons olive oil
- 3 tablespoons marinade (above)
- ¼ teaspoon salt
- 3 cups cooked rice
- ½ each red and yellow sweet peppers, chopped
- 2 scallions, trimmed and thinly sliced
- 1 tablespoon chopped cilantro

① Chicken: Place orange juice, lime juice, tequila, canola oil, salt and pepper in a large resealable plastic food-storage bag. Add chicken and seal. Marinate in refrigerator for 4 hours or overnight.

② Heat gas grill to medium-high or prep charcoal grill with medium-hot coals and set up one side for indirect grilling. Lightly coat grill rack with oil or nonstick cooking spray.

③ Remove chicken from plastic bag and pour marinade into a small saucepan. Boil for 1 minute and reserve. Place chicken on direct heat and grill for 5 minutes per side. Remove to indirect heat and grill for 20 minutes or until internal temperature registers 165°F on an instant-read thermometer. Baste every 5 minutes with reserved marinade.

④ Rice Salad: In a large bowl, whisk olive oil, 3 tablespoons of marinade and salt. Stir in rice, peppers, scallions and cilantro. Serve at room temperature with chicken.

PER SERVING 405 calories; 18 g fat (3 g sat.); 25 g protein; 31 g carbohydrate; 1 g fiber; 568 mg sodium; 110 mg cholesterol

SWITCH IT UP

Sub in swordfish for chicken; marinate 20 minutes before grilling.

chicken burgers

MAKES 4 servings   **PREP** 10 minutes   **GRILL** 12 minutes

¼ cup fat-free mayonnaise

1 tablespoon chopped parsley

1 tablespoon chopped basil, plus 4 large, whole basil leaves

1 teaspoon lemon juice

1 pound ground chicken

1 small onion, finely chopped

3 tablespoons part-skim ricotta cheese

3 tablespoons seasoned bread crumbs

4 hamburger buns

1 small tomato, sliced

① Stir together mayonnaise, ½ tablespoon parsley, ½ tablespoon chopped basil and lemon juice in a small bowl; set aside.

② Heat gas grill to medium-high or prepare charcoal grill with medium-hot coals.

③ In a large bowl, stir together remaining ½ tablespoon each parsley and basil, chicken, onion, ricotta cheese and bread crumbs until combined. Form into four 4-inch patties. Grill for 6 minutes per side or until internal temperature registers 165°F on an instant-read thermometer.

④ Remove burgers from grill and place on buns. Top with a basil leaf, a slice of tomato and 1 tablespoon mayonnaise mixture.

Broiler Method: Heat broiler. Coat a broiler pan with nonstick cooking spray. Broil burgers 5 to 6 minutes per side. Proceed with Step 4 above.

PER SERVING 370 calories; 16 g fat (5 g sat.); 26 g protein; 32 g carbohydrate; 3 g fiber; 520 mg sodium; 140 mg cholesterol

TEST KITCHEN TIP

Store ground chicken in the refrigerator for 1 to 2 days, in the freezer 3 to 4 months. Be sure to use separate cutting boards for raw meats and cooked meats or vegetables and fruits. Wash utensils with hot, soapy water after each use.

grilled turkey caprese

MAKES 6 servings **PREP** 15 minutes **REFRIGERATE** 4 hours or overnight **GRILL** 45 minutes **COOK** 8 minutes

3 tablespoons olive oil

3 tablespoons balsamic vinegar

1 tablespoon light-brown sugar

1 teaspoon salt

½ teaspoon black pepper

1 boneless, skinless turkey breast half (2½ to 3 pounds)

1½ pounds heirloom or vine-ripened tomatoes

¼ cup fresh basil, shredded

2 cloves garlic, peeled and sliced

½ pound whole-grain penne

4 ounces part-skim mozzarella cheese, cut into small cubes

① In a small bowl, whisk together olive oil, vinegar, brown sugar, ½ teaspoon of salt and ¼ teaspoon of pepper. Place 2 tablespoons of mixture and turkey breast into a resealable plastic food-storage bag. Shake bag to evenly coat turkey, seal and refrigerate for 4 hours or overnight. Reserve remaining oil and vinegar mixture.

② Heat half of a gas grill to medium-high or prepare a grill with medium-hot coals for indirect grilling. Season turkey with remaining ½ teaspoon of salt and ¼ teaspoon of pepper. Lightly grease grates and place turkey on side of gas grill that is not on or side of grill opposite coals. Cover and grill for 40 to 45 minutes or until internal temperature registers 160°F on an instant-read thermometer. Turn halfway through cooking.

③ While grill is heating, cut tomatoes into bite-size pieces and place in a large bowl. Stir in basil, garlic and reserved oil-and-vinegar mixture. Cover and refrigerate 1 hour.

④ Cook pasta, following package directions, about 8 minutes. Drain. Stir in mozzarella cheese and half of tomato mixture.

⑤ Thinly slice turkey and serve with penne. Serve remaining tomato mixture on the side.

PER SERVING 481 calories; 12 g fat (3 g sat.); 56 g protein; 37 g carbohydrate; 6 g fiber; 593 mg sodium; 136 mg cholesterol

grilled vegetable fajitas

MAKES 4 servings   **PREP** 15 minutes   **MICROWAVE** 1 minute   **GRILL** 16 minutes

- 3 tablespoons lime juice
- 2 teaspoons ground cumin
- 2 teaspoons chili powder
- ½ teaspoon salt
- ⅛ teaspoon cayenne pepper
- 1 medium-size red onion, cut into ½-inch-thick rings
- 1 pound asparagus spears, trimmed
- 1 large green, yellow and red pepper, each cut into ½-inch-thick slices
- 1 medium-size yellow squash, cut diagonally into ½-inch-thick slices
- 1 medium-size zucchini, cut diagonally into ½-inch-thick slices
- 8 small (6 inches) 96% fat-free flour tortillas
- 1 can (16 ounces) refried beans, heated
- ½ cup reduced-fat shredded Mexican cheese blend
- Prepared guacamole
- Prepared tomato salsa

① Heat gas grill to medium-high or prepare charcoal grill with medium-hot coals. In a small bowl, stir lime juice, cumin, chili powder, salt and cayenne.

② Place onion rings on large plate; brush both sides with some of lime juice mixture. Microwave on HIGH for 1 minute. Set aside.

③ Place asparagus in a large resealable plastic food-storage bag, peppers in a second bag and squash and zucchini in a third. Divide remaining lime juice mixture among 3 bags. (Can be done 2 hours ahead.)

④ Coat all vegetables with nonstick spray and grill, covered. Grill asparagus for 10 minutes, turning often, and onion for 8 minutes, turning once. In a grill basket, cook single layer of peppers for 10 minutes, turning often; remove. Add squash in a single layer; grill for 6 minutes, turning once. Place all vegetables on a platter.

⑤ Heat tortillas according to package directions. Spread each with 2 tablespoons hot refried beans, then ¾ cup mixed grilled vegetables. Top with 1 tablespoon *each* cheese and guacamole and 2 tablespoons salsa. Fold in half. Repeat with remaining filling and tortillas, and serve.

PER SERVING 216 calories; 2 g fat (0 g sat.); 11 g protein; 40 g carbohydrate; 7 g fiber; 762 mg sodium; 1 mg cholesterol

HOW-TO

Fire-roasting vegetables brings out their natural sweetness. Brush your favorites with oil or a marinade before grilling to seal moisture in and keep them from sticking to the rack. Place veggies over medium heat and cook 5 to 10 minutes, turning once, until fork-tender.

maple-glazed salmon with grilled vegetables

MAKES 4 servings **PREP** 10 minutes **REFRIGERATE** 40 minutes **MICROWAVE** 5 minutes **GRILL** 20 minutes **COOK** 5 minutes

- ¼ cup low-sodium soy sauce
- ¾ cup low-calorie pancake syrup
- 4 salmon fillets (about 6 ounces each)
- 4 long sweet potatoes (about 1½ pounds total), scrubbed
- 2 medium-size onions, sliced into ½-inch-thick rings
- 1 pound asparagus, trimmed
- ½ teaspoon salt
- ½ teaspoon black pepper

① Shake soy sauce and syrup in resealable plastic food-storage bag to mix. Add salmon. Close; refrigerate 40 minutes.

② Microwave sweet potatoes on HIGH for about 5 minutes, until slightly tender; let cool. Cut diagonally across into ¼- to ½-inch-thick slices; coat slices on both sides with nonstick cooking spray. Set aside.

③ Heat gas grill to medium-high or prepare charcoal grill with medium-hot coals. Remove salmon from marinade; pour marinade into small saucepan and set aside. Grill salmon for about 5 minutes per side, or until opaque in center; remove and keep warm. Add sweet potatoes and onions and grill for about 5 minutes. Note: If not using a grill basket, secure onion slices with a toothpick. Turn and add asparagus; cook vegetables another 5 minutes, turning asparagus frequently. Test doneness of sweet potato slices with a knife. Sprinkle salmon and vegetables with salt and pepper.

④ Meanwhile, boil marinade in saucepan over high heat for 5 minutes, until thickened. Brush salmon and vegetables with marinade.

PER SERVING 408 calories; 11 g fat (2 g sat.); 40 g protein; 37 g carbohydrate; 8 g fiber; 676 mg sodium; 94 mg cholesterol

TEST KITCHEN TIP

Sweet Potatoes—A nutrition powerhouse, sweet potatoes are a good source of vitamins A and C. There are two types: The sweet, moist orange-fleshed variety is more common than the drier, less-sweet boniato type. Sweet potatoes are frequently mislabeled "yams," a different species, not often sold in U.S. markets.

Choose firm, smooth sweet potatoes without wrinkles, bruises, sprouts or decay. The skin can vary from brown to soft red to purple; white sweet potatoes have a rough, mottled skin. Handle gently; they bruise easily. Buy only what you plan on eating within a few days or put in a cool, well-ventilated place. Do not refrigerate.

pacific rim cedar plank salmon

MAKES 4 servings **PREP** 10 minutes **COOK** 6 minutes **GRILL** 25 minutes

1   cedar plank (see tip)

¼   cup packed light-brown sugar

2   tablespoons soy sauce

3   cloves garlic; 1 minced, the other 2 sliced

½   teaspoon sesame oil

1¼   pounds salmon fillet (1 piece)

1   tablespoon olive oil

1   pound baby bok choy, trimmed and chopped

⅛   teaspoon salt

⅛   teaspoon black pepper

① Soak plank in cool water for 10 minutes, weighing down with a heavy object to keep submerged.

② Heat gas grill to medium or charcoal grill to medium coals.

③ In a small bowl, stir together brown sugar, soy sauce, clove of minced garlic and sesame oil. Set aside 2 tablespoons sauce for serving.

④ Once plank is done soaking, place salmon fillet on plank, skin-side down, and brush with half of remaining sauce. Transfer plank to grill and cover. Grill 10 minutes; if plank chars too much, mist with water.

⑤ Uncover grill; baste salmon with remaining sauce. Cover grill and continue to cook 15 minutes or until fish registers 130°F on an instant-read thermometer and flakes easily with a fork.

⑥ Meanwhile, heat oil in a large nonstick skillet over medium heat. Add 2 sliced garlic cloves and cook 1 to 2 minutes. Add bok choy, salt and pepper and cook an additional 2 to 4 minutes, until tender and cooked through.

⑦ Slide a spatula between fillet and skin and transfer to a platter. Drizzle with 2 tablespoons reserved sauce; serve with bok choy on the side.

PER SERVING 339 calories; 14 g fat (2 g sat.); 34 g protein; 17 g carbohydrate; 2 g fiber; 324 mg sodium; 90 mg cholesterol

TEST KITCHEN TIP

Grilling on cedar planks is an easy way to infuse food with a delicious smoky flavor. Visit madeinoregon.com to buy a 3-pack of cedar planks for $13.

easy salmon burgers

MAKES 4 burgers **PREP** 10 minutes **GRILL** 10 minutes

4 tablespoons light mayonnaise

2 tablespoons chopped fresh dill

1 pound salmon fillet, skin removed

⅓ cup bread crumbs

2 scallions, thinly sliced

¼ teaspoon salt

¼ teaspoon black pepper

4 whole-wheat hamburger buns, toasted

① Heat gas grill to medium-high or prepare charcoal grill with medium-hot coals. In a small bowl, stir together mayonnaise and 1 tablespoon of dill; set aside.

② In bowl of a food processor, pulse remaining tablespoon dill, salmon, bread crumbs, scallions, salt and pepper until combined. Form into four 3-inch round burgers and coat both sides with nonstick cooking spray.

③ Grill burgers for 5 minutes per side or until cooked through. Place burgers on buns and spread each with 1 tablespoon dill mayonnaise.

PER SERVING 365 calories; 15 g fat (2 g sat.); 28 g protein; 30 g carbohydrate; 4 g fiber; 591 mg sodium; 68 mg cholesterol

TEST KITCHEN TIP

For a coarser texture, the salmon can be chopped by hand. If using a food processor, pulse the machine on and off but be sure not to puree the mixture.

Chilling the salmon beforehand until it is very cold helps the salmon retain its shape when chopping, by hand or in the food processor.

greek-style swordfish kabobs

MAKES 6 servings   **PREP** 25 minutes   **REFRIGERATE** 30 minutes   **GRILL** 10 minutes

¼   cup vegetable oil

4   cloves garlic, chopped

¼   cup lemon juice

2   tablespoons grated lemon zest

2   tablespoons chopped fresh oregano

2   tablespoons chopped fresh mint

½   teaspoon salt

¼   teaspoon black pepper

2   pounds swordfish steak, cut into 1-inch pieces

24   cherry tomatoes

2   medium-size zucchini, cut into ¾-inch pieces

1   large green pepper, cored, seeded and cut into ¾-inch pieces

① In a medium-size bowl, whisk oil, garlic, lemon juice, lemon zest, oregano, mint, salt and pepper. Pour into a large resealable plastic food-storage bag.

② Add swordfish, tomatoes, zucchini and green pepper to bag, seal and shake, making sure all pieces are coated. Marinate in refrigerator for 30 minutes, shaking bag once.

③ Heat gas grill to medium-high or prepare charcoal grill with medium-hot coals. Lightly coat grill rack with oil or nonstick cooking spray.

④ Thread 6 metal skewers with fish, tomatoes, zucchini and pepper, reserving marinade. Grill kabobs, covered, for 5 minutes, basting with reserved marinade once or twice. Turn and grill for another 5 minutes, basting once. Remove from grill and serve warm or at room temperature.

PER SERVING 247 calories; 14 g fat (2 g sat.); 23 g protein; 9 g carbohydrate; 2 g fiber; 301 mg sodium; 40 mg cholesterol

TEST KITCHEN TIP

Cut cleanup in half by marinating meat, storing prepped ingredients and even saving leftovers in resealable plastic food-storage bags. Heavy-duty ones can be washed with soapy water and reused (except when raw meat is involved).

grilled tuna steak sandwiches

MAKES 4 sandwiches **PREP** 10 minutes **REFRIGERATE** 30 minutes **GRILL** 6 minutes

Soy Marinade:

- 2 tablespoons plus 1 teaspoon reduced-sodium soy sauce
- 1 tablespoon dark sesame oil
- 1 tablespoon fresh lemon juice
- 4 teaspoons chopped fresh ginger

Sandwiches:

- 4 tuna steaks (each about 4 ounces)
- 2 tablespoons light mayonnaise
- 8 slices sourdough bread
- 4 leaves red-leaf lettuce
- ½ avocado, peeled, pitted and lightly mashed

① Soy Marinade: In a small bowl, whisk 2 tablespoons of soy sauce, sesame oil, lemon juice and 3 teaspoons of ginger.

② Sandwiches: Place tuna in a large resealable plastic food-storage bag; add marinade. Refrigerate 30 minutes, turning once. In a small bowl, mix mayonnaise and remaining 1 teaspoon *each* ginger and soy sauce. Refrigerate alongside tuna.

③ Prepare grill with medium-hot coals or heat gas grill to medium-high; coat rack with cooking spray.

④ Remove tuna from marinade; pat dry with paper towels. Grill 3 minutes per side for medium. Transfer to platter; tent with foil. Top bread with lettuce, then mashed avocado, tuna and flavored mayonnaise.

PER SERVING 430 calories; 15 g fat (2 g sat.); 34 g protein; 40 g carbohydrate; 3 g fiber; 742 mg sodium; 58 mg cholesterol

TEST KITCHEN TIP

Amber-colored and aromatic, dark sesame oil is made from roasted sesame seeds. It burns easily and loses flavor when overheated, so it is used mostly as a condiment or flavoring for dressings, soups and stir-fries. Store in fridge.

soy-glazed tuna steaks with baby bok choy

MAKES 4 servings **PREP** 10 minutes **GRILL** 10 minutes **COOK** 5 minutes

- 3 tablespoons reduced-sodium soy sauce
- 5 teaspoons mirin
- 2 tablespoons grated fresh ginger
- 2 tablespoons sugar
- 2 cloves garlic, minced
- 1 teaspoon cornstarch
- 6 baby bok choy (about 1½ pounds), halved lengthwise, washed and large leaves removed
- 4 tuna steaks (about 4 ounces each, ¾ to 1 inch thick)

① In a small saucepan, combine ¼ **cup water**, 2 tablespoons of soy sauce, mirin, ginger, sugar and garlic. Bring to a boil over medium-high heat. Stir together remaining tablespoon soy sauce and cornstarch, then stir into saucepan. Cook for 3 minutes over medium heat or until thickened. Divide sauce into 2 separate bowls, 5 tablespoons in one bowl and 3 tablespoons in other.

② Prepare grill with medium-hot coals or heat gas grill to medium-high. Brush cut-side of bok choy with about half of 5 tablespoons of sauce and place cut-side down on grill. Cook for 4 to 5 minutes per side, brushing often with sauce.

③ Meanwhile, place tuna on grill and brush with about half of 3 tablespoons of sauce from second bowl. Cook about 4 minutes per side, constantly brushing with sauce. Remove bok choy and tuna from grill and serve immediately.

PER SERVING 238 calories; 6 g fat (1 g sat.); 30 g protein; 14 g carbohydrate; 2 g fiber; 609 mg sodium; 43 mg cholesterol

HOW-TO

Grilling Fish

- Tuna, salmon, snapper and swordfish are best for the grill—their flesh holds together on the grate.

- For easy flipping, make sure surface is clean and hot before adding fish.

- Brush grill grate with oil or coat with nonstick spray before you add fillets.

- Don't move fish around—just flip one time during cooking.

grilled tuna & smashed potatoes

MAKES 4 servings **PREP** 15 minutes **REFRIGERATE** 20 minutes **COOK** 15 minutes **GRILL** 8 minutes

Tuna:

- 2 tablespoons extra-virgin olive oil
- 2 tablespoons lemon juice
- 2 cloves garlic, chopped
- 2 teaspoons fresh thyme
- 4 tuna steaks (5 to 6 ounces each, about 1 inch thick)

Potatoes:

- 1¼ pounds Yukon Gold potatoes, peeled and cut into 1-inch pieces
- 3 tablespoons extra-virgin olive oil

- 2 scallions, trimmed and thinly sliced
- 2 cloves garlic, chopped
- 1 teaspoon fresh thyme
- ¾ teaspoon salt
- ½ teaspoon black pepper

① Tuna: In a large resealable plastic food-storage bag, mix 2 tablespoons oil, lemon juice, garlic and thyme. Add tuna and seal. Shake to coat all of tuna with mixture. Marinate for 20 minutes in refrigerator.

② Potatoes: While tuna is marinating, cook potatoes. Place potatoes in a medium-size pot and cover with cold, lightly salted water. Bring to a boil and simmer for 15 minutes or until tender. Drain and place in large bowl.

③ Heat 3 tablespoons oil in a small skillet or saucepan. Add scallions, garlic and thyme. Cook for 1 minute. Mash potatoes and add in warm olive oil and garlic mixture. Add ½ teaspoon of salt and ¼ teaspoon of black pepper. Continue to mash potatoes until desired consistency.

④ Heat gas grill to medium-high or prepare a charcoal grill with medium-hot coals. Lightly coat grill rack with oil or nonstick cooking spray. Season tuna steaks with remaining ¼ teaspoon salt and ¼ teaspoon black pepper. Grill for 4 minutes per side for medium. Serve tuna with smashed potatoes.

PER SERVING 400 calories; 17 g fat (3 g sat.); 40 g protein; 21 g carbohydrate; 2 g fiber; 509 mg sodium; 80 mg cholesterol

NUTRITION NOTE

An excellent source of protein, tuna is rich in a variety of important nutrients, including selenium, magnesium and potassium; niacin, B1 and B6; and perhaps most important, the beneficial Omega-3 essential fatty acids.

east coast flounder packets & grilled corn

MAKES 6 servings **PREP** 10 minutes **GRILL** 40 minutes

6 ears corn, silks removed, husks left on

6 flounder fillets (about 2 pounds total)

¾ teaspoon Old Bay seasoning

1½ teaspoons olive oil

6 slices lemon

Butter (optional)

① Place corn in a sink full of cold water; weigh down with a heavy bowl and soak 30 minutes.

② Meanwhile, heat gas grill to medium-high heat, or charcoal grill to medium-hot coals (mounding slightly on one side).

③ Transfer soaked corn to heated grill. Grill corn, turning frequently, 20 minutes. If using gas grill, move corn to warming tray. If using charcoal, transfer corn to a large platter and cover with a clean cloth to keep warm.

④ Tear off six 10-inch-square pieces of foil. Place 1 flounder fillet in center of 1 foil square. Season with ⅛ teaspoon of Old Bay seasoning. Tuck ends under fillet, top with ¼ teaspoon of olive oil and 1 lemon slice. Seal foil tightly to form packet; repeat with remaining fish, Old Bay, oil and lemon.

⑤ Reduce heat to medium on a gas grill. Place fish packets on grill; on charcoal grill, group packets on side with less charcoal. Grill packets 18 to 20 minutes or until fish is white throughout. Serve with corn and butter alongside, if desired.

PER SERVING 241 calories; 5 g fat (1 g sat.); 33 g protein; 20 g carbohydrate; 3 g fiber; 206 mg sodium; 73 mg cholesterol

grilled shrimp pitas

MAKES 6 servings   **PREP** 20 minutes   **REFRIGERATE** 15 minutes   **GRILL** 6 minutes

Sauce:

- 1 container (7 ounces) reduced-fat plain Greek yogurt (such as Fage)
- 4 ounces herb-seasoned feta cheese, crumbled
- ½ seedless cucumber, peeled, halved and thinly sliced
- 1 tablespoon lemon juice

Shrimp:

- 3 tablespoons olive oil
- 2 tablespoons lemon juice
- 2 tablespoons chopped fresh mint
- 2 tablespoons chopped fresh oregano
- 2 cloves garlic, finely chopped
- ½ teaspoon salt
- ¼ teaspoon black pepper
- 1½ pounds large shrimp, peeled and deveined
- 6 salt-free or regular whole-wheat pitas, about 6-inch diameter
- 3 cups iceberg salad mix

   Sliced red onion and plum tomatoes (optional)

① Sauce: In a medium-size bowl, stir together yogurt, crumbled feta, cucumber and lemon juice. Cover and refrigerate until ready to use.

② Shrimp: Combine olive oil, lemon juice, mint, oregano, garlic, salt and pepper in a large resealable plastic food-storage bag. Add shrimp, seal bag and shake to coat shrimp with marinade. Refrigerate for 15 minutes.

③ Heat gas grill to medium-high or prepare a charcoal grill with medium-hot coals. Lightly coat grill rack with oil or nonstick cooking spray. Place shrimp in a grilling basket and grill for 3 minutes. Baste once with remaining marinade. Turn shrimp and grill for an additional 2 to 3 minutes or until shrimp is cooked through.

④ Equally divide salad, sauce and shrimp over each pita. Add onion and tomato, if desired.

PER SERVING 406 calories; 15 g fat (5 g sat.); 31 g protein; 40 g carbohydrate; 5 g fiber; 632 mg sodium; 183 mg cholesterol

TEST KITCHEN TIP

Add another layer of taste to this dish by brushing pitas with garlic-flavored oil and grilling for a minute or two before serving.

sunday dinner on the grill

MAKES 6 servings **PREP** 20 minutes **REFRIGERATE** 4 hours **GRILL** 70 minutes

4   tablespoons olive oil

2   tablespoons balsamic or sherry wine vinegar

3   cloves garlic, peeled and chopped

1   teaspoon dried oregano

1   teaspoon dried thyme

1½ teaspoons Montreal steak seasoning (McCormick)

1   eye round roast (about 2½ pounds)

1½ pounds small white potatoes, halved

1   pound peeled baby carrots

1   container (10 ounces) Brussels sprouts, trimmed and halved

½   teaspoon salt

① In a large resealable plastic food-storage bag, mix together olive oil, vinegar, garlic, oregano, thyme and steak seasoning. Add eye round and close bag. Shake to completely coat meat. Place on a plate and refrigerate for at least 4 hours.

② Heat gas grill to medium-high, or light charcoal grill to medium-hot coals stacked up on one side of grill. Lightly coat grill rack with oil.

③ Remove roast from bag, reserving marinade. Brown eye round on grill on all sides, about 10 minutes. Transfer roast to a 15¾ x 11¼ x 3-inch disposable roasting pan. Place potatoes and carrots around meat and toss with marinade reserved from meat.

④ Reduce gas grill heat to medium-low. Place pan on grill, and cook, covered, for 30 minutes (for charcoal grill, place pan over side of grill without coals). Stir twice. Stir in Brussels sprouts and salt. Continue to grill, covered, for 15 minutes. Check internal temperature of meat. Take meat out of pan when internal temperature registers 135°F on an instant-read thermometer (meat will continue to cook and should reach 145°F). Keep warm. Stir vegetables and continue to cook for 15 more minutes or until all vegetables are tender.

PER SERVING 454 calories; 15 g fat (3 g sat.); 48 g protein; 28 g carbohydrate; 5 g fiber; 533 mg sodium; 77 mg cholesterol

TEST KITCHEN TIP

A Cut Above

Protein-packed beef provides B vitamins, iron and zinc, but to steer clear of too much fat and cholesterol, opt for leaner, healthier cuts, such as eye round roast and steak (per 3-ounce serving: 44 calories, 4 grams of fat).

GOURMET GRILLING

Grill beef, poultry or seafood over medium heat to avoid overcooking or charring. Use a meat thermometer or an instant-read digital thermometer inserted horizontally into the thickest part of whatever you're grilling to see if it's done.

Recommended internal temperatures:

Poultry: 165°F
Ground beef: 160°F
Pork (chops, ground, tenderloin): 145°F
Large cut pork roasts: 145°F + 3 minutes rest
Beef roasts, steaks, seafood: 145°F

honey-mustard steak with rice pilaf

MAKES 6 servings **PREP** 8 minutes **COOK** 20 minutes **GRILL** 13 minutes

1 package (6 ounces) wild-and-white-rice pilaf mix

1½ pounds sirloin steak (1 inch thick)

½ cup honey mustard

2 teaspoons freshly ground steakhouse seasoning

1 bunch asparagus

① Prepare rice pilaf mix according to package directions, cooking for about 20 minutes.

② Meanwhile, heat gas grill to medium-high or prepare charcoal grill with medium-hot coals. Brush both sides of sirloin liberally with ¼ cup of honey mustard. Sprinkle both sides with seasoning. Set aside.

③ Trim ends of asparagus; brush lightly with 1 tablespoon of honey mustard. Place on grill and cook about 5 minutes, turning to prevent burning. Remove and set aside.

④ Add sirloin to grill and cook 4 minutes per side, turning once. Let rest 5 minutes before slicing.

⑤ Cut asparagus into 1-inch pieces. Stir into pilaf along with remaining 3 tablespoons honey mustard. Slice sirloin across grain. Serve over pilaf.

PER SERVING 345 calories; 10 g fat (3 g sat.); 31 g protein; 34 g carbohydrate; 2 g fiber; 783 mg sodium; 74 mg cholesterol

TEST KITCHEN TIP

Look for fresh asparagus bunches with firm, tightly closed tips, and plump—not dry or wrinkly—ends. Store upright in 1 inch of water in a glass or measuring cup. Before cooking, rinse thoroughly in water. Thick? Thin? Both are equally good. Use thick spears for poaching or steaming, thin for grilling or roasting.

grilled steak & pasta salad

MAKES 6 servings   **PREP** 5 minutes   **COOK** 10 minutes   **REFRIGERATE** 1 hour   **GRILL** 10 minutes

¼   cup rice vinegar

2   tablespoons light mayonnaise

2   tablespoons extra-virgin olive oil

1   teaspoon salt

½   teaspoon dried oregano

½   teaspoon ground cumin

¼   teaspoon cayenne pepper

12   ounces flank steak

½   teaspoon Montreal steak seasoning (McCormick)

½   pound bow tie pasta

2   large tomatoes, cut into 1-inch pieces

1   medium-size sweet onion, quartered and thinly sliced

2   cups corn kernels (from 2 ears of corn)

⅓   cup fresh flat-leaf parsley, chopped

⅓   cup fresh basil, chopped

8   cups mixed salad greens

① In a medium-size bowl, whisk vinegar, mayonnaise, oil, salt, oregano, cumin and cayenne until well blended. Set aside.

② Heat a gas grill to medium-high or prepare a grill with medium-hot coals. Bring a large pot of water to a boil.

③ Sprinkle steak with seasoning. Grill 4 to 5 minutes per side or until internal temperature registers 145°F on an instant-read thermometer for medium-rare. Let rest 10 minutes, then cut into thin slices.

④ Cook pasta in boiling water. Drain; rinse under cold water.

⑤ In serving bowl, toss pasta with dressing. Add steak, tomatoes, onion, corn, parsley and basil to bowl; toss to combine. Chill 1 hour, then serve over greens.

PER SERVING 328 calories; 12 g fat (3 g sat.); 19 g protein; 39 g carbohydrate; 4 g fiber; 605 mg sodium; 25 mg cholesterol

TEST KITCHEN TIP

"Across the grain" means to cut across the fibers of the meat, rather than with them. Cutting across the fibers makes them shorter so the meat is easier to chew. For most flank steaks, this means slicing across the width of the steak rather than its length.

grilled skirt steak & wheat berry pilaf

MAKES 6 servings **PREP** 15 minutes **REFRIGERATE/SOAK** overnight **COOK** 75 minutes **GRILL** 8 minutes

Marinade/Steak:

- **2 tablespoons red wine vinegar**
- **1 teaspoon Dijon mustard**
- **½ teaspoon salt**
- **¼ teaspoon black pepper**
- **3 tablespoons olive oil**
- **1 tablespoon chopped fresh oregano**
- **1¼ pounds skirt steak**

Pilaf:

- **2 cups wheat berries**
- **1 can (14.5 ounces) reduced-sodium beef broth**
- **½ cup chopped onion**
- **½ cup dried cherries**
- **2 tablespoons red wine vinegar**
- **1 tablespoon chopped fresh oregano**
- **½ teaspoon salt**
- **¼ teaspoon black pepper**

① In a medium-size bowl, whisk together 2 tablespoons vinegar, mustard, ½ teaspoon salt and ¼ teaspoon pepper. Gradually whisk in olive oil. Stir in 1 tablespoon oregano. Reserve 2 tablespoons for pilaf. Place remaining marinade and steak in a large resealable plastic food-storage bag. Shake bag to coat steak. Refrigerate overnight. Place wheat berries in a large bowl and cover with water. Soak overnight.

② Drain wheat berries. Set aside ¼ cup broth. Into a medium-size saucepan, add remaining broth, **4 cups water** and wheat berries. Bring to a boil. Reduce heat and simmer, covered, for about 75 minutes, stirring occasionally, until tender and most liquid has been absorbed.

③ Heat reserved broth and add onion and cherries. Simmer 1 minute and add to wheat berries. Stir in reserved marinade, 2 tablespoons red wine vinegar, 1 tablespoon oregano, ½ teaspoon salt and ¼ teaspoon pepper.

④ Heat a gas grill to medium-high or prepare a grill with medium-hot coals. Lightly grease grates and grill steak for 3 to 4 minutes per side for medium-rare. Let steak rest 5 minutes before slicing. Serve with wheat berry pilaf.

PER SERVING 478 calories; 16 g fat (4 g sat.); 31 g protein; 53 g carbohydrate; 7 g fiber; 609 mg sodium; 54 mg cholesterol

all-american cheeseburgers

MAKES 6 servings **PREP** 10 minutes **BAKE** at 400°F for 10 minutes **GRILL** 6 minutes

6   whole-wheat hamburger buns

1½ pounds ground sirloin or ground round

1   tablespoon Worcestershire sauce

½   teaspoon garlic powder

½   teaspoon salt

½   teaspoon dried Italian seasoning

¼   teaspoon freshly ground black pepper

6   2% American cheese slices

1   medium-size red onion, thinly sliced

2   medium-size tomatoes, cored and sliced

Ketchup and mustard (optional)

① Heat grill or grill pan to medium-high heat. Heat oven to 400°F. Wrap hamburger buns in foil and place in lower part of oven. Bake 10 minutes.

② Meanwhile, in a large bowl, mix together ground beef, Worcestershire, garlic powder, salt, Italian seasoning and pepper. Shape into 6 patties and grill 3 minutes. Flip burgers over and grill another 2 minutes. Top with cheese slices and cook 1 minute more for medium.

③ Transfer cheese-topped patties to warmed hamburger buns and add sliced red onion and tomato. Serve with ketchup and mustard, if desired.

PER SERVING 308 calories; 10 g fat (4 g sat.); 30 g protein; 28 g carbohydrate; 4 g fiber; 755 mg sodium; 60 mg cholesterol

TEST KITCHEN TIP

For best burgers:

- Handle meat gently and as minimally as possible.
- If using onions, grate them, then incorporate.
- Refrigerate shaped burgers briefly.
- Brush the grill grate lightly with vegetable oil.
- Toast, grill or warm up the buns.

grilled pork with sweet pepper relish

MAKES 4 servings   **PREP** 15 minutes   **REFRIGERATE** 2 hours   **GRILL** 35 minutes

1   **pork tenderloin (1 pound)**

½   **teaspoon black pepper**

2   **cloves garlic, minced**

1   **tablespoon plus 2 teaspoons chopped fresh rosemary**

1   **medium-size onion, cut into ½-inch slices**

1   **large sweet red pepper, halved and seeded**

1   **large yellow pepper, halved and seeded**

2   **teaspoons plus 2 tablespoons olive oil**

1   **tablespoon white wine vinegar**

1   **tablespoon honey**

1   **teaspoon salt**

① Sprinkle pork with ¼ teaspoon of pepper, garlic and 1 tablespoon of rosemary. Cover and refrigerate 2 hours.

② Prepare a charcoal grill with medium-hot coals or heat a gas grill to medium-high. Coat grill rack with nonstick cooking spray for grilling. Brush onion and peppers with 2 teaspoons of oil and grill, turning often, for 8 to 10 minutes, until lightly charred and crisp-tender. Cool vegetables slightly and chop.

③ In a large bowl, whisk vinegar, honey, remaining ¼ teaspoon pepper, remaining 2 teaspoons rosemary and ½ teaspoon of salt. Whisk in remaining 2 tablespoons olive oil. Add chopped onions and peppers. Set aside.

④ Sprinkle pork with remaining ½ teaspoon salt and grill, turning often, 20 to 25 minutes or until internal temperature registers 145°F on an instant-read thermometer. Let rest 3 minutes. Let stand 10 minutes before slicing. Serve pork with relish.

PER SERVING 275 calories; 12 g fat (2 g sat.); 29 g protein; 13 g carbohydrate; 2 g fiber; 642 mg sodium; 67 mg cholesterol

TEST KITCHEN TIP

Pork tenderloin is the leanest and most tender cut of pork. Because of its leanness, care should be taken so that it is not overcooked. Use an instant-read thermometer to test for doneness; begin testing 5 minutes before suggested cooking time.

grilled pork & onion couscous

MAKES 4 servings **PREP** 10 minutes **MICROWAVE** 3 minutes **GRILL** 38 minutes

½   cup apricot preserves

1   tablespoon grainy Dijon mustard

2   tablespoons ketchup

1   medium-size red onion

1   large pork tenderloin (1¼ pounds)

1½   cups chicken broth

1   teaspoon hot pepper flakes

1   box (5.8 ounces) plain couscous

1   cup frozen peas, thawed

① In a small bowl, stir ⅓ cup of preserves with mustard and ketchup. Cut onion into ½-inch-thick slices. Place toothpicks through slices. Microwave on HIGH for 3 minutes.

② Heat gas grill to medium-high or prepare charcoal grill with medium-hot coals. Brush onion slices lightly with some of flavored preserve mixture. Grill onion 3 minutes, turn and grill 2 more minutes or until lightly browned. Remove and set aside.

③ Grill pork 25 minutes, turning occasionally. Remove half of flavored preserve mixture to a separate small bowl and set aside. Brush pork with remaining mixture. Grill 5 to 8 more minutes, turning often, until an instant-read thermometer registers 145°F. Let rest 3 minutes.

④ While pork cooks, place broth and hot pepper flakes in small saucepan; bring to a boil. Stir in couscous, peas and remaining apricot preserves (about 3 tablespoons); cover and remove from heat. Let stand 5 minutes.

⑤ Chop onion and stir into couscous. Slice pork and serve with couscous and reserved flavored preserve mixture.

PER SERVING 485 calories; 6 g fat (2 g sat.); 38 g protein; 70 g carbohydrate; 5 g fiber; 644 mg sodium; 92 mg cholesterol

grilled pork chops & tomatoes with mashed potatoes

MAKES 4 servings   **PREP** 15 minutes   **REFRIGERATE** 20 minutes   **MICROWAVE** 6 minutes   **GRILL** 7 minutes

- 4 **boneless center-cut pork chops (1 pound total)**
- ½ **cup plus 2 tablespoons reduced-calorie vinaigrette dressing**
- 1½ **teaspoons Montreal seasoning or other grill rub**
- ½ **teaspoon black pepper**
- 4 **plum tomatoes, halved lengthwise**
- 4 **cups cooked diced potatoes**
- ¾ **cup fat-free milk**
- 2 **tablespoons unsalted butter, cut in pieces**
- 2 **scallions, finely chopped**
- ¼ **teaspoon salt**

① In a large bowl, marinate pork chops in ½ cup of vinaigrette for 20 minutes in refrigerator. Heat grill to medium-high/medium-hot coals.

② Remove pork from marinade and pat dry. Season with 1 teaspoon of Montreal seasoning and ¼ teaspoon of pepper.

③ In a large bowl, toss tomatoes and remaining 2 tablespoons dressing. Place potatoes in a large glass bowl. Add remaining Montreal seasoning and milk.

Cover with plastic wrap, venting one side. Microwave for 3 minutes on HIGH. Uncover and mash. Stir in butter, remaining ¼ teaspoon pepper, scallions and salt. Re-cover bowl; microwave 3 minutes.

④ Meanwhile, grill pork chops and tomatoes for 4 minutes. Carefully turn over; brush tomatoes with any dressing from bowl. Grill 3 more minutes, until pork registers 145°F on an instant-read thermometer. Let rest 3 minutes. Serve warm.

PER SERVING 396 calories; 17 g fat (7 g sat.); 29 g protein; 33 g carbohydrate; 3 g fiber; 789 mg sodium; 83 mg cholesterol

italian-style grilled pork

MAKES 4 servings   **PREP** 10 minutes   **MARINATE** 10 minutes   **GRILL** 15 minutes   **COOK** 5 minutes

2 tablespoons oil

2 tablespoons balsamic vinegar

2 cloves garlic

1 tablespoon packed fresh rosemary leaves

2 tablespoons packed fresh basil leaves

4 boneless pork chops (about 5 ounces each, 1 inch thick)

3 medium-size ripe tomatoes, quartered

¾ cup instant polenta

¾ teaspoon salt

2 tablespoons milk

2 tablespoons freshly grated Parmesan cheese

① Prepare a charcoal grill with hot coals or heat a gas grill to high. Place oil, vinegar, garlic, rosemary and basil in a food processor; pulse until thoroughly blended. Remove 2 tablespoons; set aside. Place remaining marinade in a resealable plastic food-storage bag; add pork and marinate at room temperature for 10 minutes. Toss reserved 2 tablespoons marinade with tomatoes; set aside.

② To cook, remove pork from marinade, spray with nonstick cooking spray and place on grill. Grill for a total of 15 minutes, turning once, halfway through.

③ Meanwhile, bring **3 cups water** to a boil; slowly add polenta and salt. Cook, stirring constantly, over medium heat until cooked, about 5 minutes. Remove from heat; stir in cream (or milk) and Parmesan cheese. Serve pork with polenta and tomatoes.

PER SERVING 430 calories; 18 g fat (6 g sat.); 33 g protein; 30 g carbohydrate; 2 g fiber; 570 mg sodium; 85 mg cholesterol

mediterranean pork in packets

MAKES 4 servings **PREP** 15 minutes **GRILL** 20 minutes

1 tablespoon olive oil

1 tablespoon chopped fresh rosemary

2 tablespoons lemon juice

½ plus ⅛ teaspoon black pepper

4 thin boneless center-cut pork chops (about 1 pound total)

1 large tomato, cored and cut into 8 wedges

1 medium-size yellow squash, halved lengthwise and thinly sliced

1 medium-size zucchini, halved lengthwise and thinly sliced

1 can (14-ounces) artichoke hearts, drained, quartered and patted dry

1 tablespoon capers, drained

¼ teaspoon salt

1 medium-size loaf Italian bread

① Prep charcoal grill with medium-hot coals or heat gas grill to medium-high heat.

② Using 12-inch-wide heavy-duty aluminum foil, cut 4 pieces 32 inches long; fold each piece in half to make a 16 x 12-inch rectangle. Generously coat foil pieces with nonstick cooking spray.

③ In a large bowl, stir oil, rosemary, lemon juice, and ½ teaspoon of pepper. Brush onto both sides of pork; toss remaining mixture with tomato, squash, zucchini, artichokes and capers.

④ Evenly place vegetable mixture on one half of each foil piece. Season pork with salt and remaining ⅛ teaspoon pepper. Top vegetables with pork.

⑤ Create a packet: Fold second half of foil over pork and vegetables. Tightly seal sides and front edges, leaving space for steam to build. Place packets on grill rack. Grill 20 minutes; 5 minutes before packets are finished, slice bread and grill on both sides. Carefully open packets; transfer contents to 4 serving plates. Serve with grilled bread.

Note: Packets can be baked at 450°F for 20 minutes.

PER SERVING 335 calories; 9 g fat (2 g sat.); 29 g protein; 35 g carbohydrate; 5 g fiber; 762 mg sodium; 68 mg cholesterol

pork & veggie kabobs

MAKES 4 servings **PREP** 15 minutes **GRILL** 10 minutes **REFRIGERATE** 1 hour

3 tablespoons olive oil

2 cloves garlic, chopped

Zest and juice of 1 lemon

2 tablespoons chopped flat-leaf parsley

1 tablespoon chopped fresh rosemary

1 teaspoon chopped fresh thyme

1 teaspoon sugar

¾ teaspoon salt

¼ teaspoon black pepper

1 pound thick-cut boneless pork chops (about ½ pound each, ¾ to 1 inch thick), cut into 1-inch pieces

2 medium-size zucchini, cut into ½-inch slices

2 medium-size summer squash, cut into ½-inch slices

12 cherry tomatoes

① In a small bowl, whisk oil, garlic and lemon zest and juice. Stir in parsley, rosemary, thyme, sugar, ½ teaspoon of salt and the pepper.

② Place pork in a large resealable plastic food-storage bag and spoon in 4 tablespoons of herb-oil mixture. Place zucchini, squash and tomatoes in another large resealable bag; pour rest of herb-oil mixture into it. Seal both bags and shake to coat ingredients. Refrigerate for 1 hour, turning after 30 minutes.

③ Heat gas grill to medium-high or prepare a charcoal grill with medium-hot coals.

④ Thread metal skewers separately with pork, zucchini, squash and tomatoes. Grill zucchini and squash about 5 minutes per side, pork about 3 minutes per side or until internal temperature registers 145°F on an instant-read thermometer. Let rest 3 minutes. Grill tomatoes about 3 minutes per side.

⑤ Sprinkle kabobs with remaining ¼ teaspoon salt before serving.

PER SERVING 310 calories; 18 g fat (4 g sat.); 23 g protein; 11 g carbohydrate; 4 g fiber; 500 mg sodium; 60 mg cholesterol

TEST KITCHEN TIP

It's easier to control the degree of doneness when you grill each ingredient on its own individual skewer.

A slow cooker is the handiest sous chef a busy cook could ask for. All you do is put the ingredients together and it takes care of the work. Best of all, when you come home, dinner is ready to be served.

This method is also economical—inexpensive cuts of meat like chuck and round steak are ideal for the slow cooker. Low temperatures, lots of liquid and a long cook time make these typically tougher cuts of beef tender and juicy. Cooking tips:

- Pick recipes like soups, chilis or stews that have a fair amount of liquid.

- Fill the pot at least halfway but no more than two-thirds full; place vegetables in first, then meat.

- Pour liquid on top.

slow cooker

- Thaw meat completely in the fridge before putting it in the slow cooker. If meat thaws as it cooks it will be in the bacterial danger zone—40° to 140°F—too long to be safe to eat.

- Allow all ingredients to finish at the same time by cutting ingredients that take longer to cook such as vegetables into small, uniform pieces. Or put these ingredients around the sides and on the bottom of the insert close to the heat source.

- You can save valuable minutes in the morning by prepping ingredients the night before and then refrigerating them overnight.

- Although not a necessary step, browning meat and poultry beforehand adds flavor and color.

- Avoid cracking by letting the insert cool completely before cleaning.

lemon & caper chicken

MAKES 4 servings   **PREP** 15 minutes   **SLOW-COOK** on HIGH for 3 hours or LOW for 5 hours   **COOK** 3 minutes

1	**large lemon**
¼	**cup low-sodium chicken broth**
1½	**tablespoons capers, chopped**
2½	**teaspoons dried oregano**
¼	**teaspoon garlic salt**
¼	**teaspoon black pepper**
5	**boneless, skinless chicken thighs**
4	**cups broccoli florets**
¼	**cup low-fat cream cheese, softened**

① Grate zest from lemon. Cut lemon in half; juice one half, thinly slice other half.

② Combine 3 tablespoons juice, 1 tablespoon zest, broth, capers, oregano, garlic salt and pepper.

③ Place thighs in slow cooker; drizzle with 4 tablespoons juice mixture. Place lemon slices on top of each thigh. Cover; cook on HIGH for 3 hours or on LOW for 5 hours.

④ Add broccoli to center of slow cooker for last 15 minutes on HIGH or 30 minutes on LOW. In a small bowl, whisk together remaining juice and cream cheese.

⑤ Remove chicken and broccoli to a platter; keep warm. Discard lemon. Pour liquid from slow cooker, juice mixture and cheese into a saucepan. Cook, stirring, over medium heat for 3 minutes. Drizzle over chicken and broccoli and serve.

PER SERVING 309 calories; 14 g fat (5 g sat.); 43 g protein; 6 g carbohydrate; 3 g fiber; 414 mg sodium; 203 mg cholesterol

chicken with cashews

MAKES 6 servings **PREP** 15 minutes **SLOW-COOK** on HIGH for 3 hours or LOW for 5 hours, plus 30 minutes

- 1 pound boneless, skinless chicken breasts, cut into 1-inch chunks
- 2 cups baby carrots
- ½ cup low-sodium chicken broth
- 4 tablespoons ginger-flavored soy sauce (such as House of Tsang) or regular low-sodium soy sauce
- 8 ounces snow peas, trimmed
- 2 cans (8 ounces each) pineapple tidbits, drained, and 2 tablespoons juice reserved
- 1 sweet red pepper, seeded and thinly sliced
- 3 tablespoons cornstarch
- ½ cup roasted cashews
- 3 cups cooked brown rice (optional)

① In slow cooker bowl, stir together chicken, carrots, broth and 2 tablespoons soy sauce. Cover and cook on HIGH for 3 hours or on LOW for 5 hours.

② Remove cover and stir in snow peas, pineapple and red pepper and cook an additional 20 minutes.

③ In a small bowl, stir together remaining 2 tablespoons soy sauce, 2 tablespoons pineapple juice and cornstarch. Stir into liquid in slow cooker bowl. Stir in cashews and cook an additional 10 minutes or until liquid has thickened. Serve over rice, if desired.

PER SERVING 249 calories; 7 g fat (1 g sat.); 22 g protein; 23 g carbohydrate; 3 g fiber; 366 mg sodium; 44 mg cholesterol

chicken simmered with mushrooms & tomatoes

MAKES 6 servings **PREP** 15 minutes **COOK** 18 minutes **SLOW-COOK** on HIGH for 3½ hours or LOW for 5 hours

1   package chicken pieces (about 4½ pounds), skin removed, trimmed of excess fat

¼   cup all-purpose flour

1   tablespoon olive oil

2   cups thinly sliced mushrooms

1   large green pepper, seeded and chopped

1   large onion, chopped

1   carrot, peeled and chopped

2   cups canned diced tomatoes, drained

½   cup white wine

1   teaspoon Italian seasoning

2   tablespoons chopped fresh basil leaves

½   teaspoon black pepper

¼   teaspoon salt

① Pat chicken dry with paper towels. Place flour on a plate. Coat chicken in flour, shaking off excess. Heat oil in a large nonstick skillet over medium-high heat. Cook chicken for 12 minutes or until browned, turning halfway.

② Remove chicken from skillet and place in slow cooker bowl. Place mushrooms in skillet; cook over medium-high heat for 6 minutes.

③ Add mushrooms to slow cooker, along with green pepper, onion, carrot, tomatoes, wine and Italian seasoning. Cook on HIGH for 3½ hours or LOW for 5 hours. Stir in basil, pepper and salt and serve immediately.

PER SERVING 392 calories; 10 g fat (2 g sat.); 55 g protein; 13 g carbohydrate; 2 g fiber; 493 mg sodium; 172 mg cholesterol

TEST KITCHEN TIP
Serve it with fettuccine or egg noodles.

chicken & bean stew

MAKES 6 servings **PREP** 10 minutes **SLOW-COOK** on HIGH for 3 hours or LOW for 5 hours, plus 30 minutes

1 pound boneless, skinless chicken thighs, trimmed

1 large onion, sliced

1 can (14.5 ounces) diced tomatoes with pepper, celery and onions (such as Hunt's), drained

¾ cup low-sodium chicken broth

⅛ teaspoon cayenne pepper

½ teaspoon salt

½ teaspoon black pepper

¾ cup frozen corn

¾ cup frozen lima beans

1 tablespoon Dijon mustard

4 cups prepared mashed potatoes (optional)

① In slow cooker bowl, stir together chicken, onion, tomatoes, broth, cayenne and ¼ teaspoon *each* salt and pepper. Cover and cook on HIGH for 3 hours or LOW for 5 hours.

② Remove chicken from slow cooker and cut into 1-inch pieces. Return chicken to slow cooker and stir in remaining ¼ teaspoon *each* salt and pepper, frozen corn and lima beans (no need to thaw) and mustard. Cook 30 minutes more.

③ Serve with mashed potatoes, if desired.

PER SERVING 158 calories; 4 g fat (1 g sat.); 17 g protein; 12 g carbohydrate; 3 g fiber; 588 mg sodium; 74 mg cholesterol

TEST KITCHEN TIP
Be sure to taste before serving. Because of the long cooking time, you may want to adjust the seasonings.

tex-mex chicken

MAKES 7 cups filling **PREP** 15 minutes **SLOW-COOK** on HIGH for 3½ hours or LOW for 4½ hours, plus 10 minutes

1 can (14.5 ounces) diced tomatoes with jalapeños, drained

1¼ cups salsa verde (such as Herdez)

1 tablespoon ground cumin

3 cloves garlic, minced

½ teaspoon salt

½ teaspoon black pepper

3 pounds boneless, skinless chicken thighs (10 to 12 thighs), fat removed

1 large red pepper, seeded and sliced

1 large yellow pepper, seeded and sliced

1 medium-size onion, sliced

1 can (14.5 ounces) black beans, drained, rinsed and coarsely mashed

1 can (14.5 ounces) corn, drained

For Tacos:

12 hard taco shells

¾ cup shredded Monterey Jack cheese

Avocado, thinly sliced

① In a 5- to 5½-quart slow cooker, combine tomatoes, ¾ cup of salsa verde, cumin, garlic, salt and pepper. Add chicken, peppers and onion; stir to coat. Cover and cook on HIGH for 3½ hours or LOW for 4½ hours.

② Remove chicken from slow cooker to a cutting board and let cool slightly.

③ Strain mixture over a large bowl or measuring cup; set liquid aside. Return vegetable mixture to slow cooker; stir in black beans and corn. Cover and cook on HIGH for 10 minutes.

④ Meanwhile, shred chicken and stir back into slow cooker with remaining ½ cup salsa verde and 1 cup of reserved liquid (or more, if desired).

⑤ For Tacos: Set aside half of mixture (3½ cups). Heat shells according to package directions. Divide mixture evenly among shells; top each with 1 tablespoon Monterey Jack cheese and 1 or 2 avocado slices. Freeze remaining mixture for future use. Mixture can be used in a quesadilla or wrapped in a flour tortilla.

PER TACO 217 calories; 10 g fat (3 g sat.); 16 g protein; 17 g carbohydrate; 4 g fiber; 380 mg sodium; 53 mg cholesterol

TEST KITCHEN TIP

Don't Lift the Lid During Cooking So much heat will escape that you'll need to add 20 minutes to total time. Serve it up with sour cream and jarred salsa.

fruity chicken tagine

MAKES 4 servings **PREP** 10 minutes **SLOW-COOK** on HIGH for 2½ hours or LOW for 5 hours

1¾   **pounds boneless, skinless chicken thighs, trimmed and cut into 1-inch pieces**

2   **large onions, thinly sliced**

½   **cup dried apricots, coarsely chopped**

⅓   **cup raisins**

1¼   **cups low-sodium chicken broth**

2   **tablespoons tomato paste**

2   **tablespoons lemon juice**

2   **tablespoons all-purpose flour**

1½   **teaspoons ground cumin**

1½   **teaspoons ground ginger**

1   **teaspoon ground cinnamon**

½   **teaspoon black pepper**

2   **cups cooked couscous**

① Place chicken, onions, apricots and raisins in slow cooker bowl.

② In a small bowl, whisk together chicken broth, tomato paste, lemon juice, flour, cumin, ginger, cinnamon and pepper. Pour over chicken in slow cooker. Cover and cook on HIGH for 2½ hours or LOW for 5 hours.

③ Serve over cooked couscous.

PER SERVING 482 calories; 11 g fat (3 g sat.); 45 g protein; 54 g carbohydrate; 5 g fiber; 345 mg sodium; 195 mg cholesterol

TEST KITCHEN TIP

A tagine dish is a ceramic or clay cooking vessel popular in North Africa. The bottom is a wide, circular shallow dish, while the top of the tagine is distinctively shaped into a cone. The shape allows the stew in the base to cook closer to the heat, while the couscous placed above it absorbs the steam from the stew below it.

The word tagine also refers to the delicious food cooked in the clay dish. Typically a tagine is a rich stew of meat, chicken or fish, and most often includes vegetables or fruit.

jambalaya

MAKES 6 servings **PREP** 10 minutes **SLOW-COOK** on HIGH for 4 hours or LOW for 6 hours, plus 15 minutes

1   medium-size onion, chopped

2   stalks celery, cut into ¼-inch slices

1   can (14.5 ounces) no-salt-added diced tomatoes

2   cups low-sodium chicken broth

1   pound boneless, skinless chicken thighs, cut into 1-inch pieces

½   pound light kielbasa, cut into ½-inch slices

¼   teaspoon cayenne pepper

1   small green pepper, seeded and chopped

½   pound large shrimp, peeled and deveined

2   cups frozen, cut okra

½   teaspoon Cajun seasoning

3   tablespoons cornstarch

¼   teaspoon salt

Dash hot pepper sauce

Hot cooked white rice (optional)

① In a 4- to 6-quart slow cooker, stir onion, celery, tomatoes, broth, chicken, kielbasa and cayenne together. Cover and cook on HIGH for 3 hours or LOW for 5 hours.

② Stir in green pepper, shrimp, okra and Cajun seasoning and cook for 1 hour or until shrimp is cooked through.

③ Remove ¼ cup of liquid from slow cooker and place in a small bowl; stir cornstarch into liquid. Stir back into insert and cook an additional 15 minutes or until thickened. Stir in salt and hot sauce; serve with rice, if desired.

PER SERVING 280 calories; 11 g fat (3.5 g sat.); 32 g protein; 14 g carbohydrate; 3 g fiber; 710 mg sodium; 155 mg cholesterol

SWITCH IT UP

Substitute turkey sausage or chicken sausage for kielbasa.

cassoulet

MAKES 8 servings **PREP** 15 minutes **SLOW-COOK** on HIGH for 4 hours or LOW for 7½ hours

1   medium-size onion, chopped

2   cloves garlic, crushed

1   can (14.5 ounces) no-salt-added tomatoes, drained

1½   cups low-sodium chicken broth

1   cup white wine

2   pounds chicken thighs, skin and excess fat removed

¾   pound boneless pork shoulder, trimmed and cut into 1-inch pieces

1   tablespoon tomato paste

2   sprigs fresh thyme

1   bay leaf

1   cup bread crumbs

2   cans (15 ounces) cannellini beans, drained and rinsed

½   pound kielbasa, halved lengthwise and cut into ½-inch-thick slices

½   teaspoon chopped fresh thyme

¼   teaspoon salt

½   teaspoon black pepper

① In a 5- to 6-quart slow cooker, combine onion, garlic, tomatoes, broth, wine, chicken, pork, tomato paste, thyme and bay leaf, and cook on HIGH for 4 hours or on LOW for 7½ hours.

② Remove thyme sprigs and bay leaf and discard. Stir in ¾ cup of bread crumbs, beans, kielbasa, fresh thyme, salt and pepper. Sprinkle each serving with ½ tablespoon crumbs and serve.

PER SERVING 442 calories; 17 g fat (6 g sat.); 36 g protein; 28 g carbohydrate; 3 g fiber; 766 mg sodium; 132 mg cholesterol

SWITCH IT UP

Substitute white kidney beans or navy beans for cannellini.

turkey & curried vegetables

MAKES 6 servings **PREP** 15 minutes **SLOW-COOK** on HIGH for 4½ hours or LOW for 8 hours, plus 10 minutes

1 tablespoon curry powder

2 teaspoons ground ginger

½ teaspoon salt

¼ teaspoon black pepper

1 cup chicken broth

1 tablespoon sugar

8 medium-size cauliflower pieces (from a 2-pound head)

1 can (15 ounces) chickpeas, drained and rinsed

½ cup dried apricots, coarsely chopped

½ cup golden raisins

1 cinnamon stick

1 bone-in turkey breast half (about 2½ to 3 pounds), skin removed

1 box (10 ounces) frozen green beans, thawed

2 tablespoons cornstarch mixed with 2 tablespoons water

1 jar (12 ounces) mango chutney (optional)

Cooked rice (optional)

① In a small bowl, stir together curry powder, ginger, salt and pepper. Stir 2 teaspoons spice mix into chicken broth along with sugar.

② Place cauliflower, chickpeas, apricots and golden raisins in a 6-quart slow cooker. Tuck in cinnamon stick. Rub remaining spice mix into turkey breast. Place on top of vegetables. Pour broth around meat. Cover. Cook on HIGH heat for 4½ hours or on LOW heat for 8 hours.

③ Remove turkey to a cutting board, cover loosely with foil and let stand for 10 minutes. If necessary, increase heat to HIGH. Stir green beans and cornstarch-water mixture into slow cooker; cover and cook 10 minutes or until beans are tender.

④ Cut turkey into ¼-inch-thick slices. Pour a little juice on top; serve with vegetables plus chutney and rice, if desired.

PER SERVING 423 calories; 4 g fat (1 g sat.); 54 g protein; 44 g carbohydrate; 7 g fiber; 621 mg sodium; 130 mg cholesterol

TEST KITCHEN TIP

Store spices, such as ginger, cinnamon and curry powder, in a cool, dark place away from the stove, light and humidity. Ground spices will retain optimum flavor for a year and whole spices will last up to 5 years, if stored properly.

A new way to make lasagna—in the slow cooker! Although cooked in a pot, it should firm up similarly to when it's oven-roasted, so simply cut into servings with a metal spatula and carefully lift them out.

turkey lasagna

MAKES 8 servings **PREP** 10 minutes **COOK** 10 minutes **SLOW-COOK** on HIGH for 4 hours or LOW for 5 hours

- 1 **medium-size onion, chopped**
- 2 **cloves garlic, minced**
- 1¼ **pounds ground turkey**
- 1 **teaspoon dried oregano**
- ¼ **teaspoon salt**
- ¼ **teaspoon black pepper**
- 1 **container (15 ounces) low-fat ricotta cheese**
- 1 **cup shredded Italian cheese blend**
- 12 **lasagna noodles (12 ounces) broken in half**
- 1 **package (10 ounces) frozen chopped broccoli, thawed and drained**
- 1 **jar (26 ounces) chunky tomato sauce**

① In a large nonstick skillet, cook onion and garlic over medium-high heat for 4 minutes or until softened. Add turkey to skillet and cook, breaking up large chunks, for about 6 minutes or until no longer pink; drain fat. Season turkey with oregano, salt and pepper. Set aside.

② In a small bowl, combine ricotta cheese and ½ cup of shredded Italian cheese.

③ In a 5- to 6-quart slow cooker, layer half uncooked noodles, overlapping as necessary. Spread half of both meat mixture and broccoli over noodles, then top with about half of tomato sauce and ¼ **cup water**. Gently spread ricotta mixture on top, and continue layering with remaining noodles, meat, broccoli, sauce and an additional ¼ **cup water**.

④ Cover and cook on HIGH for 4 hours or LOW for 5 hours. Sprinkle remaining ½ cup of Italian cheese on top for last 15 minutes of cooking time or until melted.

PER SERVING 429 calories; 14 g fat (6 g sat.); 30 g protein; 44 g carbohydrate; 4 g fiber; 757 mg sodium; 85 mg cholesterol

SWITCH IT UP
Substitute frozen spinach for broccoli.

easy salmon & bok choy

MAKES 4 servings **PREP** 10 minutes **SLOW-COOK** on HIGH for 1 hour or LOW for 2 hours

1½ pounds salmon, patted dry

3 tablespoons finely chopped fresh ginger

2 cloves garlic, minced

½ cup low-sodium chicken broth

3 tablespoons rice vinegar

2 tablespoons sugar

2 tablespoons low-sodium soy sauce

1 medium-size head bok choy, trimmed and cut into 1-inch pieces, stems and leaves separated (4 cups each)

1 teaspoon hoisin sauce

¼ cup thinly sliced scallions

Fully cooked brown rice (optional)

① Coat a 5- to 6-quart slow-cooker bowl with nonstick cooking spray and arrange salmon in it, tucking thin end of fillet underneath. Sprinkle ginger and garlic over salmon.

② In a medium-size saucepan, bring broth, vinegar, sugar and soy sauce to a boil over high heat. Pour liquid around salmon, not over, and cook on HIGH for 1 hour or LOW for 2 hours.

③ Stir bok choy stems into slow cooker for last 30 minutes of cooking time on HIGH or last hour of cooking time on LOW. Add leaves to slow cooker for final 10 minutes of cooking time on HIGH or final 30 minutes of cooking time on LOW.

④ Carefully remove salmon from slow cooker with a wide spatula; set aside and keep warm. Stir hoisin into liquid. Sprinkle salmon with scallions and serve with bok choy, brown rice if desired, and liquid.

Note: While this dish can be cooked on HIGH, the color will be more vibrant and the flavor more delicate if cooked on LOW.

PER SERVING 312 calories; 12 g fat (2 g sat.); 38 g protein; 14 g carbohydrate; 3 g fiber; 515 mg sodium; 94 mg cholesterol

TEST KITCHEN TIP

Hoisin sauce, also called Chinese barbecue sauce, is a fragrant, pungent sauce used frequently in Asian stir-fries and marinades. Made from a combination of fermented soy, garlic, vinegar, chiles and sweetener, hoisin is dark in color and thick in consistency. It is described as sweet, salty and spicy.

shrimp stir-fry

MAKES 6 servings **PREP** 10 minutes **SLOW-COOK** on HIGH for 1¾ hours or LOW for 3½ hours

1   pound carrots, peeled and cut diagonally into ½-inch slices

1   medium-size sweet red pepper, seeded and cut into ½-inch slices

¾   cup low-sodium chicken broth

¼   cup low-sodium teriyaki sauce

2   tablespoons cornstarch

1   tablespoon oyster sauce

2   teaspoons sugar

1   pound shrimp, peeled and deveined

8   ounces snow peas, trimmed

1   can (8 ounces) bamboo shoots

     Sliced scallions (optional)

3   cups cooked brown rice

① Place carrots and red pepper slices in a 5- to 6-quart slow cooker. In a small bowl, blend broth, teriyaki, cornstarch, oyster sauce and sugar. Pour into slow cooker and cook on HIGH for 1¾ hours or LOW for 3½ hours.

② Stir shrimp, snow peas and bamboo shoots (drained) into slow cooker for final 20 minutes of cook time. Sprinkle stir-fry with scallions, if desired, and serve with brown rice.

PER SERVING 277 calories; 3 g fat (1 g sat.); 21 g protein; 42 g carbohydrate; 6 g fiber; 349 mg sodium; 115 mg cholesterol

HOW-TO

Slice a Pepper

- Grasp pepper at stem end; use sharp knife to cut into quarters from stem to bottom along the curve.

- Lay pepper pieces skin-side down. Trim away and discard any inner white membranes.

- Slice pieces lengthwise into strips of desired width.

beef & barley soup

MAKES 6 servings **PREP** 15 minutes **COOK** 19 minutes **SLOW-COOK** on HIGH for 4 hours or LOW for 7½ hours

1 pound chuck steak, trimmed and cut into ½-inch pieces

2 medium-size carrots, cut into ½-inch pieces

1 large onion, chopped

10 ounces mushrooms, thinly sliced

1 tablespoon tomato paste

4 cups low-sodium beef broth

1 can (14.5 ounces) petite cut diced tomatoes

¾ teaspoon dried thyme

¾ cup barley

½ teaspoon salt

½ teaspoon black pepper

① Place a stovetop-safe 5- to 6-quart slow cooker insert over medium-high heat on stove. Add meat; cook 5 minutes, stirring occasionally, until browned. Remove with slotted spoon and set aside.

② Place carrots and onion in slow cooker insert and cook for 5 minutes or until browned, stirring occasionally. Add mushrooms and cook for another 7 minutes. Stir in tomato paste and cook for 2 minutes, stirring constantly. Take insert from stovetop and place in slow-cooker base.

③ Add browned beef, low-sodium beef broth, diced tomatoes and thyme to slow cooker. Cook on HIGH for 3 hours or on LOW for 6½ hours. Stir in barley and cook for an additional 1 hour (keep slow cooker on same setting). Stir in salt and pepper immediately before serving. Taste and adjust seasonings, if desired.

PER SERVING 338 calories; 14 g fat (6 g sat.); 22 g protein; 30 g carbohydrate; 6 g fiber; 386 mg sodium; 51 mg cholesterol

TEST KITCHEN TIPS

• When adding herbs to a slow-cooker dish, stir in dried at the start and fresh at the end.

• Use a saucepan to brown beef if you don't have a stovetop-ready slow cooker.

tangy beef stew

MAKES 4 servings **PREP** 10 minutes **SLOW-COOK** on HIGH for 4 hours or LOW for 6 hours

1 large onion, cut into 1-inch pieces

1 pound boneless beef chuck, cut into 1-inch cubes

1 tablespoon ground ginger

¼ teaspoon salt

3 medium-size carrots, cut into 1-inch slices

2 large celery stalks, cut into 1-inch slices

1 large beef bouillon cube

2 tablespoons red wine vinegar

¼ cup raisins

¼ teaspoon black pepper

2 tablespoons cornstarch

Cooked egg noodles (optional)

① In slow cooker insert, layer onion, beef, ginger, salt, carrots and celery. Add bouillon cube, **2 cups water**, vinegar and raisins. Cover and cook on HIGH for 4 hours or LOW for 6 hours.

② Remove cover and stir in pepper. Using a ladle, remove 3 tablespoons liquid from slow cooker and place in a small bowl. Whisk in cornstarch. Whisk cornstarch mixture back into slow cooker and stir to combine.

Continue stirring until liquid has thickened. Turn off slow cooker and serve with noodles, if desired.

PER SERVING 250 calories; 5 g fat (2 g sat.); 27 g protein; 24 g carbohydrate; 3 g fiber; 653 mg sodium; 50 mg cholesterol

TEST KITCHEN TIP

Slow cooking is good even for your energy bill. It costs about 2 cents per hour to use a slow cooker—just 16 cents for 8 hours! An oven costs about 50 cents per hour, or $4 for 8 hours.

beef with mushrooms & red wine

MAKES 4 servings   **PREP** 15 minutes   **COOK** 13 minutes   **SLOW-COOK** on HIGH for 5 hours or LOW for 7 hours, plus 30 minutes

1 tablespoon olive oil

1 pound chuck steak (1-inch thick), trimmed and cut into 1-inch pieces

1 package (10 ounces) cremini mushrooms, cleaned and quartered

2 cloves garlic, chopped

½ teaspoon salt

½ teaspoon black pepper

2 tablespoons tomato paste

3 tablespoons all-purpose flour

1 package (1 pound) frozen pearl onions

1½ cups low-sodium beef broth

¾ cup dry red wine

¾ teaspoon dried thyme

8 ounces green beans, trimmed

6 ounces cholesterol-free egg noodles, cooked (optional)

① Heat oil in a large nonstick skillet over medium-high heat. Add steak to skillet and cook 5 minutes, stirring occasionally, until browned. Remove with a slotted spoon to slow cooker bowl.

② Add mushrooms and garlic to skillet and sprinkle with ¼ teaspoon *each* salt and pepper. Cook, stirring occasionally, 5 minutes. Stir in tomato paste and cook, stirring, 2 minutes. Add flour and cook, stirring constantly, 1 minute.

③ Scrape contents of skillet into slow cooker bowl with beef. Stir in onions, broth, red wine and ½ teaspoon of thyme. Cover and cook on HIGH for 5 hours or LOW for 7 hours.

④ Remove lid and stir in remaining ¼ teaspoon *each* salt and pepper, ¼ teaspoon dried thyme and green beans. Cover and cook an additional 30 minutes. Serve over egg noodles, if desired.

PER SERVING 383 calories; 16 g fat (5 g sat. fat); 28 g protein; 23 g carbohydrate; 4 g fiber; 420 mg sodium; 75 mg cholesterol

TEST KITCHEN TIP

Adapting for a Slow Cooker You can convert your favorite recipes using these tips:

- Decrease total liquid added to 1 to 2 cups of the liquid called for, to prevent sauce from being too thin.

- Place all ingredients in slow cooker at the beginning (the only exceptions are milk, sour cream, cream or seafood, which should be stirred in during the last hour of cooking).

- Cook noodles, macaroni and other pasta before adding. If using raw rice (long-grain is preferable), stir in about 1 cup extra liquid per 1 cup of raw rice.

- If traditional oven-cooked recipes take 35 to 45 minutes, plan 6 to 10 hours on low heat, 3 to 4 on high; for those taking 50 minutes to 3 hours, plan 8 to 10 hours on low and 4 to 6 hours on high.

beef tostadas

MAKES 12 tostadas **PREP** 15 minutes **SLOW-COOK** on HIGH for 6 hours or LOW for 8 hours **MICROWAVE** 1½ minutes

1½ **pounds boneless beef round steak**

½ **teaspoon salt**

½ **teaspoon black pepper**

¼ **cup lime juice**

3 **cloves garlic, finely chopped**

1 **jalapeño, seeded and finely chopped**

1 **large onion, chopped**

1 **tablespoon chili powder**

¼ **teaspoon cumin**

⅛ **teaspoon cayenne pepper**

12 **packaged tostadas or hard taco shells**

¾ **cup fat-free refried beans**

1½ **cups shredded iceberg lettuce**

1 **cup reduced-fat shredded Mexican cheese blend**

¾ **cup salsa**

① Sprinkle steak with salt and black pepper. Place 3 tablespoons of lime juice, garlic, jalapeño, onion, chili powder, cumin and cayenne in a slow cooker. Place beef on top and cook on HIGH for 6 hours or on LOW for 8 hours.

② Remove beef to a cutting board and when cool enough to handle, shred using 2 forks. Place shredded beef in a large bowl.

③ Strain remaining liquid in slow cooker over a bowl or measuring cup, discarding solids. Add strained liquid and remaining 1 tablespoon lime juice to beef in bowl and stir to combine. Cover; keep warm.

④ Warm tostada shells in oven according to package directions. While tostadas are baking, heat refried beans in microwave for 1½ minutes on HIGH, stirring halfway through until warm and spreadable.

⑤ Spread each tostada with 1 tablespoon refried beans. Place ⅓ cup beef over beans and divide lettuce equally among tostadas. Top each with 1 heaping tablespoon Mexican cheese blend and 1 tablespoon salsa.

PER TOSTADA 187 calories; 8 g fat (3 g sat.); 18 g protein; 13 g carbohydrate; 2 g fiber; 152 mg sodium; 41 mg cholesterol

SWITCH IT UP
Substitute flank steak for round.

chili con carne

MAKES 6 servings **PREP** 10 minutes **COOK** 12 minutes **SLOW-COOK** on HIGH for 4 hours or LOW for 6 hours

1 tablespoon plus 1 teaspoon olive oil

2 pounds boneless beef round steak, trimmed and cut into ½-inch cubes

3 cloves garlic, minced

1 large onion, finely chopped

3 tablespoons plus 1 teaspoon chili powder

3½ teaspoons cumin

1 teaspoon salt

½ teaspoon cayenne pepper

1 package (10 ounces) frozen corn

3 tablespoons finely ground cornmeal

Sour cream (optional)

Avocado, sliced (optional)

① Heat 1 tablespoon oil in a large nonstick skillet over medium-high heat. Add beef to skillet and cook, stirring occasionally, for 8 minutes, draining any fat if it accumulates. Remove beef to slow cooker and reduce heat to medium. Add 1 teaspoon olive oil to skillet then add garlic and onion to pan; cook, stirring often, for 2 minutes. Stir in 3 tablespoons chili powder, 2 teaspoons cumin, ½ teaspoon salt and ¼ teaspoon cayenne; cook 1 minute, stirring constantly.

② Scrape skillet contents into slow cooker bowl and add corn and **3¾ cups water** (enough to cover by 1 inch). Cover and cook on HIGH for 4 hours or on LOW for 6 hours.

③ When there is 1 hour cook time remaining, stir together cornmeal and **3 tablespoons water** to make a thick paste. Stir in cornmeal paste, remaining 1 teaspoon chili powder, 1½ teaspoons cumin, ½ teaspoon salt and ¼ teaspoon cayenne; continue to cook for 1 more hour or until thickened. Spoon sour cream over top and serve with sliced avocado, if desired.

PER SERVING 374 calories; 17 g fat (5 g sat.); 36 g protein; 21 g carbohydrate; 4 g fiber; 536 mg sodium; 60 mg cholesterol

beef ragu with beans

MAKES 12 cups **PREP** 15 minutes **SLOW-COOK** on HIGH for 6 hours or LOW for 9 hours

2 large carrots, peeled and coarsely chopped

2 large ribs celery, coarsely chopped

1 large onion, coarsely chopped

4 cloves garlic, peeled

2 pounds ground beef

2 cans (14.5 ounces each) diced tomatoes

2 cups beef broth

3 tablespoons tomato paste

2 teaspoons sugar

1 can (15.5 ounces) cannellini beans, drained and rinsed

1½ teaspoons dried Italian seasoning

1½ teaspoons salt

1 teaspoon red pepper flakes

1 pound rigatoni, cooked

Grated Parmesan cheese (optional)

① Place carrots, celery, onion and garlic in a food processor; pulse until finely chopped.

② In a large bowl, mix vegetables, ground beef, diced tomatoes, beef broth, tomato paste, sugar and beans. Add half of *each*: Italian seasoning, salt and red pepper flakes. Stir until combined.

③ Place mixture in a 6-quart slow cooker and cook on HIGH for 5½ hours or on LOW for 8½ hours.

④ Stir in remaining Italian seasoning, salt and red pepper flakes. Cook for an additional 30 minutes.

⑤ For 8 servings, toss half of meat sauce with rigatoni; serve with grated Parmesan cheese, if desired. Reserve other half of sauce for future meals. May be frozen, tightly covered, for up to 2 months.

PER ½ CUP SERVING WITH PASTA
359 calories; 8 g fat (3 g sat.); 22 g protein; 52 g carbohydrate; 4 g fiber; 505 mg sodium; 47 mg cholesterol

pork roast with peach sauce

MAKES 8 servings **PREP** 10 minutes **SLOW-COOK** on HIGH for 3 hours or LOW for 6 hours

1   boneless pork loin roast (about 3 pounds), tied

¼   teaspoon onion salt

¼   teaspoon black pepper

1   can (15.25 ounces) sliced peaches in heavy syrup

½   cup chili sauce

⅓   cup packed light brown sugar

3   tablespoons apple cider vinegar

1   teaspoon pumpkin pie spice

1   tablespoon cornstarch mixed with 2 tablespoons water

Cooked egg noodles (optional)

① Coat a 6-quart slow cooker with nonstick cooking spray. Place roast into slow cooker; season with onion salt and pepper.

② Drain peaches, reserving syrup. In a medium-size bowl, whisk syrup, chili sauce, brown sugar, vinegar and pumpkin pie spice. Pour over meat; scatter peach slices over roast.

③ Cook 3 hours on HIGH or 6 hours on LOW.

④ Remove meat and allow to rest for 10 minutes. Spoon out peach slices and reserve. Place liquid in a small saucepan and bring to a boil over medium-high heat. Stir in cornstarch mixture and cook, stirring, for about 30 seconds until sauce thickens.

⑤ Slice meat and scatter reserved peach slices over top. Serve with sauce on the side and egg noodles, if desired.

PER SERVING 363 calories; 12 g fat (5 g sat.); 37 g protein; 25 g carbohydrate; 1 g fiber; 368 mg sodium; 103 mg cholesterol

SWITCH IT UP

Sub apricots or pineapple for the peaches.

italian pork roast

MAKES 8 servings **PREP** 15 minutes **COOK** 1 minute **SLOW-COOK** on HIGH for 3 hours or LOW for 5½ hours

1 **boneless pork loin roast (about 3 pounds), trimmed and tied**

3 **teaspoons Italian seasoning**

1 **can (14.5 ounces) diced tomatoes with basil, oregano and garlic, drained**

⅓ **cup plus 2 tablespoons low-sodium chicken broth**

¾ **teaspoon salt**

½ **teaspoon black pepper**

1 **large green pepper, seeded and chopped**

2 **tablespoons cornstarch**

1½ **teaspoons balsamic vinegar**

① Rub pork with 1 teaspoon of Italian seasoning and place in slow cooker bowl.

② Scatter tomatoes around pork. Pour ⅓ cup of broth in bowl; top with 1½ teaspoons Italian seasoning, ½ teaspoon of salt and ¼ teaspoon of pepper. Cook on HIGH for 3 hours or on LOW for 5½ hours.

③ Add green pepper to slow cooker for last 45 minutes of cook time.

④ In a small bowl, blend remaining 2 tablespoons broth, cornstarch and balsamic vinegar. Set aside. Remove pork to a serving platter; keep warm. Strain liquid from slow cooker into a small saucepan and place vegetables around pork on serving platter.

⑤ Bring liquid to a boil over medium-high heat. Whisk in cornstarch mixture, remaining ½ teaspoon Italian seasoning and ¼ teaspoon *each* salt and black pepper; cook 1 minute. Spoon sauce over pork.

PER SERVING 242 calories; 7 g fat (3 g sat.); 37 g protein; 5 g carbohydrate; 1 g fiber; 460 mg sodium; 107 mg cholesterol

TEST KITCHEN TIP

Serve it with instant polenta flavored with Parmesan.

pulled pork sandwiches

MAKES 6 servings **PREP** 10 minutes **REFRIGERATE** at least 1 hour **COOK** 2 minutes
SLOW-COOK on HIGH for 6 hours or LOW for 8 hours

2½ tablespoons packed
  dark-brown sugar

1 tablespoon paprika

1 teaspoon chili powder

1 teaspoon ground cumin

1 teaspoon black pepper

1 boneless pork butt or
  shoulder (about 2½ pounds),
  trimmed

1 cup low-sodium chicken
  broth

2 tablespoons cider vinegar

2 tablespoons ketchup

6 hamburger buns

① In a small bowl, stir together 1 tablespoon of sugar, paprika, chili powder, cumin and pepper; set aside.

② Lay pork on work surface and sprinkle all sides with spice rub; rub well into meat. Wrap in plastic wrap and refrigerate for 1 hour or overnight.

③ Unwrap pork and place in slow cooker with chicken broth. Cover and cook on HIGH for 6 hours or LOW for 8 hours. Remove pork from slow cooker and cut into large chunks; let stand for 20 minutes or until cool enough to handle.

④ While pork is cooling, pour cooking liquid into a fat separator. Pour de-fatted liquid into small saucepan. Heat over medium-high heat. Whisk in vinegar, ketchup and remaining 1½ tablespoons brown sugar. Cook until sugar has dissolved, about 2 minutes; set aside.

⑤ Using forks or your hands, pull meat into shreds, discarding excess fat and place in bowl. Stir in sauce and put ½ cup meat on each bun. Serve immediately.

PER SERVING 366 calories; 12 g fat (4 g sat.); 39 g protein; 22 g carbohydrate; 1 g fiber; 424 mg sodium; 114 mg cholesterol

TEST KITCHEN TIP

Serve it with store-bought coleslaw.

pork goulash

MAKES 6 servings **PREP** 15 minutes **SLOW-COOK** on HIGH for 3½ hours or LOW for 5 hours

1 boneless pork loin roast (about 1¾ pounds), trimmed and cut into ½-inch pieces

3 medium-size parsnips, peeled and cut into ½-inch coins

2 large carrots, peeled and cut into ½-inch coins

1 large onion, chopped

4 tablespoons sweet paprika

2 cups low-sodium chicken broth

½ pound green beans, trimmed and cut into 1-inch pieces

½ cup reduced-fat sour cream

2 tablespoons cornstarch

½ teaspoon salt

½ teaspoon black pepper

① Place pork, parsnips, carrots and onion in slow cooker. Sprinkle with 2 tablespoons of paprika; stir to coat. Pour in broth. Cover and cook on HIGH for 3 hours or LOW for 4½ hours.

② Add green beans; cook 30 minutes.

③ In a small bowl, blend remaining 2 tablespoons paprika, sour cream, cornstarch, salt and pepper. Stir into slow cooker bowl until thickened.

PER SERVING 274 calories; 6 g fat (3 g sat.); 34 g protein; 21 g carbohydrate; 6 g fiber; 678 mg sodium; 85 mg cholesterol

TEST KITCHEN TIP
Serve it up with poppy seed noodles: Toast 2 teaspoons poppy seeds in a dry skillet over low heat 2 minutes. Toss 8 ounces cooked noodles with 2 tablespoons softened butter. Add poppy seeds and stir to combine.

pork chops with red cabbage

MAKES 4 servings   **PREP** 5 minutes   **SLOW-COOK** on HIGH for 3½ hours or LOW for 7 hours

1 small head red cabbage, core removed and shredded (about 8 cups)

2 Fuji apples, peeled, cored and diced

½ cup red wine vinegar

2 tablespoons packed light brown sugar

2 teaspoons caraway seeds

½ teaspoon salt

½ teaspoon black pepper

4 bone-in pork loin chops (about 2 pounds)

2 tablespoons cornstarch

① Place cabbage and apples in slow cooker. Stir in vinegar, sugar, caraway seeds, and ¼ teaspoon *each* salt and pepper.

② Place pork chops in slow cooker over cabbage and sprinkle with ¼ teaspoon pepper. Cover and cook on HIGH for about 3½ hours or LOW for 7 hours or until cabbage is softened.

③ Remove pork from slow cooker and keep warm. Using a ladle, remove 2 tablespoons liquid from slow cooker and place in a small bowl. Whisk cornstarch into liquid in bowl. Clear cabbage aside in slow cooker and whisk cornstarch mixture back into slow cooker. Using tongs, toss thickened liquid with cabbage and stir in remaining ¼ teaspoon salt. Serve immediately with pork.

PER SERVING 335 calories; 8 g fat (3 g sat.); 32 g protein; 35 g carbohydrate; 6 g fiber; 412 mg sodium; 71 mg cholesterol

HOW-TO

Cut Cabbage

- Remove loose outer leaves and discard. Then cut cabbage in half through stem end. Next, cut into quarters.

- With each cabbage quarter, cut out tough stem end by first separating one side and then the other. Discard stem.

- Turn one quarter on one of its cut edges. Slice to desired thickness, repeating with all cabbage pieces.

- Look for heads of cabbage that are compact and firm with fresh, crisp, blemish-free leaves.

pork posole & corn bread stew

MAKES 8 servings **PREP** 15 minutes **COOK** 16 minutes **SLOW-COOK** on HIGH for 4½ hours or LOW for 6½ hours

3 pounds boneless pork shoulder, well trimmed and cut into 1-inch chunks

½ teaspoon black pepper

1 tablespoon canola oil

4 large carrots, cut into ¼-inch pieces

2 onions, chopped

¼ teaspoon salt

2 tablespoons all-purpose flour

3 teaspoons chili powder

1 teaspoon dried oregano

4 cloves garlic, minced

1½ cups low-sodium chicken broth

1 box (8.5 ounces) corn muffin mix

2 eggs

Zest of 1 lime

2 tablespoons plus 1 teaspoon chopped cilantro

1 can (15 ounces) white hominy, rinsed and drained

1 tablespoon lime juice

① Sprinkle pork with ¼ teaspoon of pepper. Heat oil in a large skillet over medium-high heat. Cook pork for 5 minutes, stirring often, in 2 batches until browned. Remove pork to slow cooker.

② Add carrots and onions to skillet and sprinkle with ¼ teaspoon *each* salt and pepper; cook for 5 minutes, stirring often. Stir in flour, chili powder, oregano and garlic; cook 1 minute then remove to slow cooker. Add broth to skillet and bring to a boil; pour into slow cooker. Cover; cook on HIGH for 4½ hours or LOW for 6½ hours.

③ When there is 1 hour cook time remaining, stir together corn muffin mix, eggs, lime zest, 1 teaspoon cilantro and ¼ cup water. Remove cover; stir in hominy, lime juice and 2 tablespoons cilantro. Dollop corn muffin mixture on top. Place cotton dish towel over slow cooker bowl then top with cover; cook for remaining cook time or until top is firm.

PER SERVING 455 calories; 17 g fat (6 g sat.); 37 g protein; 38 g carbohydrate; 3 g fiber; 795 mg sodium; 159 mg cholesterol

TEST KITCHEN TIP

Hominy are hulled corn kernels that have been stripped of their bran and germ. Southern cooks usually boil whole or ground hominy until it's tender and then serve it in much the same way that Northern cooks would serve potatoes. Hominy is more tender and creamy than regular corn and can be served in many of the same ways as potatoes.

pork ragu with pasta

MAKES 8 servings **PREP** 30 minutes **COOK** 10 minutes **SLOW-COOK** on HIGH for 5½ hours or LOW for 7 hours

3 teaspoons vegetable oil

2 carrots, sliced

2 ribs celery, sliced

1 large onion, chopped

4 cloves garlic, chopped

2 pounds boneless country-style pork ribs

1 cup beef broth

2 tablespoons tomato paste

1 can (28 ounces) crushed tomatoes

1½ teaspoons dried Italian seasoning

½ teaspoon black pepper

½ teaspoon salt

Cooked bow tie pasta

① Heat 1½ teaspoons of oil in a large skillet over high heat. Add carrots, celery, onion and garlic; cook and stir about 5 minutes or until vegetables are browned. Remove from skillet. Add remaining 1½ teaspoons oil and pork ribs; cook about 5 minutes or until ribs are browned.

② Transfer ribs to 5-quart slow cooker. Top with vegetables. In small bowl, stir together beef broth and tomato paste; add to slow cooker. Stir in tomatoes with their juices, half of Italian seasoning and half of pepper. Cook on LOW for 7 hours or on HIGH for 5½ hours.

③ Skim off fat. Using a slotted spoon, remove pork ribs to a platter, reserving cooking liquid; let pork ribs cool. Stir remaining Italian seasoning, pepper and salt into cooking liquid in slow cooker. Using 2 forks, pull meat apart into shreds. Stir shredded pork into reserved cooking liquid in slow cooker. Serve over hot cooked pasta.

PER SERVING 459 calories; 13 g fat (4 g sat.); 32 g protein; 55 g carbohydrate; 6 g fiber; 503 mg sodium; 73 mg cholesterol

TEST KITCHEN TIP

Bow ties or other shaped pastas are ideal for trapping this chunky meat-and-vegetable sauce.

mexican tortilla casserole

MAKES 8 servings **PREP** 15 minutes **SLOW-COOK** on HIGH for 3 hours or LOW for 5½ hours

1 head cauliflower, cored

3 plum tomatoes, chopped

1 can (15.5 ounces) 50% less salt added black beans, rinsed and drained

1 cup frozen corn

⅓ cup chopped cilantro

2 teaspoons chili powder

2 teaspoons ground cumin

3½ cups shredded Monterey Jack cheese

1 jar (16 ounces) tomatillo salsa

6 fajita-size flour tortillas

Sour cream (optional)

① Cut cauliflower into florets and slice them into ½-inch-thick slices (you should have about 6 cups). Place cauliflower, tomatoes, beans, corn and cilantro in a large bowl. Sprinkle with chili powder and cumin and stir to combine.

② Coat inside of oval slow cooker bowl with nonstick cooking spray. Spread a scant 3 cups cauliflower mixture over bottom of slow cooker, then sprinkle with 1 cup Monterey Jack cheese and a generous ½ cup salsa over top.

Place 2 tortillas on top. Repeat layering two more times, setting aside last 2 tortillas. Cut these tortillas into 2-inch pieces and scatter over top.

③ Cover and cook on HIGH for 3 hours or on LOW for 5½ hours or until cauliflower is tender. Top with remaining ½ cup cheese.

Cover and cook another 30 minutes or until cheese has melted. Let sit for 10 minutes, then serve with sour cream, if desired.

PER SERVING 277 calories; 14 g fat (8 g sat.); 15 g protein; 25 g carbohydrate; 5 g fiber; 800 mg sodium; 35 mg cholesterol

Enjoying the food we eat is one of life's greatest pleasures. And eating healthy should never mean depriving yourself of the foods you love.

Satisfying your sweet tooth by treating yourself to something wonderful at the end of a meal is essential to sticking to a healthy eating plan. The recipes that follow (except for the frozen fruit desserts, which are naturally low in fat) are slimmed-down versions of classics—low in fat and calories but high in flavor and satisfaction. At no more than 200 calories per recipe with 6 grams of fat, these are guilt-free indulgences.

Fresh fruit is not only good for you (it contains important vitamins, antioxidants and fiber), but it also forms the basis for fabulous desserts. Buy fruit in season

desserts

when it's at its peak and least expensive. Frozen desserts, like our Strawberry Sorbet (page 338) or Mango Granita (page 340), highlight the intense flavor of fruit in its simplest form. Grilling fruit, as in our Grilled Georgia Peaches (page 344), is another easy way to bring out fruit's essential goodness.

Thought of as the ultimate indulgence, we now know chocolate is also good for you. The cocoa bean is filled with powerful antioxidants that can help circulation, improve skin quality and even boost brain power. Whenever possible, choose dark chocolate, as it's high in antioxidants. So go ahead—indulge in one of our luscious Chocolate Truffles (page 350) or Chocolate-Walnut Turnovers (page 352). They're good for you.

Enjoy the intense flavor of strawberries in every spoonful of this sorbet. This quick and easy recipe is best made when strawberries are in season and at their most flavorful.

strawberry sorbet

MAKES 6 cups **PREP** 10 minutes **COOK** 1 minute **FREEZE** 6½ hours

¾ cup sugar

2 quarts strawberries, hulled (about 8 cups)

½ cup lemon-lime soda

Chocolate-lined wafers (such as Pirouline) or mint (optional)

① In a medium-size heavy-bottom saucepan, stir together ¾ **cup water** and sugar. Bring to a boil over medium-high heat. Boil for 1 minute. Turn off heat and stir until sugar is dissolved. Allow to cool.

② In a food processor, purée strawberries and soda. Add in sugar syrup and process until combined. Pour into a 13 x 9 x 2-inch metal baking pan and freeze for 4 to 4½ hours, until frozen solid.

③ Scrape into a food processor and process briefly until smooth but not melted. Spoon back into metal pan and freeze for an additional 1 to 2 hours before serving.

④ Form into balls with an ice cream scoop; serve in dessert dishes with chocolate wafers or mint leaves, if desired.

PER SERVING 130 calories; 1 g fat (0 g sat.); 1 g protein; 35 g carbohydrate; 4 g fiber; 4 mg sodium; 0 mg cholesterol

TEST KITCHEN TIP

Look for well-shaped, plump, bright red berries with fresh, green caps. Avoid any with green or white around the cap. Remove strawberries from their container and place in a bowl. Store berries in the coldest part of the refrigerator loosely covered with plastic wrap for up to 3 days. Do not wash until ready to use.

mango granita

MAKES 6 servings **PREP** 10 minutes **COOK** 3 minutes **FREEZE** 3 to 4 hours

⅓ cup sugar

Juice of 1 lime

3 mangoes, peeled and cut into 1-inch pieces

½ cup mango-lime juice (such as Dole Mango Lime Fiesta) or orange juice

Lime slices (optional)

① Place ½ cup **cold water** and sugar in a small saucepan and bring to a simmer over medium heat. Stir until sugar dissolves, about 3 minutes. Remove from heat and pour into a large bowl and allow to cool. Stir in lime juice.

② Place mangoes and mango juice into a blender and purée. Add to sugar syrup and stir. Pour into a shallow metal pan and freeze for 3 to 4 hours. Stir mixture every hour, spooning ice crystals from the side of pan into the middle.

③ When mixture is frozen, place in food processor and pulse for about 5 seconds until you get a snow-like consistency.

④ Spoon into dessert dishes and garnish with lime slices, if desired.

PER SERVING 122 calories; 0 g fat (0 g sat.); 1 g protein; 32 g carbohydrate; 2 g fiber; 5 mg sodium; 0 mg cholesterol

HOW TO CUT A MANGO

Packed with fiber, vitamin C and beta-carotene, mangoes are the world's sweetest superfruit. Enjoy their island flavor!

Cut the "cheeks" off either side of the mango pit.

Slice the flesh into a checkerboard pattern.

Slice cubes from skin and eat as is, or dice.

frozen tiramisu

MAKES 9 servings **PREP** 10 minutes **FREEZE** 4 hours or overnight

1 pint coffee-flavored frozen yogurt

3 tablespoons chocolate sauce (such as Hershey's)

1 tablespoon instant regular or decaf coffee granules

1 container (8 ounces) frozen light whipped topping, thawed

1 package (3 ounces) soft ladyfingers

1 tablespoon cocoa powder

① Soften frozen yogurt on countertop for 10 minutes.

② Meanwhile, in a small bowl, combine chocolate sauce, coffee granules and **1 tablespoon warm water**.

③ In a large bowl, beat frozen yogurt with ⅔ cup of whipped topping until good spreading consistency. Place half of ladyfingers on bottom of an 8 x 8 x 2-inch baking dish, spreading to cover as much as possible. Drizzle with 2 tablespoons of chocolate mixture. Working quickly, spread with 1 cup of frozen yogurt mixture. Top with 1 cup whipped topping. Repeat layers (ladyfingers, chocolate sauce mixture, frozen yogurt, whipped topping).

④ Dust top with cocoa; cover with plastic wrap. Freeze at least 4 hours or overnight. Let soften slightly before serving.

PER SERVING 198 calories; 5 g fat (4 g sat.); 5 g protein; 33 g carbohydrate; 0 g fiber; 93 mg sodium; 49 mg cholesterol

grilled georgia peaches

MAKES 6 servings **PREP** 5 minutes **GRILL** 5 minutes

3 **peaches, halved and pitted**

3 **tablespoons unsalted butter, melted**

3 **tablespoons packed dark-brown sugar**

⅛ **teaspoon ground cinnamon**

Vanilla ice cream (optional)

① Heat gas grill to medium-high heat, charcoal grill to medium-hot coals. Brush cut sides of peaches with a little butter. In small bowl, blend remaining butter, sugar and cinnamon.

② Grill peaches, cut side down, 3 minutes. Flip over and carefully brush with butter mixture (remove from grill to do this). Return peaches to grill, cut side up. Grill 2 minutes, until butter is bubbly. Serve warm, with ice cream, if desired.

PER SERVING 98 calories; 6 g fat (4 g sat.); 1 g protein; 12 g carbohydrate; 1 g fiber; 4 mg sodium; 15 mg cholesterol

SWITCH IT UP

Substitute nectarines, pineapple or pears for the peaches. Let the seasons dictate your choice.

tropical parfaits

MAKES 6 servings **PREP** 20 minutes **COOK** 5 minutes

Fruit:

- 1 ripe mango, peeled, pitted and diced (see page 340)
- 1 cup pineapple chunks, diced
- 1 cup raspberries
- 1 cup blueberries
- 2 kiwi, peeled and diced
- 2 tablespoons honey

Yogurt Layer:

- 1½ cups 2% plain Greek yogurt (such as Fage)
- 2 tablespoons honey
- 6 tablespoons sweetened shredded coconut
- 6 rolled cookies (optional)

① Fruit: In a large bowl, combine mango, pineapple, raspberries, blueberries, kiwi and honey. Stir gently to combine and set aside.

② Yogurt Layer: In a medium-size bowl, whisk together yogurt and 2 tablespoons honey. Chill until layering.

③ Place coconut in a small nonstick skillet. Heat over medium heat until toasted, stirring occasionally, 3 to 5 minutes. Remove from heat and cool.

④ Spoon 2 tablespoons fruit into bottom of an 8-ounce glass. Top with 1 tablespoon yogurt and a little coconut. Repeat layering one more time, finishing with coconut. Garnish with a cookie, if desired.

Layer 5 more glasses with remaining fruit, yogurt, coconut and cookies and serve.

PER SERVING 184 calories; 4 g fat (3 g sat.); 6 g protein; 36 g carbohydrate; 4 g fiber; 36 mg sodium; 3 mg cholesterol

ricotta mousse with berries

MAKES 4 servings **PREP** 15 minutes **REFRIGERATE** 1 to 24 hours **STAND** 15 minutes

1 cup light ricotta cheese

2 tablespoons orange liqueur

½ teaspoon finely shredded orange peel

½ cup sliced fresh strawberries

½ cup fresh blueberries

½ cup fresh raspberries

½ cup fresh blackberries

1 teaspoon lemon juice

½ to 1 teaspoon heat-stable granular sugar substitute (such as Splenda) or 2 teaspoons honey

Fresh mint leaves (optional)

① In a small bowl, whisk together ricotta cheese, 1 tablespoon of orange liqueur and orange peel. Cover and chill for at least an hour or overnight.

② In a medium-size bowl, combine berries, lemon juice and remaining 1 tablespoon liqueur. Cover and let stand at room temperature 15 minutes to develop flavors.

③ Divide fruit mixture among 4 dessert dishes, spooning any juices onto fruit in dishes. Top with ricotta mixture. Sprinkle individual servings with sugar substitute or drizzle with honey. If desired, garnish with mint leaves.

PER SERVING 112 calories; 3 g fat (2 g sat.); 6 g protein; 13 g carbohydrate; 3 g fiber; 56 mg sodium; 15 mg cholesterol

NUTRITION NOTE

Loaded with disease-fighting antioxidants and fiber, raspberries are high in vitamin C and low in calories (only 60 in 1 cup). But the best part is their appealing, sweet flavor. Pick plump, evenly colored berries without dents, dark spots or broken tiny bumps (known as "druplets"). Keep these highly perishable berries as dry as possible; refrigerate for 2 days max. Do not wash until using.

strawberry banana s'mores

MAKES 12 servings **PREP** 10 minutes **MICROWAVE** 45 seconds

12 graham cracker boards

6 ounces milk chocolate

12 large marshmallows, cut in half crosswise

6 large strawberries, hulled and thinly sliced

1 large banana, thinly sliced on the diagonal

12 teaspoons strawberry preserves

① Break each graham cracker in half along perforation to form 2 squares.

② Place 12 squares on a flat work surface. Layer a ½-ounce piece of chocolate and 2 marshmallow halves on each cracker. In batches of 4, place them on a microwave-safe plate and microwave for 15 seconds, until marshmallows puff up.

③ Place a few strawberry slices and a banana slice on top of each square. Spread 1 teaspoon of preserves on one side of each remaining graham cracker and place, preserve side down, over fruit. Press down gently; serve immediately.

PER SERVING 198 calories; 6 g fat (3 g sat.); 2 g protein; 34 g carbohydrate; 2 g fiber; 70 mg sodium; 3 mg cholesterol

NUTRITION NOTE

Bananas are a great source of potassium, vitamin B6 and fiber. Store bananas at room temperature.

If you are going to indulge, make it with something truly satisfying. You can use semisweet or bittersweet chocolate—or both—depending how intensely flavored your family likes chocolate desserts.

chocolate truffles

MAKES 3 dozen truffles **PREP** 10 minutes **COOK** 5 minutes **REFRIGERATE** 1¾ hours

⅔ **cup heavy cream**

3 **tablespoons almond-flavored liqueur (such as Amaretto) or your favorite flavor**

12 **ounces semisweet or bittersweet chocolate**

2 **ounces unsweetened chocolate**

⅔ **cup confectioners' sugar**

3 **tablespoons unsweetened cocoa powder**

① Line an 8-inch square baking pan with nonstick foil, leaving a small overhang on 2 sides. Line a large baking sheet with waxed paper. Heat cream and liqueur in a small saucepan just to a simmer.

② Process chocolates and confectioners' sugar in food processor 1 to 2 minutes, until finely chopped. With machine running, add cream-liqueur mixture in steady stream. Process until smooth. Scrape into foil-lined pan. Refrigerate just until thick enough to hold shape, 1 to 1½ hours.

③ Lift chocolate from pan using foil. Cut chocolate into 36 pieces. With hands, quickly shape into balls. Place on waxed paper-lined baking sheet. Refrigerate 15 minutes. Reroll truffles to smooth out surface, if needed.

④ Sift cocoa into small bowl. Add truffles, 3 at a time, tossing to coat. Refrigerate in airtight containers up to 1 month, placing each in a small paper or foil candy cup, if desired.

PER TRUFFLE 77 calories; 5 g fat (3 g sat.); 1 g protein; 9 g carbohydrate; 0 g fiber; 3 mg sodium; 6 mg cholesterol

TEST KITCHEN TIP

Look for paper candy cups at a well-equipped kitchenware store or confectioneryhouse.com.

HOW TO MAKE CHOCOLATE TRUFFLES

Process both kinds of chocolate and confectioners' sugar in food processor until finely chopped.

In a continuous stream, with machine running, add warm cream-liqueur mixture to chocolate.

Working quickly, roll chilled, cut squares of chocolate into balls; mixture will begin to melt in your hands.

Gently toss 3 truffles at a time in sifted cocoa powder. Refrigerate; serve at room temperature.

chocolate-walnut turnovers

MAKES 18 turnovers **PREP** 15 minutes **BAKE** at 400°F for 14 minutes

2   **eggs**

½   **cup part-skim ricotta cheese**

⅓   **cup plus 1 tablespoon granulated sugar**

2   **teaspoons vanilla extract**

1   **tablespoon cocoa powder**

1   **tablespoon all-purpose flour**

2   **ounces semisweet chocolate, finely chopped**

⅔   **cup chopped walnuts**

1   **package (17.3 ounces) puff pastry sheets, thawed**

    Confectioners' sugar, for dusting

① Heat oven to 400°F. In a small bowl, whisk together 1 egg and **1 tablespoon water**; set aside.

② In a large bowl, mix ricotta cheese, ⅓ cup of sugar, vanilla and remaining egg. Stir in cocoa powder and flour, then chocolate and walnuts.

③ On a lightly floured surface, roll out puff pastry sheets into 12-inch squares. With a sharp knife, cut each sheet into 9 equal squares (each 4 inches per side).

④ Spoon 1½ tablespoons chocolate-walnut filling into center of one square. Brush edges with egg mixture; fold in half diagonally to form a triangle. Press well to seal edges; transfer to an ungreased baking sheet. Repeat with remaining pastry squares and filling.

⑤ Brush tops with egg mixture and sprinkle with remaining 1 tablespoon granulated sugar. Bake at 400°F for 14 minutes or until browned on top. Cool turnovers on rack. Dust with confectioners' sugar.

PER SERVING 100 calories; 6 g fat (2 g sat.); 3 g protein; 9 g carbohydrate; 1 g fiber; 39 mg sodium; 26 mg cholesterol

HEALTH BENEFITS OF CHOCOLATE

• Chocolate's natural antioxidants help keep the blood vessels smooth and pliable, and naturally thin the blood, making it less likely to clot.

• Preliminary studies show that cocoa anti-oxidants can help blood flow throughout the body, resulting in improved skin quality and even a boost in your brain power.

• You don't need to overindulge. Eating about 30 calories a day—that's less than half an ounce of dark chocolate—was associated with a lowering of blood pressure without weight gain or other adverse effects.

cookies 'n' cream mini cupcakes

MAKES 36 mini cupcakes **PREP** 15 minutes **BAKE** at 350°F for 15 minutes

1½ cups all-purpose flour

2 teaspoons baking powder

¼ teaspoon salt

½ cup (1 stick) unsalted butter, softened

¾ cup granulated sugar

2 large eggs

½ cup reduced-fat sour cream

2 tablespoons milk

½ teaspoon vanilla extract

5 chocolate sandwich cookies (such as Oreos), broken up

Frosting:

2 cups confectioners' sugar

¼ cup (½ stick) unsalted butter, softened

¼ cup reduced-fat sour cream

¼ teaspoon vanilla extract

Crushed sandwich cookies (optional)

① Heat oven to 350°F. Line 36 indents of mini muffin pans (using 3 pans total) with paper or foil liners. If you have only 1 or 2 pans, bake batter in batches.

② In a small bowl, whisk flour, baking powder and salt. In a large bowl, beat butter until smooth. Beat in granulated sugar until fluffy. Beat in eggs, one at a time.

③ On low speed, alternately beat flour mixture and sour cream into butter mixture, beginning and ending with flour. Add milk and vanilla; fold in cookie pieces. Divide batter among prepared cups; for ease, place batter in a resealable plastic food-storage bag, snip off a corner and pipe into cups.

④ Bake at 350°F for 15 minutes, until tops spring back when lightly pressed. Remove cupcakes to a rack; let cool.

⑤ Frosting: In a medium-size bowl, beat confectioners' sugar, butter, sour cream and vanilla until good spreading consistency.

⑥ Once cupcakes have cooled, spread with frosting, about 2 teaspoons for each. Top with cookie crumbs, if desired. Refrigerate until serving, up to 2 days.

PER MINI CUPCAKE 114 calories; 5 g fat (3 g sat.); 1 g protein; 16 g carbohydrate; 0 g fiber; 68 mg sodium; 24 mg cholesterol

TEST KITCHEN TIP

The Real Deal on Extracts Look for pure vanilla extract which has more than 250 components that contribute to its flavor and aroma. Less expensive "imitation vanilla" uses only one of the elements, vanilla; while this does provide a strong characteristic scent, it can't duplicate the complexity and richness of the real thing.

raspberry cheesecake bars

MAKES 32 bars **PREP** 15 minutes **BAKE** at 350°F for 50 minutes **REFRIGERATE** at least 2 hours

1 box (18.25 ounces) lemon cake mix

½ cup cornflake crumbs

1 egg plus 3 egg whites

¼ cup (½ stick) unsalted butter, melted

2 packages (8 ounces each) Neufchâtel cream cheese, softened

¼ cup sugar

1 teaspoon almond extract

1 cup seedless raspberry preserves

½ cup sliced almonds

① Heat oven to 350°F. Line a 13 x 9 x 2-inch baking pan with nonstick foil.

② Set aside ½ cup of cake mix. In a medium-size bowl, stir together remaining cake mix, cornflake crumbs, 1 egg and ¼ cup of butter. Press into bottom and partially up sides of prepared baking pan.

③ In a medium-size bowl, beat cream cheese, sugar, almond extract and egg whites; spread over crust. Dollop cream cheese mixture with preserves and gently spread over cream cheese.

④ Sprinkle reserved cake mix over top and drizzle with **4 tablespoons water**. Bake at 350°F for 25 minutes. Sprinkle with sliced almonds and bake an additional 25 minutes or until set.

⑤ Cool completely in pan on cooling rack. Refrigerate for at least 2 hours. Cut into 32 bars and serve slightly cool.

PER SERVING 160 calories; 6 g fat (4 g sat.); 3 g protein; 23 g carbohydrate; 0 g fiber; 181 mg sodium; 43 mg cholesterol

TEST KITCHEN TIP

Bar Cookie Basics

- Line your baking pan with nonstick aluminum foil, leaving enough overhang to grab so you can lift out the whole baked bar in one motion. This also makes cleanup effortless.

- To press dough evenly into the pan without mess, wrap plastic around your hand.

- Feel free to use a different size pan than specified; simply adjust baking time accordingly. A smaller pan will require a few minutes more in the oven, a larger one, a little less time.

- For neat, clean sides, cut baked bar only after it has cooled completely.

coconut marshmallow patties

MAKES 36 pieces **PREP** 10 minutes **COOK** 7 minutes **BAKE** at 350°F for 18 minutes **STAND** 3 hours

1 bag (7 ounces) shredded coconut

½ cup confectioners' sugar

⅓ cup cornstarch

2 envelopes unflavored gelatin

1⅓ cups granulated sugar

⅔ cup light corn syrup

⅛ teaspoon salt

1 teaspoon coconut extract

① Heat oven to 350°F. Place coconut on a baking sheet and bake for about 18 minutes, stirring occasionally, until lightly browned. Set aside.

② Sift confectioners' sugar and cornstarch into a small bowl. Line a 13 x 9 x 2-inch baking pan with nonstick foil. Coat with nonstick cooking spray. Sift 2 tablespoons of sugar-cornstarch mixture into pan, tilting to coat sides.

③ Place ⅔ **cup water** in a large bowl and sprinkle gelatin over top. Let soften 5 minutes.

④ In a medium-size heavy-bottomed saucepan, heat sugar, corn syrup and salt over medium heat for about 7 minutes, until sugar dissolves. Stir occasionally. Strain into bowl with gelatin and stir in coconut extract.

⑤ Beat on high speed with an electric mixer until light and fluffy and beaters leave tracks in mixture, about 12 to 14 minutes. Spread into prepared pan and smooth top. Sprinkle ¼ cup of toasted coconut over top. Let set at room temperature for 2 hours.

⑥ Lift marshmallow from pan using foil. With a wet knife, cut into 6 squares. Spread remaining sugar-cornstarch mixture onto a baking sheet. Carefully dip bottoms of each marshmallow square in mixture on sheet. Cut each into 6 pieces. Dip cut sides in remaining coconut. Set on a sheet; allow to set for an additional hour. Store loosely covered at room temperature.

PER PIECE 84 calories; 2 g fat (1 g sat.); 1 g protein; 18 g carbohydrate; 1 g fiber; 28 mg sodium; 0 mg cholesterol

butter-pecan cupcakes

MAKES 36 mini cupcakes **PREP** 15 minutes **BAKE** at 350°F for 22 minutes

Cupcakes:

- 2 **cups cake flour (not self-rising)**
- 2 **teaspoons baking powder**
- ¼ **teaspoon salt**
- 10 **tablespoons unsalted butter, softened**
- ¾ **cup granulated sugar**
- 2 **eggs**
- ⅔ **cup milk**
- 1 **teaspoon imitation butter flavor (such as McCormick)**
- ⅓ **cup pecan pie-flavored glazed pecans (such as Emerald) or regular pecans, chopped**

Frosting:

- 2½ **cups confectioners' sugar**
- ¼ **cup (½ stick) unsalted butter, softened**
- 2 **tablespoons milk (plus additional, if necessary)**
- ½ **teaspoon imitation butter flavor**
- 36 **pecan pie-flavored glazed pecan halves**

① Heat oven to 350°F. Line 3 mini cupcake pans with 12 foil or paper liners each (total of 36).

② Cupcakes: In a medium-size bowl, whisk flour, baking powder and salt. Set aside.

③ In a large bowl, with mixer, beat butter and sugar. Add eggs 1 at a time. Beat until light and smooth, 3 minutes. Add half of flour mixture, followed by milk, then remaining flour mixture. Stir in butter flavoring and chopped pecans.

④ Spoon batter into prepared cups. Bake at 350°F for 18 to 22 minutes or until browned. Remove from pan; cool on rack.

⑤ Frosting: On low speed, beat confectioners' sugar, butter, milk and flavoring until smooth (adding more milk if necessary). Spread onto cupcakes; garnish with pecans.

To make standard-size cupcakes: Line 2 standard cupcake pans with 20 foil or paper liners. Spoon batter into cups; bake at 350°F for 24 to 26 minutes. Frost as directed.

PER MINI CUPCAKE 110 calories; 6 g fat (3 g sat.); 1 g protein; 13 g carbohydrate; 0 g fiber; 54 mg sodium; 5 mg cholesterol

gingersnap apple crisp

MAKES 8 servings **PREP** 20 minutes **BAKE** at 375°F for 1 hour

4   Fuji apples, peeled, cored and cut into ¼-inch-thick slices (about 5 cups)

⅓   cup sweetened dried cranberries

2   tablespoons lemon juice

2   tablespoons packed light brown sugar

2   tablespoons cornstarch

12 gingersnap cookies, coarsely chopped

⅓   cup quick-cook oats

2   tablespoons unsalted butter, softened

① Heat oven to 375°F. Coat 2½-quart baking dish with nonstick cooking spray.

② In large bowl, combine apples, dried cranberries, lemon juice, brown sugar and cornstarch. Toss to combine and spoon into prepared dish.

③ In medium-size bowl, stir together cookie crumbs and oats. Mix in softened butter until mixture is crumbly. Sprinkle evenly over apple mixture. Cover with aluminum foil.

④ Bake at 375°F for 30 minutes. Remove foil and bake 30 minutes more, until apples are tender. Allow to cool 15 minutes before serving.

PER SERVING 175 calories; 5 g fat (2 g sat.); 1 g protein; 33 g carbohydrate; 2 g fiber; 37 mg sodium; 8 mg cholesterol

NUTRITION NOTE

Fuji apples contain heart-healthy antioxidants and offer many immune system–boosting vitamins and minerals. They are low in calories, low in fat and provide a complex carbohydrate that won't spike blood sugar levels too quickly.

apple cake

MAKES 8 servings **PREP** 12 minutes **BAKE** at 350°F for 25 minutes

1 cup all-purpose flour

1 teaspoon baking powder

½ teaspoon baking soda

½ teaspoon ground cinnamon

½ teaspoon salt

2 large eggs

⅔ cup granulated sugar

½ cup unsweetened applesauce

2 tablespoons vegetable oil

1 teaspoon vanilla extract

1 Granny Smith apple, peeled, cored and thinly sliced (set aside a few slices for garnish, if desired)

1 tablespoon confectioners' sugar (optional)

① Heat oven to 350°F. Coat a 9-inch round baking pan with nonstick cooking spray.

② In a small bowl, whisk flour, baking powder, baking soda, cinnamon and salt. In a large bowl, whisk eggs, sugar, applesauce, oil and vanilla extract. Stir in sliced apple.

③ Stir flour mixture into apple mixture until blended. Turn into prepared pan; spread evenly. Bake at 350°F for 25 minutes or until toothpick inserted in center comes out clean.

④ Let cool in pan on wire rack 5 minutes. Invert on rack to cool completely. If desired, place a doily on top of cake; sift confectioners' sugar over doily to make design on top; garnish with fresh apple slices.

PER SERVING 190 calories; 5 g fat (1 g sat.); 3 g protein; 34 g carbohydrate; 1 g fiber; 289 mg sodium; 55 mg cholesterol

PHOTO CREDITS

Peter Ardito: Roasted Veggie & Shrimp Salad, pg. 27; Scallop Couscous Paella, pg. 93; Chickpea and Brown Basmati Curry, pgs. 81, 97; Kasha Picadillo Peppers, pg. 99; Wheat Berry Salad Cups, pg. 101; Wild Rice & Tofu Toss, pg. 103; Smoky Beef & Hominy Stew, pg. 105; Rainbow Chard & Bean Casserole, pg. 135; Garam Masala Lentils, pgs. 107, 137; Mom's Pot Roast, pg. 189; Jerk-Rubbed London Broil, pgs. 187, 191; Cube Steak & Onion Gravy, pg. 196; Southwest Meatloaf, pg. 201; Lobster Roll, pg. 253; Smoky BBQ Chicken, pg. 256; Grilled Turkey Caprese, pg. 267; Skirt Steak & Wheat Berry Salad, pg. 287

James Baigrie: herbs (10), pg. 36; Tortellini Soup, pg. 41; All'amatriciana, pg. 73; 2-Bean and Corn Salad, pg. 113; Zucchini & Chickpea Ratatouille, pg. 121; Vegetable Curry, pg. 125; Risotto with Edamame, pgs. 107, 129; Vegetable Medley, pg. 122; Chicken Scallopine al Marsala, pg. 145; Filet with Mushroom Sauce, pgs. 187, 195; Shrimp how-tos, pg. 250; Grilled Pork with Pepper Relish, pgs. 255, 291; Pork & Veggie Kabobs, pg. 297; Jambalaya, pg. 307; Turkey Lasagna, pg. 311; Easy Salmon & Bok Choy, pg. 313; Shrimp Stir-fry, pgs. 299, 315; Tangy Beef Stew, pg. 317; Beef Ragu with Beans, pg. 325

Marty Baldwin: Cavatappi with Chicken and Veggies, pgs. 39, 65; Vidalia Chicken how-to (left), pg. 257

Hallie Burton: Tilapia with Lemony Herb Salad, pg. 221; Red Snapper with Gazpacho Salsa, pgs. 219, 223; Salmon & Israeli Couscous, pg. 231; Cod & Ratatouille Packets, pg. 245; Baked Flounder with Crabmeat Filling, pg. 247; Tuna Steaks with Baby Bok Choy, pg. 277

Mike Dieter: Vidalia Chicken how-to (right), pg. 257

Jason Donnelly: Risotto how-tos, pg. 94

Alexandra Grablewski: Red Lentil Soup, pg. 109; Assorted potatoes, pg. 126; Jerk Chicken & Rice, pgs. 139, 153; Chicken Curry & Brown Basmati, pgs. 139, 161; Stuffed Flank Steak, pg. 193; Flank steak how-tos, pg. 192; Fruity Chicken Tagine, pgs. 299, 305; Cassoulet, pg. 309; Chili con Carne, pg. 323; Pork Goulash, pg. 330

Brian Hagiwara: Chicken with Apricot BBQ Sauce, pgs. 255, 261; Grilled Tuna Steak Sandwiches, pg. 275

Lisa Hubbard: Frozen Tiramisu, pg. 343

Mike Jensen: Eggplant how-to, pg. 117

Yunhee Kim: Mediterranean Orzo, pg. 70; Pork Fried Rice, pg. 83; Bulgur with Chickpeas, pg. 84; Bulgur-Stuffed Squash, pgs. 81, 85; Turkey Quinoa Alfredo, pg. 87; Chicken & Barley Salad, pg. 89; Polenta with Cauliflower & Marinara, pg. 131; Chicken how-tos, pg. 158; Beef Kabobs Over Couscous, pg. 195; Strawberry Sorbet, pg. 339; Strawberry Banana S'mores, pg. 349

Scott Little: Ricotta Mousse, pg. 347

Mark Lund: Pantry stocking, pg. 54; Linguine with Clam Sauce, pg. 55; Sausage and Lentil Salad, pg. 167

Andy Lyons: Stack of chocolate bars, pg. 352

Rita Maas: Pasta Primavera, pg. 47; Tropical Fruit Parfaits, pg. 345

Kate Mathis: Soba Noodles with Spicy Veggie Stir-Fry, pg. 53; Sweet & Savory Pasta Salad, pg. 59; Chipotle Chicken Wagon Wheels, pgs. 39, 68; Stuffed Chicken & Cherry Tomatoes, pg. 155; Maple Pork & Sweet Potatoes, pgs. 187, 209; Lemony Flounder & Roast Zucchini, pg. 229; Teriyaki Salmon & Glazed Broccoli, pg. 233; Sauteed Shrimp & Red Chard, pgs. 219, 245; Pulled Pork Sandwiches, pg. 329

Meredith: Slicing peppers, pg. 314

Alison Miksch: Lettuce silos (4), pg. 10; Thai Peanut Chicken, pg. 151; Quick Pork Schnitzel, pg. 213; Beef Tostadas, pg. 321; Mango how-tos, pg. 340

Ellie Miller: Mango Granita, pgs. 337, 341

Blaine Moats: Thermometer how-to, pg. 282

Kana Okada: Lemon-Basil Arugula Salad, pg. 11; Frisee with Pears and Pecans, pgs. 9, 13; Panzanella, pg. 15; Crispy Tofu Peanut Salad, pg. 17; Spinach Niçoise, pg. 19; Chinese Shrimp Salad, pg. 23; Mexican Chicken Salad, pgs. 9, 30; Romaine with Turkey and Cranberries, pg. 35; Vietnamese Pork Salad, pg. 37; Steak Salad, pg. 33; Ultimate Turkey Burger, pgs. 139, 179; Sausage Bolognese, pg. 181; Italian Pork Roast, pg. 327; Pork Posole with Cornbread, pg. 333

David Prince: Penne with Sausage and Peas, pgs. 39, 61; Ravioli with Spinach and Squash, pg. 79; Baked Potato Florentine, pg. 127; Chicken Tortilla Soup, pg. 169; Sloppy Joes, pg. 203; Quick Meat Sauce & Shells, pg. 63; Cheeseburger-Zucchini Pie, pg. 205; Citrusy Tequila Chicken Thighs with Rice Salad, pg. 263; Cedar Plank Salmon, pg. 271; Grilled Shrimp Pitas, pgs. 255, 281; All-American Cheeseburgers, pg. 289

Alan Richardson: Butter-Pecan Cupcakes, pg. 359

Alexandra Rowley: Rigatoni Siciliana, pg. 44

Tina Rupp: Orange silos (3), pg. 20; Shrimp Salad with Scallion Dressing, pg. 25; Cobb Salad, pg. 28; Celentani with Ham, pg. 74; Shrimp & Barley Pilaf, pg. 91; Risotto with Sugar Snap Peas, pgs. 81, 95; Easy Minestrone, pg. 108; Greek-Style Veggie Burgers, pgs. 107, 115; Harvest Chili, pg. 123; Ligurian-Style Pasta, pg. 51; Roast Chicken & Veggies, pg. 141; Chicken Noodle Soup, pg. 143; Chicken Cacciatore, pg. 156; Arroz con Pollo, pg. 159; Baked Greek Chicken, pg. 162; Turkey & Broccoli Salad, pg. 171; Penne & Turkey Sausage, pg. 69; Fish Tacos, pg. 227; Mustard-Basil Chicken with Grilled Corn, pg. 259; Chicken Burgers, pg. 265; Easy Salmon Burgers, pg. 273; Sunday Dinner on the Grill, pg. 283; Chicken with Cashews, pg. 301; Chicken & Bean Stew, pg. 303; Beef with Mushrooms & Red Wine, pg. 319; Mexican Tortilla Casserole, pgs. 299, 335; Chocolate Truffles, pgs. 337, 351; Chocolate-Walnut Turnovers, pg. 353; Truffle how-tos, pg. 350

Lucy Schaeffer: Penne with Escarole, pg. 43; Reduced-Fat Mac, pg. 49; Spaghetti with Basic Marinara, pg. 76; Cheesy Meximac, pg. 48; Pork & Sweet Potato Stir-Fry, pg. 215; cutting sweet potatoes, pg. 213; Oven Roasted Cod with Tomato Relish, pg. 235; Creamy Salmon & Rotini, pg. 57; Gingersnap Apple Crisp, pg. 360

Charles Schiller: Scallop & Orange Salad, pgs. 9, 21; Chicken with Broccolini, pg. 67; Salad Pizza, pg. 110; Stuffed Peppers, pg. 183; Curried Salmon & Mint Raita, pgs. 219, 237; Panko-Crusted Tilapia, pg. 241; Mediterranean Fish Casserole, pgs. 233, 243; Grilled Tuna & Smashed Potatoes, pg. 278; Grilled Pork Chops & Tomatoes, pg. 293; Cookies 'n' Cream Minis, pgs. 337, 355; Vinaigrette, pg. 14; Eggplant Rollatini, pg. 119

Ann Stratton: Lemony Chicken with Orzo, pg. 148; Turkey Tetrazzini, pg. 173; Harvest Pot Pie, pg. 177; Asian Beef & Noodles, pg. 207; Gingered Tilapia & Swiss Chard, pg. 225; Gingered Cod & Carrots, pg. 237; Coconut Marshmallow Patties, pg. 357

Kirsten Strecker: Chicken with Balsamic Succotash, pg. 147

index

Page numbers in *italics* indicate photos.